PRINCETON SERIES ON THE MIDDLE EAST

Bernard Lewis and András Hámori, Editors

THE REVOLT OF AFRICAN SLAVES IN IRAQ
IN THE 3rd/9th CENTURY

In memory of my father,
Toma Lj. Popović
(1889–1953)

THE REVOLT OF
AFRICAN
SLAVES
IN IRAQ

in the 3rd/9th Century

Alexandre Popovic

With a new introduction by
Henry Louis Gates, Jr.

Translated from French by
Léon King

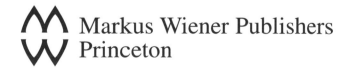 Markus Wiener Publishers
Princeton

THE TRANSLATION OF THEIS BOOK INTO ENGLISH WAS SUPPORTED BY A GRANT FROM THE FRENCH MINISTÈRE DE LA CULTURE ET DE LA COMMUNICATION.

FOR INFORMATION WRITE TO: MARKUS WIENER PUBLISHERS
231 NASSAU STREET, PRINCETON, NJ 08542

COVER DESIGN BY CHERYL MIRKIN
COPY EDITING BY SUSAN VAN DOREN
THIS BOOK HAS BEEN COMPOSED IN TIMES ROMAN BY CMF GRAPHIC DESIGN.

LIBRARY OF CONGRESS CATALOGING-IN-PUBLICATION DATA
POPOVIC, ALEXANDRE
[RÉVOLTE DES ESCLAVES EN IRAQ AU IIIᴱ, IXᴱ SIÈCLE. ENGLISH]
THE REVOLT OF AFRICAN SLAVES IN IRAQ IN THE 3RD/9TH CENTURY
BY ALEXANDRE POPOVIC;
TRANSLATED FROM FRENCH BY LÉON KING; INTRODUCTION
TO THE ENGLISH EDITION BY HENRY LOUIS GATES, JR.
INCLUDES BIBLIOGRAPHICAL REFERENCES AND INDEX.
ISBN 1-55876-162-4 HARDCOVER
ISBN 1-55876-163-2 PAPERBACK
1. IRAQ—HISTORY—ZANJ REBELLION, 868–883   I. TITLE.
DS76.4.P6613   1998
956.7'02—DC21   98-35899   CIP

Contents

Preface

As is often the case with an author's first book, this work is intimately linked to my own personal journey. Most of the important events in my life have occurred suddenly and quite unexpectedly. I was preparing to take the examination for the diploma in classical Arabic at the École Nationale de Langues Orientales Vivantes de Paris, when my professor, Charles Pellat, asked me: "What do you intend to do later?" I was non-plussed by the question and must have mumbled something like, "I don't know," to which he replied: "Would you like to do a thesis with me at the Sorbonne? Choose a subject and come to see me sometime this week."

That was in June 1957. My concerns at the moment were far from academic. I was merely trying to survive and find a job less pathetic than my previous employment. To get a job, one needed a work permit. To obtain a work permit, one must already have a job. In an attempt to sort things out, I took a long walk along the Seine.

I had fled Yugoslavia and the régime there in 1954, after having spent my childhood and youth in Belgrade where, under the direction of Fehim Bajraktarevic, at the University, I had just earned my B.A. in Oriental Philology. Life in Paris seemed fantastic to me: I was living by my wits, of course, but I was studying under leading authorities and playing on the team of a well-known Parisian basketball club with good friends. Nevertheless, the enormous problems confronting me every day seemed insurmountable.

In these conditions, it would clearly be insane to undertake a dissertation. Yet. The challenge intrigued me. I decided to do it but to take my time. That very afternoon, I glanced through Brockelmann's *Geschichte der islamischen Völker* in search of a subject. I chose one with little hesitation. A few days later, when I informed Professor Pellat of my choice, he replied: "I knew you would choose the Zanj." His remark put to rest any doubts I might have had about my choice. In answer to his question about how I intended to proceed, I told him that, with no personal thesis to defend, I would not do the usual dissertation and that what had appeared on the subject so far, in the part of the world I had just left, was rather annoying. I wanted to examine closely every scrap of information that existed on the subject in order to create as complete a body of knowledge as possible on the revolt of the Zanj, even if it took ten years. His response was simplicity itself: "We agree, then. Come to see me from time to time." In the end the project took up eight years of my life. I passed my orals in 1965, but that is another story. Twelve years later, in 1976, the book was published by Editions Geuthner in Paris. Having come full circle, I turned to other projects.

It is easy to imagine, I suppose, the excitement I felt when, twenty years later, Markus Wiener telephoned from Princeton to suggest that he publish an English translation of my book, which would ensure it of a wider readership. So, with Léon King's *maestria* and expertise, we have deleted some scholarly references and comments (specialists will find them in the French edition), provided additional notes and explanations for the nonspecialist reader, and simplified the transliteration.

Now it is time to let you read this true story of events that occurred more than eleven centuries ago.

Introduction to the English Edition

by Henry Louis Gates, Jr.

Western historians have long presumed that the great natural expanses of the Indian Ocean and the Sahara desert proved to be unsurpassable barriers to the Africans who lived in proximity to them. They assumed incorrectly that Africans, unlike all other human beings, would not see these natural wonders as conduits, as highways through which to connect to other civilizations and other human beings. Trade is the enemy of distance. It is also the godfather of movements among peoples that result in captivity and enslavement.

Eleven centuries ago, slaves from East Africa—the "Zanj"—at Basra engaged in a war against their masters in Baghdad. Between 869 and 883 C.E., these slaves struck their blows for freedom against the Abbasid Empire (762–1258 C.E.). For fourteen years they succeeded, achieving remarkable military victories and even building their own capital. Their achievement is all the more impressive considering that the Abbasid Empire was one of the world's most powerful states at its height, presiding directly over Iraq, Mesopotamia, and western Persia and indirectly over territories from North Africa to Central Asia and from the Caspian Sea to the Red Sea.

The Zanj were commonly found as slaves in Muslim countries. Like all slaves, they were stereotyped as thieves, rapists, devoid of reason, and lacking memory. Nevertheless, these brutally oppressed slaves—forcibly packed into camps by the hundreds and thousands, without family or hope, and given meager rations of food—under Ali b. Muhammad's leadership rose up against their masters, and fought to the death for their freedom. As detailed in these pages their uprising brings to mind the revolts of Eunus (140 B.C.E.) and of Spartacus (73–71 B.C.E.) against Rome, as well as those of Toussaint L'Ouverture in Haiti and the strikes of the

Indian coolies in Natal led by Gandhi against European colonialism (1906–13).

Dr. Popovic's fascinating study of this curious historical event is an important contribution to historical scholarship, in general, to the scholarship of slavery, and to African and Islamic Studies, more specifically. This book helps us to understand the complexity of the relations between black Africa and the Middle East long before the age of European discovery, as well as the degree of agency that these Africans manifested as they fought, and died, before the Magna Carta.

Cambridge, September 1998.

Foreword to the French Edition

It is not for me to discuss the merits or flaws of this work, but the few preliminary remarks that follow do not seem inappropriate.

In more than one place in this study, the reader might find that I take a tentative position on the Zanj revolt. It could not be otherwise on such a delicate subject for which there continues to be a lack real of information. Rather than advance plausible but unverifiable hypotheses, I have chosen not to attempt a valid response to problems that cannot be solved or for which there are several possible solutions. The general rule guiding me has been to say less rather than more. Similarly, in reviewing works and opinions of various scholars, I have tried to avoid discussing errors and questionable judgments as much as possible, preferring instead to write about facts. I was more concerned with bringing together all the information available to us rather than interpreting it at all costs. Hesitation in establishing dates and facts was inevitable. I kept to the chronological order of events, even though it cannot be proven to be always correct. As for the bibliography, there are undoubtedly omissions, but it is obvious that they are unavoidable and can only be corrected later. I believe it is largely a question of modern works, however, and that few older works have been neglected. Finally, I must emphasize how much the present study owes to Claude Cahen, particularly his *L'histoire économique et sociale de l'Orient musulman mediéval*. With it constantly in mind, it would be difficult for me to be wholly satisfied with the present effort.

This study could not have been carried out without a great deal of support. I wish to thank first of all Charles Pellat who, during all these years of research, has given me reliable and invaluable assistance through his advice, his constant encouragement, and his kindness. May he find here assurance of my gratitude and profound respect. My thanks go also to

Claude Cahen and Maxime Rodinson who, at different times, read and commented on my manuscript, as well as to Robert Brunschvig for his criticism and suggestions. I am also grateful to George Vajda, whose friendship and interest in my work were demonstrated on more than one occasion. It gives me special pleasure to acknowledge emphatically Pierre Rondot's generosity and confidence, particularly in difficult moments. I sincerely thank him. I am also grateful to G. C. Miles and J. T. P. De Bruijn for the information they were good enough to send me, as well as to Ms. D. Stamboli and Messrs. Otto Spies, N. Špiric. V. Jagodic and A. Olabi, who allowed me to consult a certain number of manuscripts or published works. I am indebted, too, to Mme. C. Meuvret and to Mme. G. Bouchon, whose understanding made my work much easier. To Mr. George Douillet who reread and commented on my manuscript, I offer my most sincere gratitude. I am also profoundly grateful to Mr. Henri Laoust for accepting my work in his Library of Islamic Studies and to Mme. Janine Sourdel-Thomine and Mr. Dominique Sourdel, for their invaluable understanding and assistance.

Finally, it is my very agreeable duty to acknowledge my debt to Milorad Stjepanovic who oversaw the final editing of this book with devotion and competence.

Clichy-sous-Bois
July 1974

Introduction

I. THE PROGRAM OF THE BOOK

For a long time we have attempted to explain historical facts solely through the acts of a handful of illustrious men whose accomplishments or failures are held to be the main causes of all events. Yet, in parts of the world another method has been preponderant for some time now. It attempts to explain events by the economic situation of the masses and considers the role played by great men of secondary importance. Unfortunately, this method is often applied with a point of view that misrepresents the problem. Attempts are made to explain certain peoples, environments, or civilizations of the past through ideas or emotions completely alien to them, since they did not come into existence or take shape until many centuries later and in other climes.[1] The oversimplification that this method produces must be viewed with great caution, because events become distorted when they are packed into unchanging, ready-made frameworks. We must also be careful about witticisms such as, "History is a battalion of consequences led by chance." There is certainly a measure of truth to such remarks, but we must keep in mind that all great changes have often complex but very real causes. It is obvious that we make the fewest errors in judgment when we attempt to see history as a whole, free of preconceptions. When all is said and done, that is the way we become mindful that historical truth must be the product of a certain number of factors, all of which are important.

In the case of the Zanj revolt this means that, if it is almost certain that without the extraordinary configuration of the Basra region and the very weak situation in which the central power found itself at the time, the Zanj insurrection would never have lasted as long nor been as widespread as we know it; but it is also highly probable that, without the personality of 'Alî b. Muhammad, events would not have unfolded as they did, in spite of the incredible misery of the slave population.

In medieval Islamic history there were many revolts for various causes: political, ideological, national, economic, and obviously religious. We must not forget that among Muslims there is no act that is not directly related to religion and that it would be unthinkable to rebel without claiming to be a "better Muslim."

> In a state in which the temporal and the spiritual, politics and religion are intimately linked, most political movements have a religious basis and vice versa, and it is impossible to separate the two elements. Here, religion will outweigh politics, there, the latter will have the principal role, not without relying on a religiously based doctrinal system; further, foreigners will introduce heretical dogmas into Islam and incur punishment in the name of orthodoxy, while the main objective of their action would be to come to power by roundabout or by direct means.[2]

This rule applies to the revolt of the slaves of Basra. It is not pointless to emphasize here and now we must be careful about assigning a definite label to it, as these few passages show:

> This revolt is very important, because it is a typical class war, a genuine 'social war' against Baghdad, as those of Eunus (140 B.C.) and of Spartacus (73–71 B.C.) were against Rome. As were those of Toussaint Louverture in Haiti (1794–1801), and the strikes of Indian coolies in the Natal led by Ghandi (1906–1913) against European colonialism.[3]

> To consider the evolutionary aspect of economic and social history is to also call to mind the antagonisms, the conflicts manifest in this history. Was there in the Muslim world a "class struggle," in the most subtle meaning of the term? There are the Zanj, naturally: but there is little sense in blowing this episode out of all proportion if we do not give it its place, which is exceptional, in medieval Islamic history as a whole.[4]

> The central government's weakness, manifested in the corrupt

economy and the incessant changes in regimes, is most clearly evident in a state run by bandits which was able to grow under its eyes and almost at the gates of its capital.[5]

The claims of the chosen race and the expectation of the Mahdi, who would come from this race, were useful as pretext and means to the agitators, whose disruption of the empire and the resultant economic unrest favored action. Thus was born the terrible Zanj revolt, which between 877 and 883, sowed the seeds of Lower Mesopotamia's ruin.[6]

Even this semi-barbarian movement was marked enough by the dominant tendency of Islamic society to seek a religious expression.[7]

. . . moreover, economic development introduced into the country masses quite prepared to allow themselves to become fanaticized by their agitators at the required moment, as was the case at the time of the uprising of the Zanj, who had been imported from East Africa.[8]

. . . proletarian movement based on a coherent politico-religious doctrine.[9]

Considering these diverse opinions, I wanted to take my bearings on all the information concerning the revolt, sort out the facts and dates, and put together as complete a bibliography as possible, while leaving the field open to interpretation.

As far as the distinctive character of the movement is concerned, the revolt occupies a very special place in medieval Islamic history because, as we shall see, it suppressed the unique attempt to transform domestic slavery into colonial slavery. It is for this reason, above all, that it deserves our attention.

II. STUDIES OF THE REVOLT

The revolt of the slaves of Basra, commonly called the revolt of the

Zanj, has been taken up in a great number of books that differ in their use-fulness. For the most part, they are either works dealing with a much broader subject, or works on various subjects with only a slight connection to the Zanj. In both cases, all we have is information about details, a quick sketch of the problem or a personal opinion. This rarely takes up more than a few pages, indeed, a few lines. Works devoted entirely to the Zanj revolt are scarce.

The earliest such work is Theodor Nöldeke's *Ein Sklavenkrieg im Orient*, which is part of his *Orientalische Skizzen*. As the title suggests, it is a thirty-page outline, with no notes or bibliography, in which the author gives his view of the problem and a synopsis of the events. If we cannot always agree with his view of the problem, given the progress that has been made in historiography since 1892, his synopsis of the events is perfectly acceptable inasmuch as it is based on the latest sources. It should be particularly underlined that Nöldeke was the first to draw attention to Hamza al-Isfahânî's Leyden manuscript regarding a version of 'Alî b. Muhammad's death.

'Abd al-'Azîz al-Dûrî also devotes about thirty pages to the Zanj revolt. He makes use of a limited bibliography and accompanies his rapid survey of the events with a few remarks.

We should mention next Abdul Karim Khalifa's three-part unpublished thesis. In his bibliography, the author mentions a hundred ancient and modern works, without indicating page numbers. His choice is rather arbitrary, all the more so since he ignores passages by al-Mas'ûdî (*Tanbîh*), Abû l-'Alâ' al-Ma'arrî, Ibn Hazm, etc. In his foreword, the author briefly assesses the four main sources, namely, al-Tabarî, al-Mas'ûdî (*Murûj*), Ibn al-Athîr, and Ibn Abî l-Hadîd. He interprets the facts and gives his point of view on the question in his Introduction, but, above all, elaborates on the problem of class warfare in Abbasid society. Moreover, his work has the following dedication: "To all of the oppressed in their struggles against their exploiters." In spite of the extent of this part of the study (fifty pages of a large format book), it deals less with the problems of the Zanj revolt itself than one might expect. It is surprising to find in the work such flagrant omissions as the failure to mention even the existence of Zanj money pieces: "On the other hand, there is no mention of coins being struck especially for use by the insurgents." The third part of the work is by far the most important. We find there a complete translation of all of the passages in which al-Tabarî refers to the revolt of the Zanj. The translation is accompanied by many notes. They are part translation of complementary information drawn from different sources and part identification of the names of persons and places. I refer to these notes from time to time in the present work.

Faysal al-Sâmir's doctoral thesis, *Thawrat al-Zanj*, written at the University of Cairo and published in Baghdad, is a thorough study that attempts to look at the various aspects of the revolt. The work's different chapters do not all have the same value. The study contains omissions, imperfections, inaccuracies, and a few questionable judgments; nevertheless, Faysal al-Sâmir's book is testimony to the commendable effort he devoted to the study of the problem.

Then there is the work of Ahmed S. Olabi, entitled *La révolte des Zanj et son chef 'Alî b. Muhammad*, which appeared in 1961, in Beyrouth (Beirut). Drawing on an expanded bibliography, the author is first of all concerned with interpretation of the facts. His foreword contains the following sentence: "What claim to originality can the present study make? As far as possible, we have avoided subjects already developed in previous studies. In the present endeavor, we have done our best to delve more deeply into subjects that have already been studied and judge them. This has led us to conclusions that we believe are closer to the truth." It is regrettable, however, after reading the first chapter, which is so complete, that the author then limited himself to taking up only certain points, thus condemning his work to remain a "complementary study." In addition to the bibliography of sources, there is a very useful bibliography of works and articles on the Middle East that have appeared of late.

The most recent book on the subject is Heinz Halm's remarkable work. Bearing in mind that my study already included all of the existing documentation,[10] and following the texts more closely, the author undertook a critical examination of the sources. The result is a careful and intelligent work that can at least give us a whole new perspective, if not drastically change our earlier notions. Nevertheless, as seductive as these hypotheses may appear, they need confirmation by documentation that is still lacking. This fact will obviously come up several times in the pages that follow.

III. THE SOURCES

Although a great many authors of the Middle Ages mention the Zanj revolt, those who contribute new information or sound opinions are rare. Most of them merely pass on information compiled and abridged from the works of predecessors and are therefore of little interest.

By far the most important primary sources are the works of Arab writers and, above all, historians. First, there is al-Tabarî, valued as much for the quality as for the quantity of his information, then there are al-Mas'ûdî and Ibn al-Athîr. Some information can also be gleaned from geographers (Ibn Rustah, al-Muqaddasî) and poets (Ibn al-Rûmî, al-Buhturî, Ibn al-Mu'tazz). But it is, above all, in the secondary sources (works of *adab,* or general culture, and sundry) that we find the abundant complementary information that can enrich the material handed down by the historical chroniclers (Ibn al-Nadîm, al-Husrî, Abû l-'Alâ al-Ma'arrî, Ibn Hazm, al-Najâshî, al-Tûsî, Ibn Abî l-Hadîd, al-Safadî, etc.). Persian authors also mention the revolt of the Zanj and give a few details (the anonymous *Hudûd al-'âlam,* the anonymous *Tarikhe Sîstân,* the anonymous *Mujmal al-tawârîkh,* Nizâm al-Mulk, Hamdallâh Mustawfî Qazwînî, Mirkhwând, Khwândamîr, etc.). It is also mentioned by Syrian authors (Barhebraeus). As far as Armenian and Byzantine authors are concerned, there were no positive results from my perusals of their works. On the other hand, Turkish historians are too late and they only hand down scraps of compilations, of no interest (Ahmad b. Yûsuf al-Qaramânî).

As far as studies of Orientalists are concerned, they will be cited fairly often in the present work, so it is not necessary to speak of them here. A list of various works that touch on the Zanj revolt, more or less, will be found in the bibliography. It would be useless to emphasize their importance.

It is the same for the publications of Oriental scholars like Ahmad Amîn, Zaky Muhammad Hassan, 'A. 'A. al-Dûrî, Saleh Ahmed el-'Ali, and the others.

NOTES

1. This situation was denounced, in no uncertain terms by Maxime Rodinson: "There is no reason to blame people of the past for not having achieved an ideal that did not correspond to the conditions of their times. It is equally absurd to transpose our ideal back to this epoch and artificially seek to discover it there. Likewise, to reduce the claims of today's conscience to the demands of a bygone era is, in the strict sense, a reactionary undertaking. Neither the justice conceived by the Qur'an, nor that conceived under its influence by Muslims of the Middle Ages fits the modern ideal's definition of the concept. We should be aware of this."
2. Charles Pellat.
3. Louis Massignon.
4. Claude Cahen.
5. C. Brockelmann.
6. G. Marçais.
7. Bernard Lewis.
8. R. Hartmann.
9. Charles Pellat.
10. It is a question of the mimeographed edition of my 1965 thesis.

CHAPTER I

Origins of the Revolt

The Abbasid Empire was founded in 750, by Abû al-'Abbâs al-Saffâh (descendant of 'Abbâs, uncle of the Prophet Muhammad) who, with the aid of Persian troops, seized power and put an end to the Umayyad dynasty (661–750). Baghdad, founded in 762, became their residence. The caliphs, thirty-seven in number, reigned until 1258, when Hûlâgû, a grandson of Genghis Khân, brought their empire to an end. Their chief interest was in the Asian part of the empire, for, as soon as they arrived to power, first Spain had slipped from their grasp and then North Africa, where only the the Ifriqiyya (Tunisia and the eastern part of Algeria) remained nominally submitted to them. In the time of Hârûn al-Rashîd, the Abbasid Empire was one of the principal centers of world civilization, and Baghdad dazzled the world with its splendor and prosperity. Nevertheless, following troubles brought on by Turkish mercenaries, the seat of the caliphate was moved, in 836, to Sâmarrâ which remained the capital until the year 892. At the beginning of the tenth century, continuing domestic troubles and growing decadence obliged the caliph to yield temporal power to a sort of "palace mayor," while the governors became practically independent of the central power . . . Temporal power then passed into the hands of the Seljuk sultans (Turks) until February 10, 1258, the day Hûlâgû's Mongols seized and devastated Baghdad, putting an end to the Abbasid dynasty, whose last caliph was strangled to death.

However, at the time of the revolt of the Zanj (869–883), the Abbasid Empire was still a great world power which reigned *de facto* or *de jure* (mostly through semi-independent governors) over vast territories from

Tunisia to Central Asia and from the Caspian Sea to Yemen, but actually over hardly more than Iraq, Mesopotamia, and western Persia.

I. GEOGRAPHY

Two provinces of the Abbasid Empire were affected by the Zanj revolt: Iraq and Ahwâz (the Khuzistân).[1] Hostilities, which did not extend beyond Jarjarâyâ and Râmhurmuz, raged mostly in southern Iraq and western Ahwâz. Tremendous rivers crossed the provinces, facilitating navigation and transport and, along with caravan routes, the hundreds of canals that linked up the waterways favored intense movement of people and goods. Of special interest to us are two regions that contributed greatly to the insurrection because of the nature of their soil. They are al-Batîha and Maysân, Lower Iraq's canal region.

Al-Batîha.—The "Marshes" is the name for a basin with prairies that are almost constantly filled with mud due to regular flooding, more or less. In the Middle Ages Arab authors employed the term al-Batîha and its plural al-Batâ'ih specifically to designate Lower Iraq's swamp region, located roughly between Kûfa and Wâsit in the north and Basra in the south. These swamps were the result of annual flooding and had existed from earliest antiquity because the waters of the Tigris and the Euphrates frequently overran the extremely flat terrain and often changed course. Assyrians, Greeks, Romans, Sassanids, and Arabs had built dams, dikes, and canals in the region, but "a stable hydrographic network was impossible in the extensive flatlands of southern Mesopotamia where there were no elevations to offset the malleability of alluvion-formed soil, all the more so since the system of irrigation canals was subject to economic and political fluctuations."

Enormous growths of reeds and rushes, often several meters tall, covered the vast surface across which ran a great many more or less wide but often very shallow canals. Most of the time, they could be navigated only by small, flat boats, and this made access to al-Batîha very difficult. As a result, the region was always a perfect location for brigands, rebels, or malcontents who needed observation posts from which they could keep an eye on trade and other activities. But it could be a dangerous area. Ibn Battûta, the famous fourteenth-century Arab traveler, notes:

> . . . And, in a region known as Idhâr, we went along the Euphrates. It is a forest of reeds surrounded by water, and inhabited by Arabs, known for their excesses. They are bandits of the sect of 'Alî [that is to say Shiites]. They attacked a troop of *fakirs* (poor people) who had fallen behind our caravan and stripped them of even their sandals and goblets. They fortify themselves in these swamps and defend themselves against pursuers. There are many ferocious beasts in that place.

Al-Batîha's ordinary inhabitants engaged in tilling plots of land, and their chief crops were rice, barley, yellow corn, sorghum, millet, lentils, melons, watermelons, and onions. The reeds and rushes growing wild in the region were also gathered and put to many uses.

Fish of various kinds were plentiful and there were other fauna such as buffalo, sheep, and cows, without mentioning various types of waterfowl: gulls, wild duck, geese, swans, etc. Lions, leopards, jackals, wolves, lynx, and wildcats were also found. "Herds of wild boar still wallow in the swamp. The countless swarms of mosquitoes and gnats are a terrible scourge and the source of endemic diseases such as malaria, which must have been one of the principal causes of the region's decline."[2]

Inaccessibility, a readily available food supply, and climate which Abbasid troops found difficult and unhealthy are features which made this an ideal location for the insurgents.

The Canal Region of Lower Iraq.—We know from Arab authors of the time that the Basra region's canal system was highly developed. Among the canals particularly mentioned, on the west bank of Dijlat al-'awrâ' (the present Shatt al-'arab), are the Nahr Ma'qil, the Nahr al-Ubulla, and, about 25 km. south of Basra, the Nahr Abî l-Khasîb. There were also numerous interlinking irrigation canals in a region covered with palm trees and scattered villages. It should also be pointed out that seaworthy vessels were able to navigate the Tigris as far as Wâsit and even beyond.

Over the centuries there were many changes in the canal system until eventually a great part of it was destroyed by the Mongols. Although there were constant changes in the canals and their flow, they made it possible to irrigate land said to support populations three times larger than today.

Some of these numerous canals are known, but it is impossible to pinpoint their locations today.[3] They were Nahr al-Marâ', Nahr al-Dayr, Nahr Bithq Shîrîn, Nahr Ma'qil, Nahr al-Ubulla, Nahr al-Yahûdî, Nahr Abî l-Khasîb, Nahr al-Amîr, and Nahr al-Qindal to the west. To the east were Nahr al-Rayân and Nahr al-Bayân.[4]

This canal region and especially the Nahr Abî l-Khasîb, where the insurgent's capital, al-Mukhtâra, was located, was the heart of the Zanj state. It was the base from which the rebels launched their raids and to which they returned for safety. As emphasized by everyone who has studied the Zanj revolt, the nature of the soil lent itself very well to guerilla activity and made it easy for the insurgents to carry out their operations.

Land Renewal.—Arabs, above all, Bedouins or merchants, showed little interest in the land before the occupation of Iraq. The development of Lower Mesopotamia was only undertaken through the impetus given by al-Hajjâj (renowned Umayyad governor in the seventh and eighth centuries) and his successors.

Later the situation changed. The Abbasid Caliphs began to take an interest in the land and revived vast areas, long abandoned as a result of the rural population's exodus to the cities. These lands, which their owners had often received as rewards for services, were cultivated by servile labor, under the direction of overseers (*wakîl*) and freemen (*mawlâ*). "In these vast agricultural establishments where the subordinates who ran them were much harsher than the absentee owners . . . " there is no question that conditions became intolerable for the slaves.

Four points deserve special attention: the existence of "dead lands" in the Basra area; the possibility of acquiring these lands; the presence in Basra of people with substantial capital; the availability, thanks to slavery, of labor in great numbers to exploit the lands.

Two reasons seem to explain the "dead lands" phenomenon: the exodus from the country to the city on the one hand and the the peculiar nature of the natron-covered soil on the other.[5]

There were various ways to obtain lands of this type. If we disregard the many kinds of donation, known by the name *iqtâ'*, the problem of which has been definitely settled by Claude Cahen,[6] we must emphasize above all the special statute concerning these dead lands. I am referring to the famous hadith (tradition reporting the Prophet Muhammad's words or deeds, or his appproval of words or deeds performed in his presence) "he who rejuvenates a dead land becomes it proprietor." Thus all that one had to do to own some of this land was to make it suitable for farming by removing its layer of natron.

There is no need to dwell on the existence of the substantial capital in the hands of different people in Basra. A century before the Zanj revolt, the city was at its height and a center of commercial, financial, industrial, agricultural, intellectual, and religious life, all at the same time. There is no need either to emphasize the availability for purchase of large numbers of slaves in Basra, which was the chief port of transit for slaves from East African markets.

II. THE POPULATION (THE ZUTT, THE ZANJ)

Among the population of very diverse origins inhabiting these regions in the ninth century, two ethnic groups attract our particular attention: the Zutt and the Zanj.

The Zutt.—The Zutt lived in the swamps and engaged in violent robbery and even open revolt. They fought government troops on several occasions during the reign of al-Ma'mûn (Abbasid caliph, 813–833), disrupting communications between Baghdad and Basra. Al-Mu'tasim (Abbasid caliph, 833–842) managed to subdue them, but not without difficulty. He resettled them on the northern border of Syria, but we do not know much more about the Zutt or these events.

The Zanj.—"Jâhiz (a very important Arab prose-writer) distinguishes four categories of Zanj. Qunbula, Lanjawiyya, Naml, and Kilâb [*Bayân*, III, 36, we were not able to identify these names] were Negroes from the east coast of Africa who had been imported as slaves, at an indeterminate date."[7]

Origins of the Name "Zanj."—This name is not Arabic, even though the Arabs have treated it as a word of their language. Its composition in three letters, Z, n, j, made it easy for the Arabs to adapt. They use it as a collective word with the value of a plural, which they can also denote by the form *zonoûdj*, just as from *hind*, the singular collective denoting Hindus, they form the plural *Honoûd*.

Since the word Zanj is not of Arabic origin, there are several explanatory hypotheses for it, and opinions are very divided. L. M. Devic thinks it is a borrowed Ethiopian word: "It is obviously a foreign word. The Ethiopian language, sister of Arabic, has a verb *zanega*, meaning to prattle, to stammer, to barbarize with the noun *Zengua*, confused, absurd speech, and these words are probably etymologically related to the name of the Zendj people; but we can presume that the latter produced the Ethiopian verb and noun."

Others, such as G. Ferrand, A. Werner, and Philip K. Hitti believe in a Persian origin, but G. F. Hourani questions it. As for M. Dunlop, he writes: "The name itself has been explained as having come from the Persian *Zang, Zangî* (Pahlawi Zoroastrian *zangîk* "Negro"), but it is perhaps of local origin." This is close to the view held by W. Fitzgerald who, speaking of Zanzibar, writes: "The name is derived from two terms, one Persian, the other Indian, *viz. Zanz-bar*, which means 'Country of the Black Man'."

Some authors, among whom are A. Müller and the same G. F. Hourani, believe that the name is related to the Greek "Zingis"; but they remain extremely guarded, as for example, C. H. Becker: "The name Zandj goes back to early antiquity; Ptolemy, the famous Greek astronomer, mathematician and geographer of the second century, knew *Zingis akra* and Kosmas Indicopleustes (merchant and traveler of the sixth century) spoke of *tò Zingion*. The name itself is unexplained."

Opinions are also divided as far as interpretation of the word is concerned. L. M. Devic hesitates between Zinj, Zanj, or Zenj, therefore between *fatha* and *kasra*. F. al-Sâmir believes that three readings are possible: Zanj, Zinj, and Zunj; therefore *fatha, kasra*, and *damma*. Ibn Manzûr (author of a famous Arab dictionary, who lived in the thirteenth and fourteenth centuries) indicates only two: Zanj and Zinj, therefore, *fatha* and *kasra*. And we find the same thing in E. W. Lane's work. On the other hand, Ibn Durayd (Arab philologist, 837–933), who lived at the time of the revolt, is of a different opinion altogether and says clearly: "The Zanj are a well-known people; as for the pronunciation Zinj, it is incorrect."

D'Herbelot was the first to point out that "Rîh" instead of "Zanj" is sometimes found in texts.

The Land of the Zanj, the Sea of the Zanj.—Though all Arab geographers speak of the land and the sea of the Zanj, our information is poor and imprecise. L. M. Devic collected all the relevant pages from Arab authors. After comparing them,[8] he writes:

> . . . the geographers are misinformed. If they pass names on to us in a rather precise order, their information regarding distances are often only rough estimates or even completely contrary to the truth; they are only based on the duration of the crossings, which were undoubtedly passed on from memory to the authors by merchants more concerned with calculating their profits than counting miles and parasangs . . . [9]

To attempt to speak of the "Land of the Zanj" (which supposedly comprised territory south of Abyssinia with a part of the coast) seems all the more difficult since the term "Zanj" certainly included blacks from numerous peoples bought or seized as in ports of call all along the coast.

Their Characteristics and Way of Life.—We have said that many Arab geographers and travelers left notes on the "Bilâd al-Zanj" and the "Bahr al-Zanj." Now let us hasten to add that many more left descriptions of the Zanj themselves. Unfortunately, their information is rather anecdotal.

Here are a few examples:

> Galen, (the famous Greek doctor of the first and second centuries) says Kazouini, the Arab cosmographer and geographer of the thirteenth century, (see *Âthâr al-bilâd*, p.14) attributes ten special characteristics to the Zanj: black complexion, kinky hair, flat nose, thick lips, slender hands and feet, fetid odor, limited intelligence, extreme exuberance, cannibalistic customs. The Arab cosmographer explains the characteristic that we translate as exuberance by adding that one never sees a worried Zanj. Incapable of sorrow, they all abandon themselves to gaiety. Doctors say this is because of the equilibrium of the blood from the heart or, according to others, because the star Soheil (Canope) rises over their head every night and this star has the power to give rise to gaiety . . . "

Two centuries before Kazouini, Masoudi also mentions the attributes of blacks according to Galen's ten characteristics. His list differs on a few points from the one we have just read. Here it is grouping the characteristics in the same order, so that the difference between the two listings can be seen immediately: black complexion, kinky hair, flat nose, thick lips, thin hands and feet, smelly skin, excessive petulance, sparse eyebrows, highly developed sexual organs (*Prairies d'or,* ch. VII, t. I, p. 163–64).

Finally in keeping with De Guignes's analysis, Bakoui who, in his description of the Bilâd ez-Zendj, confines himself to the role of Kazouini's plagiarist, notes the ten characteristics of Negroes in these terms: They differ from other men by their black color, their flat nose, the thickness of their lips, the thickness of their hands, by their odor, by their quickness to anger, their lack of intellect, their habit of eating one another and their enemies.[10]

Would you like a prince of Arab philosophy's explanation for these characteristics of the Negro? Here is how al-Kendi, undoubtedly inspired by some Greek, puts it: God has established a chain of causes in all parts of creation; the cause exercises on the creature subject to it an influence which in turn becomes cause; but this purely subjective creature cannot react on its cause or its agent. Therefore, the soul being the cause and not the effect of the sphere, the sphere cannot react on the soul. But it is the soul's nature to follow the body's temperament as long as it meets no obstacle, and that is what takes place in the case of the Zendj. Since their country is very hot, the heavenly bodies exert their influence and draw the humors to the upper part of the body. Hence the eyes of these peoples, their hanging lips, their large flattened nose and the development of the head following the upward movement of the humors. The brain looses its balance, and the soul can no longer exert its complete action on it; the swell of perceptions and the absence of any act of intelligence are the result (*Prairies d'or,* ch. VII, t. I, p. 164).

This argument does not satisfy the grave Ibn Khaldoun, who was too far removed from the times of the great Arab philosophers. Here is how the author of the *Histoire des Berbères* perceives the passages just cited:

Masoudi had undertaken research into the cause of this this light-mindedness, this carelessness and extreme inclination to cheerfulness, but the only solution he found was to mention the remark by Galen and al-Kendi, according to which this character is due to a weakness of the brain from whence would come a weakness of intelligence. This explanation is worthless and proves nothing . . . (*Prolegomenes,* p.176–77).

There are a number of pages of this type in the work of Devic, that is to say, among Arab authors of the Middle Ages, and even among those who came later. They contain explanations for these characteristics, for the planets that govern the destinies of the blacks, as well as all sorts of essays and proverbs.

Here is a summary of these pages. Among other things, the Zanj are: evil, "they surpass brute animals in their unfitness and their perverse natures"; cannibals, "there are among them tribes of men with sharp teeth who eat one another"; ugly, " . . . and they are so hideous and so ugly that they appear to be the most horrible thing in the world to see. The women of this island are the ugliest in the world"; idolaters, evil and cruel; they have soothsayers remarkable for their accuracy in predicting the future; most of the time they go naked; they are great fighters, "Without the deserts and the branch of the Nile that flows into the sea, which is a natural protection for the Abyssinian frontier, the Habacha, would not have been able to remain in their country because of the numerous and violent troops of these Negroes"; they go into combat mounted on oxen; they have themselves tattooed; they have their nose pierced for the very uncommon needs due to their manner of waging war among themselves; they venerate the Arabs; they eat various kinds of millet, maize, bananas, meat, honey; they adore dates, etc.

Their political organization is simple. They have a king, who is the chief of one or several tribes, and they wage war on another.

On the other hand we can find:

The Zanj are very eloquent, and have orators who address the people in their language. Often one of the country's religious men stands in the middle of a large crowd and urges them to make themselves pleasing to God and follow his commandments, pointing out to them the punishments to which their disobedience exposes them and, reminding them of the example of their ancestors and former kings. The Zanj have no religious code; their kings confine themselves to a few traditions which lay down certain obligations of the people towards their ruler, and a few rules that the prince must observe in regard to his subjects.[11]

In studying the objects of creative activity of the language, that-is-to-say the literary monuments, al-Jâhiz remains faithful to his comparative method which he considers indispensable in other cases (*Bayân,* II, 56). He knows the literature of other peoples, not only that of the Greeks and Persians, but also that of the Hindus and the Zanj.[12]

These passages must have referred above all to the Zanj in their country of origin because, as Devic emphasizes: "Besides the reason we have given for explaining the diversity of judgments concerning the Zanj, we must consider that some of the peoples of this name had undergone the civilizing influence of the Muslims settled on their coasts, while others continued to live in a savage state."

The Zanj in Arab Countries.—We know that blacks were much appreciated as slaves in Muslim countries. From time immemorial, they constituted a large part of the population and were to be found at every level of Islamic society. The Zanj were imported as slaves at an indeterminate date, and it is not at all easy to understand this importation phenomenon in a real-life situation without being faced with the disadvantage of the "particular case." F. al-Sâmir emphasizes that the slave trade was not of Arab origin and that it was well-known at the time of the pharaohs. He insists on having it conceded that the Arabs themselves did not capture the Zanj, but acquired them from tribal chiefs. There is no doubt that the slaves were acquired in different ways and that it is impossible to generalize as to just how they were obtained. That is why we prefer the opinion of Bernard Lewis, who flatly states, ". . . they were largely Negroes from East Africa, where they had been captured, bought or obtained from subject states as tribute."

As for just when the Zanj were introduced into Iraq, it is practically impossible to give anything close to an exact date. Devic believes that the Arabs had visited Zanguebar since the new era, and in any case, from the beginning of Islam. F. al-Sâmir suggests 720 as the date for the Muslim trading posts in East Africa, and the first century of the Hegira (622–722) for date of Arab arrival in Iraq. As we have seen, Charles Pellat more cautiously prefers "an indeterminate date." That seems to us the only plausible solution. If Arab historians report Zanj revolts in 70/689–90 and 75/694–5, which proves that the Zanj had arrived at an even earlier date, there is no doubt that the boats and caravans transporting them were still arriving in the period that interests us.[13]

Arab Opinions of the Zanj.—In a preceding section (characteristics and way of life), we dealt with the Zanj in their land of origin. Now we turn to the opinions of medieval Arab authors on the Zanj in "Islamic country."

Before citing any author at all, we wish to direct attention to a certain number of points. First of all, we should eliminate the revolt and its consequences (all later judgments are known in advance); we must not forget that there are Zanj and Zanj, that some had been settled (and Islamized ?) for a century or more, and some had just arrived; we should never lose sight of their condition of absolute physical and moral destitution; we must reflect on their transplantation from an archaic culture to civilization, and on the language barrier; finally, we must not forget that, if there are no Zanj who are not black, there are many blacks who are not Zanj.

We have already said that the Zanj were highly valued as rural labor; on the other hand, they were considered to have many flaws.[14] According to a common proverb: "The hungry Zanj steals; the sated Zanj rapes"; the

Zanj was, as we would say today, stereotyped: he is stupid; he is cheerful for no apparent reason; he is a thief; he does not speak Arabic[15]; he has no memory; he is the cheapest slave in the market, etc. . . . [16]

Two passages from al-Jâhiz summarize the general opinion, which emerges from the texts:

> We know that the Zanj are the least intelligent of men, the least discerning, and the least concerned with the future. If their generosity came only from their lack of intellect and intelligence, and knowledge, it would be agreed that the Persians were greedier than the Byzantines . . .
>
> . . . He was in the habit of saying, 'I have never eaten dates with pleasure, except in the company of the Zanj and the people of Esfahan. The Negro does not choose, while I choose; as for the inhabitant of Esfahan, he takes a handful and finishes it before touching any other dates.

Few texts are favorable to them. Ahmad Amîn's attempt to group together complimentary descriptions of them concerns only a few actual or presumed individual Zanj. As for the famous treatise by al-Jâhiz,[17] Charles Pellat is definite: "Al-Jâhiz mentions them often but certainly did not have them in mind when he was writing his letter on the merits of the blacks."[18]

It must be pointed out that "racism," as the term is understood today, was never an important factor in the Muslim world of the Middle Ages. From time to time, there might be violent eruptions against unassimilable groups, such as the despised and mistreated Zutt and Zanj, but if for no reason other than the occurrence of significant intermixing among the populations, we can say that racial separation, in the strict sense, did not exist.

> Some Arabs displayed loathing for the Zanj. Taous al-Yemani, who was a lieutenant of Abdallah, son of Abbâs, refused to eat the meat of any animal killed by a Zanj, in his words, a hideous slave; and the Caliph Rhadi Billah (d. 940), son of al-Moktadir, shared this

aversion to such an extent that he would accept nothing from a black man's hand. Nevertheless, there were undoubtedly special reasons for these feelings since, in general, the Arabs harbor no sentiments of repugnance for Negroes.[19]

Be that as it may, the conditions of Zanj slaves in Iraq were wretched, and there were two uprisings before the great revolt.

The Insurrection of 70/689–90.—A first uprising occurred under the government of Halid Mus'ab b. al-Zubayr (governor of Iraq for the Umayyads). For the most part, it involved small gangs engaged in pillage and is of little importance. The government's army broke them up easily, beheading the prisoners taken and hanging their corpses on the gibbet. F. al-Sâmir, in speaking of this revolt, points out that in this early period the Zanj were already living under appalling social conditions.

The Insurrection of 75/694.—The second revolt seems to have been more important and, above all, better prepared. The Zanj had a leader, the Lion of the Zanj, and the authorities were obliged to undertake two operations to crush them. This revolt was more complicated than the first, but we have very little information about it:

> . . . A few years later, in 75/694–5, thanks to a revolt led by 'Abd Allâh ibn al-Jârûd, against al-Hajjâj (celebrated Umayyad governor), a large number of Zanj chose a certain Rabâh (Riyâh?), known as Shîr Zanjî (Lion of the Zanj) to be their leader and revolted. They even defeated a troop that was sent against them, and it was not until Ibn al-Jârûd's rebellion was suppressed that al-Hajjâj succeeded in reestablishing order . . . The true nature of this movement cannot be determined from the information we have; it would seem that it did not break out spontaneously and that the Zanj had been stirred up by propaganda, but the movement was short-lived because almost two centuries passed before the Zanj were heard from again.[20] Not without interest on this subject, [adds the author in a note] are the lines

of a maulâ (client or freed slave) of the qurayshite tribe of the Banû
Sâma ibn Lu'ayy, named Sulaih ibn Riyâh in which he praises the
Negroes and mentions a certain number of sons of Negro women
such as Ziyâd ibn 'Amr al-'Atakî and 'Abd Allâh ibn Khâzim
as-Sulamî. These lines would have been composed after the first
revolt . . .

*Other References to the Zanj in Muslim History before the Great
Revolt of 255/869.*—Apart from the two early insurrections and without
mentioning texts concerning true or false Zanj personalities, historical
sources record only an incident in 132/749–50. Under 'Abû l-'Abbâs al-
Saffâh's caliphate, a government force of four-thousand men strong was
sent to put down an uprising of the inhabitants of al-Mawsil (present-day
Mosoul, Iraqui city in northern Mesopotamia). It distinguished itself by
its fierceness and massacred, it was said, more than ten-thousand people,
men, women, and children.

The Huge Spawning Grounds of the Revolt.—Our information about
the sites on which the Zanj worked is very limited. Everything that has
been written on the subject is based on a few bits of information found in
the work of al-Tabarî (a great Arab historian, 838–923, who lived at the
time of the revolt) and on a passage from *Kitâb al-'Uyûn.* (By al-
Qayrawânî, Arab author of the eleventh and twelfth centuries).

> According to Tabarî, our principal source, the rebels were
> employed as laborers (*kassâhîn*) to prepare land of Lower-
> Mesopotamia, removing the *sebâkh* and piling it in mounds, so that
> the nitrous lands of the Shatt al-'Arab could be cultivated.[21]
> . . . They were recruited from among imported Negro slaves and
> local peasants, and grouped in camps of 500 to 5,000 workers,
> packed in without family or hope, given a few handfuls of flour,
> semolina and dates as their only food. From contact with the Islam
> of their masters, these wretches learned through the phenomenon of
> spiritual induction that they had a right to existence and minimum

justice; the influence of Muslim religious from the neighboring hermitages of 'Abbâdân (city southwest of Basra, not far from the sea) perhaps had something to do with it.[22]

These work camps were reportedly located at Furât al-Basra and on the other side of the Dujayl. It is generally believed that they were east of Basra and part of a small section of Khûzistân. Given the number of slaves employed on them, they must have been very large, and only rich persons or wealthy merchants are thought to have owned such camps.[23] The number of slaves they employed was certainly very large; al-Tabarî's figure of fifteen thousand has been repeated by other historians, but it is obvious that no figures can be verified. As already mentioned the labor in these camps was composed of Zanj and other blacks, of different names, from other regions,[24] including probably a certain number of peasants. The task was to remove the crust of natron from the surface of the land, take it away on mules, and pile it in heaps "as large as mountains." It was hard work, and overseers appointed from among emancipated slaves, eager to justify their promotion, made it even more grueling.[25]

The situation is all the more striking since slavery in Islamic countries in the Middle Ages (contrary to slavery in Rome at the time of Spartacus) was essentially domestic servitude and not much employed for large rural projects. The conditions under which the Zanj slaves lived were unquestionably unusual for medieval Muslim society.

Basra's growth was a brief, intense crisis in the rise of Arabism, as studied by Ibn Khaldûn. Basra was destined to furnish the first example of the destructive social crisis of the city in Islam, when social restraints were broken, when usury, indirect taxes, government borrowing were rampant, and the opposition was exasperated by the luxury of the wealthy; slaves for luxury and luxuriousness, expensive clothes and jewelry, African ivory, pearls from the Gulf, precious wood from India made a mockery of the working proletariat's misery on the plantations (canonically, the lands of Basra were 'amwât' ('dead lands'), under their original crust of unproductive natron or *sebâkh*), 'revived' by the coolie labor of Zanj, kassâhîn, shûrjîyîn, who were refused their claim to freedom following their conversion. In the third century of the hegira, while in other Muslim cities, the social crisis was only among large bourgeois corporations and the small craftsmen of the guilds, between 'hostile gangs' of financiers carving up the latifundia, and serfs of the land ambitious to become landowners, in Basra it ended in a fight to the death between the privileged elite of the City that wanted everything for itself, and the starved proletariat of the plantations and sand-filled oases who pounced on the City to destroy it. Babel, which was alive as long as it was a place where the exogamous exchange of values and language was carried on, became Sodom, and burned.[26]

III. THE PERIOD

There will be no attempt to present here a complete picture of the Abbasid Caliphate's situation in the middle of the ninth century. Nevertheless it is imperative that we say a few words about this period which has been referred to as "the beginning of the Caliphate's dislocation" and which gradually facilitated the growth and duration of "the Negro State." In no way is this meant to detract from 'Alî b. Muhammad's qualities as a revolutionary or from the fighting spirit of his troops.

For some time the Caliphs' authority had been steadily declining to the advantage of local governors, who were often only theoretically under their control. In several cases these governors broke away completely from the central power, creating new states and dynasties. Financial disorder, already present, grew worse. New military leaders (who, like their troops, were of Turkish origin), became more and more powerful. They controlled the ruler's court and the city, appointiing and deposing caliphs at will. In the nine years following al-Mutawakkil's murder (247/861), four caliphs succeeded one another, and all were powerless in the hands of their Turkish guards. Things did not change until the succession of al-Mu'tamid, whose brother al-Muwaffaq, the real master of the empire, restored the central government's authority somewhat. Thus, during the period that interests us, the caliphate found itself grappling with problems both in its own capital and in its provinces.

Discontent in the Capital.—Malaise in the capital was brought about by the court and its spending, despite the financial chaos and, above all, the internecine struggle between three groups at the head of the empire: "the mostly Arab dogmatic, juridical and legislative element of the ulemâs and qâdis, the mostly Persian administrative element of civil servants of the dawâwîn (ministerial offices) and the mostly Turkish military element of the leaders of the jond (the army)."

As for the civil servants:

> In the hands of clever leaders, the Shi'ism of the Imâmiyah (the majority of the Shiites, who recognize the twelve legitimate imams) had become a first-rate trump card, which they used against the government. If they were threatened with disgrace, to the advantage of Arab or Turkish officials, they cited the divine right of the 'Alids (descendants of 'Alî, cousin and son-in-law of the Prophet Muhammad). And as soon as the leader of a party, above all an 'Alid, undertook to change the social order to ensure that justice would be more prevalent, they sided with the government against him (cf. their historians' bias against the leader of the revolt of the Zinj . . .).

Other problems were presented by the army which found it difficult to recruit and, above all, keep troops because the caliphs were hard pressed to pay them. Then there was the almost unlimited power of the Turkish generals over recruits who, having no other attachment, obeyed and supported their respective chiefs in their intrigues and conflicts, sometimes to such degree that the activities of war were rendered ineffective.

The Provinces.—In the provinces controlled by governors who were nearly or completely independent, it was clearly the economic situation that prepared the ground for disturbances and upheaval. Determining just what the economic situation was like at any given moment, in any precise region, during the Muslim Middle Ages, is extremely difficult. However, for the period and region that interest us, we can indicate specifically rural impoverishment and peasant suffering. Moreover, for the nomads (Bedouins), banditry became a "complementary industry," and there were people in the cities who had everything to gain and little to lose in the turmoil. It is not difficult to imagine here the sort of solidarity that occurs between various movements when they emerge and continues to unite them as long as they are likely to be successful. This has led certain authors to speak of a class struggle of the modern type, which is, to say the least, unwise.

Since a bad economic situation was made worse by anarchy and the disorder it caused and since the central government was powerless under the supervision of Turkish officers, a bad situation was made worse.

It is interesting to note how an Armenian historian would see this period three centuries later:

> Now I want to point out the signs of the race of Ismaelites' decline. At the time of their accession to the monarchy, the Bagritides (Armenian dynasty from the ninth to the eleventh centuries) ruled with their permission but occupied, nevertheless, a great part of the universe, not, however, under the single monarchy of the emir-chief, as from Mahomet to Djafar and to his sons, but by handing authority over to certain persons, according to their whims; which is a sign of the weakness and decline of power, with unity being replaced by the distribution [of power] among several [persons]. Sofar was the master of Khorasan; Alavic Abû-Thorab, of the city of Basra; Isé, son of Sheikh, of Palestine; the sons of Abel Touph of Dilem (Daylam, region in western Iran, near the Caspian Sea) and others, of other places. There were wars, constant attempts

by one to dominate the other by force, hence the disorder which prevents the accurate reporting of these ungodly tyrants' names.[27]

Naturally, this period of anarchy, which saw the break-up of the Caliphate confirmed, gave rise to all sorts of revolts. While Ya'qûb b. al-Layth the Saffârid (founder of the Saffârid dynasty, 863–902, that reigned over part of present-day Iran and Iraq) was overthrowing the Tahirid dynasty (Iranian dynasty reigning over Khurâsân, as vassals of the Caliphate of Baghdad, 820–873), while the Samanids (Iranian dynasty that reigned in Persia and Transoxiania, 874–999) were appearing in Transoxiania (region in Central Asia, to the west of the Oxus, that is to say of the Amu Darya river), and the Tulunids were detaching Egypt from the Abbasid Caliphate, the Kharijites (followers of 'Alî, the Prophet's son-in-law, who broke away from 'Alî and formed a puritanical sect) and the 'Alids were rising up in several places, and the Qarmates (members of a branch of the Ismaelian sect founded by Hamdân Qarmat in Iraq) were emerging.

The Saffarids, the Samanids, and the Tulunids on the one hand, the Kharijits and the various Alid pretenders on the other, continuous war against Byzantium and the emergence of the Qarmat movement, were all indirectly linked to the revolt of the Zanj.

Three of these many groups were of major importance to 'Alî b. Muhammad and his supporters. They were the Saffarid, the Tulunid, and the Qarmat movements.[28]

In spite of Ya'qûb b. Layth's rejection of 'Alî b. Muhammad's proposal for an alliance,[29] there is no question about the Saffarid contribution to the Zanj cause. Without speaking of the tacit and less important agreements between detachments of the two armies in Khûzistân,[30] we must remember that the central government's struggle against the Saffarids had constant repercussions on the war against the Zanj.[31] It was only when the Saffarid question was settled that al-Muwaffaq was able to undertake the large-scale operations that would eventually crush the revolt.

The advent of the Tulunids also contributed to the expansion of the Zanj rebellion. The contribution was indirect, but it created a situation beneficial to both parties. The Zanj profited from the fact that the central government was deprived of taxes from Egypt and Syria, which would have allowed it to assemble the troops necessary to combat them, and also from the fact that the central government was obliged to detach some of its troops to fight in Syria and even put them under the command of one of its best generals, Mûsâ b. Bugâ, who until then had been fighting the Zanj.[32] As for Ibn Tûlûn, he owed part of his success to the Zanj revolt.

Although the great Qarmat period did not begin until long after the Zanj had been crushed, these two movements were also of mutual benefit to one another.[33]

Slave masses living under inhuman conditions and ready to rise up, a terrain favorable to guerrilla warfare, a country shaken by anarchy in its central region and by serious problems in its distant provinces: all that was lacking was a leader capable of stirring up the Zanj and lighting the fire.

NOTES

1. Without mentioning a detachment in Mecca that was brought to our attention.
2. On several occasions Tabarî emphasizes that diseases were rampant in the Abbasid army.
3. Medieval Arab geographers often give the fantastic number of 120,000 (!) canals, just for the Basra region.
4. Let us also add Nahr Sayhan, Nahr al-Banat, and Nahr al-Murgab in the West; Nahr al-Mubarak in the East.
5. Natron or natrum, natural crystallized sodium carbonate.
6. "There has been a great deal of discussion about the origin of the *iqta‘* and more generally of various categories of land in Muslim countries. The discussions are shaky because we are forced to rely on texts from later jurists who were trying to fit institutions that began in obscurity into precise schema."

7. Charles Pellat (*Le milieu basrien*): ". . . as for d'Herbelot, he writes, 'most of its sectarians were Zenges, in other words, people who had been picked up and whom we call Bohemians'; and also: "In Arabic this word stands for the country that today we call Zanguebar or, oppositely, the coast of Cafrerie. The people who live there are also called Zengi in Arabic and Zenghi in Persian, from which is derived the word Zenghibar, which means the country of the Zenghis, who are exactly those whom the Italians call Zinghari and the rest of us Egyptians and Bohemians."

8. As far as the works that were not known in his time are concerned, they hardly improve matters for us: "Their territory, which is bordered on the east by the western regions of India and on the west by the sea, is spongy terrain which turns to dust. It produces nothing [agriculturally] and trees cannot grow there; the region imports food and clothing and exports gold, slaves, coconuts." (Maqdisî, *Le livre de la création*).

9. L. M. Devic to whom I refer for the country's products, its climate, and its flora and fauna.

10. L. M. Devic's note. This list should be completed by Maqdisî, which was not available to Devic: "The Zandjes have black skin, flat nose, kinky hair; they are not very intelligent and are slow-witted."

11. E. Quatremère.

12. I. Kratchkovsky.

13. Heinz Halm makes good arguments for situating the beginnings of this importation in the Sassanid epoch.

14. A witness to the raids (in 334/945) on the eastern coasts of Africa, reports the perpetrators' answer to the question, 'Why did you come here to find slaves?' "They replied that it was because this land contained merchandise that would be useful in their country and in China, such as ivory, tortoise shells, panther skins and amber, and because they wanted to get Zandjs, who were strong men suitable for hard labor." (G. Ferrand).

15. "As if one spoke Arabic to a Zendj" (Beidhaoui, Arab author of the thirteenth century, cited by Devic).

16. Let us mention how the Zanj appear in popular tales: in the Arabian Nights, they are cannibals (night 301) or servants of terrifying personages (night 765).

17. *Kitâb fakhr al-sûdân*.

18. Charles Pellat.

19. Louis Marcel Devic.

20. Charles Pellat.

21. Loius Massignon.

22. Loius Massignon. The possibility that the cenobites of 'Abbâdân had an influence on the Zanj is a subtle question for which there is apparently no answer.

23. Nevertheless collective Soviet works emphasize "state lands," which our sources do

not indicate at all, quite the contrary. When Claude Cahen writes: "In Iraq the Abbasids and the great merchants of Baghdad and of Basra owned huge estates . . . ," he is obviously thinking of members of the ruling family and of the regime's high officials who were in a position to obtain these vast domains or receive them as gifts, and exploit them to their own advantage.

24. Muwaffaq was wounded in 269/882 by a Byzantine slave named Qirtâs.

25. At the beginning the revolt was turned against them and their masters, who were violently reproached by 'Alî b. Muhammad.

26. Louis Massignon.

27. Samouel d'Ani.

28. It might also be added that, if we follow closely the incessant wars with Byzantium, we will realize that the troops of Basil I won important victories in Cappadocia (central region of Asia Minor, i.e., of Anatolia) and around Melitene (an ancient city that was on the upper Euphrates) at the exact moment of the Zanj revolt. We can assume that this was an added concern for the central power.

29. We will return to this putative correspondence on several occasions.

30. See the chapters that follow which retrace the events in chronological order.

31. With mutual benefit to the two rebel parties.

32. Without mentioning Caliph al-Mu'tamid's famous attempt to escape which we will also mention again.

33. In the chapters that follow, we will return to this and particularly to the famous proposal for an alliance that Hamdân Qarmat is supposed to have made to 'Alî b. Muhammad.

CHAPTER II

'Alî b. Muhammad

We know little about the life of 'Alî b. Muhammad, the man who insti-
gated the revolt of the Zanj. Only a few phrases dealing with his birth,
parents, and family have come down to us. There is even less information
on the period he spent at the court of Samârrâ (city of Iraq on the left bank
of the Tigris, north of Baghdad). There are a few more details, but still
they are insufficient to allow us to make a definitive statement about his
sojourns in Bahrayn, Basra, and Baghdad. Even for the periods covered
by pages and pages devoted to his exploits in war, we have only frag-
mentary information or disparate details. Tabarî's nine pages and a passage in Safadî's work represent just about all we know about the person
responsible for the Zanj uprising.

'Alî b. Muhammad's Birth, His Name, His Parents, His Ancestors.—
The leader of the Zanj was apparently born in a village in the vicinity of
al-Rayy[1] called Warzanîn.[2] His true name was probably 'Alî b.
Muhammad b. 'Abd al-Rahîm,[3] and he would have been of the tribe of
'Abd al-Qays. There are two different versions of his parental back-
ground, but the one that is known and that later historians have repeated
is from Tabarî.

His mother's name was Qurra bint 'Alî b. Rahîb b. Muhammad b.
Hakîm. She was of the Banû Asad b. Khuzayma tribe and lived in
Warzanîn, where he was born and grew up. It has been recorded that, in
speaking of his family, he maintained that his maternal grandfather,
Muhammad b. Hakîm, lived in the town of Kûfa. With Zayd b. 'Alî b. al-

Husayn, he was a member of the Kharijites against Hishâm b. 'Abd al-Malik. When Zayd died, Muhammad fled Iraq and went to al-Rayy, where he settled in Warzanîn.

'Alî's paternal grandfather, 'Abd al-Rahîm, was of the 'Abd al-Qays tribe. Born in al-Tâliqân (Tâlaqân?),[4] he settled in Iraq and bought a Sindian slave. The son she bore him named Muhammad would be our 'Alî's father.

Safadî's version is much longer and disagrees with the one above:

> His mother, Qurra bint 'Abd al-Wâhid b. Muhammad al-Shâmî, recounted that her father went on the pilgrimage every year and passed through Medina where he stayed with a shaykh of Abû Talib's family who received him with honor and respect and to whom he brought gifts from Rayy every year. One year when he went on the pilgrimage carrying his gifts, the shaykh's son, Muhammad (future) father of 'Alî, was (then) ten years old, the shaykh was dead when my father arrived and only his son was left to receive my father as best he could. My father suggested that he come with him, but he refused, saying: 'My father and my sister prevent me from doing so.' My father continued on the pilgrimage and on his return found them dead (both of them), he (then) brought Muhammad back to the village of Warzanîn with him and suggested that he marry me. At first he refused saying: 'In a dream I saw myself urinating, and my urine burned half the world'; (after the dream) my father forbade me to marry him.[5] Nevertheless, he did marry me later, and I bore him two daughters who died at an early age. My father died. Then I brought 'Alî b. Muhammad into the world. After that Muhammad ['Alî's father] spent my fortune and squandered it and I separated from him because of a slave he had bought. Then he left me and took his son with him and for several years I had no news of them. Then my child came back and told me of his father's death. For a certain period, he stayed with me in Rayy and endlessly pursued everyone who knew the *adab* (necessary general culture) and the *riwâya* (the traditions, the 'narratives'), after that he left for Khurâsân and was away two or three years. He

returned, (again) stayed a little while, then left again and disappeared. (It was during this absence) that I received a letter from him from Basra, telling me what he had become and that he possessed wealth, but I did not believe (this news) because of what I knew about him, for sure.

'Alî, Master of the Zanj states: 'When I was young, I was stricken by a serious illness. My father came to visit me and found my mother sitting at my bedside. She said to him, "He is going to die." He replied, "If he dies who will lay waste to Basra?" That remained engraved in my heart (mind) until the moment I rebelled there.'

The Sojourn in Samârrâ.—After having spent his childhood in Warzanîn,[6] 'Alî b. Muhammad went to Samârrâ where he became poet (panegyrist) at the court of Caliph al-Muntasir (861–862). There he was in contact with people attached to the Caliph's family and with, among others, Gânim al-Shatranjî, Sa'îd al-Sagîr and Yusr al-Khâdim. He earned a living in the capital from his poetry and from teaching children the art of writing, grammar, and astronomy.[7]

The Sojourn in Bahrayn.—In 249/863–864, he left Samârrâ for Bahrayn, where he claimed to be an 'Alid with the following genealogy: 'Alî b. Muhammad b. al-Fadl b. al-Hasan b. 'Ubayd Allâh b. al-'Abbâs b. 'Alî b. Abî Tâlib.[8]

It was at Hajar that he began his movement by asking the residents of the town to follow him. Some of the population joined him, and some would not. Relations between the two factions became acrimonious, causing many deaths in both camps. Following these events, 'Alî b. Muhammad left Hajâr for al-Ahsâ' and went first to the tribe of Banû Tamîm, then to the Banû Sa'd, of the Banû Shammâs branch, among whom, it is said, he was considered such a prophet that the population paid taxes to him.[9]

He exercised great influence over the population and succeeded in stirring up some of the people against the Caliphate's forces. Not everyone approved of his actions, however, so he changed his location again and went into the desert with his most loyal supporters. Among those who accompanied him were a measurer of grains from al-Ahsâ', named Yahyâ b. Muhammad al-Azraq known by the nickname al-Bahrânî (who was a *mawla*, a client, an emancipated man), from the Banû Dârim;[10] a merchant from Hajar, Yahyâ b. Abî Tha'lab; and finally a black man, a *mawla*, from the Banû Hanzala[11] named Sulaymân b. Jâmi'. They went from one tribe to another in the desert. 'Alî b. Muhammad claimed to have received supernatural revelations in the form of verses of the Qur'an. He did not know how he had learned them, but they rolled off his tongue straight-away; and while he was complaining about the laxness of the desert's inhabitants, he heard a voice from heaven, in the thunder, ordering him to go to Basra.[12]

It is said that, on arriving in the desert, he claimed to be Yahyâ b. 'Umar Abû l-Husayn.[13] With desert-dwellers who joined him, he pushed on to al-Radm, where he was defeated and a great number of his followers were killed. At this juncture, the Bedouins with him withdrew and fled. In 254/868, he returned to Iraq and went to Basra.

We have scant information on the five years he spent in Bahrayn.

Bernard Lewis writes: "after a first attempt to win support in Bahrayn where he would have had family connections. . . . " He also says: "after several aborted attempts at sedition in different places . . . . " Faysal al-Sâmir's statements contribute nothing new. This is even more the case since they ignore a passage from Mas'ûdî that went completely unnoticed by Arab authors (except for A. Olabi), but which was already known to de Goeje.

As a matter of fact, speaking of the cities of al-Bahrayn, Mas'ûdî writes: "Al-Zahrân and al-Hasâ, residences of the Temimite tribe of Sa'd;—al-Juwata, placed under the command of al-'Uryân, son of al-Haytham the Rebiite. It is from him that we hear of the leader of the black slaves, 'Alî, son of Muhammad, who revolted in the province of Basra, and who, in a poem composed at the moment he took up arms in the Bahrayn at the head of Temimite, Kilâbite, Numayrite, and other tribes, before going to Basra, claimed to be a descendant of Abû Tâlib. With the tribes of 'Abd al-Qays, of 'Âmir son of Sa'sa'a, of Muhârib, son of Khasafa, son of Qays, son of Aylân and others, al-'Uryân had attacked him; after several battles, he had forced him to leave Bahrayn and the vicinity, having inflicted great loses on him. In Sammân, 'Alî b. Muhammad had noticed a little bird and had written a poem that begins as follows:

> Oh, bird of Sammân, what are you doing there all alone? Did you come to find consolation near me, or did an accident separate you from your friend?

During this piece, he says:

> May my noble horses be taken from me if I do not bring them back (to Bahrayn) mounted by armored horsemen of noble race;
> Mounted by the men of Temîm headed by the glorious, valiant men of Kulayb, son of Yarbû';
> Sa'd forming the center; Numayr and the excellent swords of Kilâb on the flanks!
> If no accident prevents me, I will surprise 'Âmir and Muhârib in the morning with a blow that will smash them.
> Does 'Uryân think that I forget my horsemen who fell on the day of the attack near the dike, when death hung from them?

In another piece, the same poet, speaking of 'Abd al-Qays's tribe, says:

> Does 'Abd al-Qays think that I have forgotten him? I will never forget him and I will not renounce my vengeance.

De Goeje speaks of this passage and draws conclusions above all about the Qarmats, which takes us away from the subject. W. Caskel summarizes the period: "During the year 249–254 (863–868), an 'Alid or a pseudo 'Alid rebelled in Bahrayn. He tried his luck first in Hadjar then with the Sa'd in al-Ahsâ'. Finally, he went to the desert and gathered an army of Tamîm and tribes recently arrived from the West. Al-'Uryân and other 'Abd al-Qays princes had difficulty driving away the rebel who, before long, would set in motion the great Zanj revolt in Basra."

The First Sojourn in Basra.—In Basra, he stayed with the Banû Dubay'a. Some of the tribe, among whom were 'Alî b. Abân al-Muhallabî (who will be mentioned a great deal in the pages that follow) and his two brothers, Muhammad and Halîl, rallied to him.

At this time the city was in turmoil because of the struggle between two tribal groups: the Balâlites and the Sa'dites. In an attempt to draw one of the parties into his camp, 'Alî b. Muhammad sent four of his men—Muhammad b. Salm al-Qassâb al-Hajarî, Buraysh al-Quray'î, 'Alî al-Darrâb, and Husayn al-Saydanânî, all faithful supporters since Bahrayn—to preach in front of the 'Abbâd mosque. Their mission was unsuccessful, and the governor of the city, Muhammad b. Rajâ al-Hidârî, drove them out.[14]

Accompanied by Muhammad b. Salm, Yahyâ b. Muhammad, Sulaymân b. Jâmi', and Buraysh al-Quray'î, 'Alî b. Muhammad left the city and fled to Baghdad. His supporters in Basra, people who had joined his ranks and certain members of his family, were thrown into prison on orders from the governor. Among his companions who were jailed were Yahyâ b. Abî Tha'lab and Muhammad b. al-Hasan al-Iyâdî. Members of his household who were imprisoned included his wife, his oldest son, his daughter, and her servant.

The Sojourn in Baghdad.—The fugitives were captured while crossing al-Batîha and taken before the governor of Wâsit, Muhammad b. Abî 'Awn. 'Alî b. Muhammad managed to extricate himself and his men from their precarious situation, and he went on to Baghdad where they remained for a year.[15] At that time, he was claiming to be a descendant of Ahmad b. 'Isâ b. Zayd. In addition, he again invoked the supernatural: he claimed to know what every one of his men was doing and thinking and to have received a message that was written automatically on a wall, in handwriting that was invisible.

During his stay in Baghdad, his supporters increased in numbers. Among his new supporters were Ja'far b. Muhammad al-Sûhânî, Muhammad b. al-Qâsim, and two of Yahyâ b. 'Abd al-Rahmân b. Khaqân's *gulâm* (young servants or freed slaves) named Mushriq and Rafîq. To Mushriq, 'Alî b. Muhammad gave the name Hamza Abû Ahmad, and to Rafîq that of Ja'far Abû al-Fadl.

Return to the Basra Region.—Meanwhile, Muhammad b. Rajâ, who had been dismissed as governor of Basra, left the city. Anarchy and disturbances broke out immediately thanks to the Balâlite and Sa'dite agitators who opened the doors of the prisons and freed the inmates. As soon as he learned of this, 'Alî b. Muhammad returned to the Basra region. This was in the month *Ramadân* 255/August–September 869, and among the supporters who accompanied him were 'Alî b. Abân al-Muhallabî (who had joined the ranks during the time in Baghdad), Yahyâ b. Muhammad, Muhammad b. Salm, Sulaymân b. Jâmi', Mushriq, Rafîq, and a deserter from the army named Abû Ya'qûb who took the name Jurbân. When they arrived at Furât al-Basra, they settled at Qasr al-Qurashî, located at Bi'r Nakhl[16] on the 'Amûd b. al-Munajjim Canal, in the saltpeter region. Now, 'Alî b. Muhammad passed himself off as a business man from a princely family and the manager of a *sabâkh* sale for one of al-Wâthiq's children. This brought him into close contact with the Zanj, and he began preparing the uprising.[17]

The first person in the region to join him was a man named Rayhân b. Sâlih. While engaged in his usual work transporting flour from Basra for distribution to the Zanj laborers in the area, he was captured near Bi'r

Nakhl and taken to 'Alî b. Muhammad who questioned him about the situation in the city. He was unable to provide the rebel leader with any information. 'Alî b. Muhammad then asked him about the workers in the saltpeter sites; he wanted to know how they were fed. He urged Rayhân to speak to the workers on his behalf and promised him a good reward and command of any he succeeded in recruiting. After having sworn to return and not to reveal to anyone 'Alî b. Muhammad's whereabouts, Rayhân was allowed to continue on his way. When he had made his delivery, he returned to 'Alî b. Muhammad and became one of his followers.

Rafîq, whom 'Alî b. Muhammad had sent to Basra, returned accompanied by a *dibs*[18] merchant named Shibl b. Sâlim. He also brought with him the silk that 'Alî b. Muhammad had ordered him to purchase to make a flag. It was to be inscribed in red and green letters,[19] with an entire verse from the Qur'an, beginning with: "Allâh purchased from believers their persons and their possessions, in exchange for a gift from the Garden. They fight in the path of Allâh. . . . ."[20] 'Alî's name and that of his father were also inscribed on the flag.

Proclamation of the Revolt.—The revolt was probably declared on Wednesday, 26 *Ramadân* 255/September 7, 869. Rebels intercepted a group of fifty slaves who were on their way to work. After binding the leader hand and foot, they went on to another work site where they did the same thing. Five-hundred slaves, including a certain Abû Hudayd, are reported to have joined them, then another 150 slaves, among whom were Zurayq and Abû l-Hanjar, and yet another 80 slaves, among whom were Râshid al-Magribî (Mugrabî?) and Râshid al-Qurmatî.[21] Such occurrences were constantly repeated, and the ranks of the insurgents continued to grow.

In due time, 'Alî b. Muhammad called together and addressed all of the men who had joined his cause. After promising them improvement in their conditions with much wealth, he solemnly swore that he would never deceive them or fail to support them.

Turning towards the slaveholders, he reminded them that they deserved death for the way they had behaved towards their slaves and for doing things forbidden by God. They replied that the slaves would leave him before long and offered him money to return them. 'Alî b. Muhammad ordered the slaves to beat their masters and overseers, and when each had received 500 blows, he released them after making them take a solemn oath[22] not to reveal to anyone his whereabouts or the number of his troops. One of the slave owners crossed the Dujayl and went to warn the overseers of the large camps where 15,000 slaves were working.

As for 'Alî b. Muhammad, he left the region after the prayer of the 'asr. He crossed the Dujayl with his men and settled on Maymûn Canal. The mosque in the middle of the market overlooking the canal housed his headquarters.

At that time (middle of *Shawwâl* 255/September, 869), he was claiming to be 'Alî b. Muhammad b. Ahmad b. 'Alî b. 'Isâ b. Zayd b. 'Alî b. al-Husayn b. 'Alî b. Abî Talib.[23]

NOTES

1. The ruins of ancient al-Rayy are eight kilometers southwest of Teheran. It is because of where he was born that so many authors took him for a Persian. The fact that he spoke the language is not mentioned anywhere. As for his parents, true or fictitious, they were related to Arab tribes, even though they lived in the cities of Persia for a long time, more or less.

2. "A town in the vicinity of Rey that is as large as a city."

3. Safadî adds the name of the paternal great-grandfather: Ibn Rujayb. In a passage that has never been mentioned anywhere, Abû 'Alâ' al-Ma'arrî points out that before the revolt, he bore the name Ahmad and claimed to be of the 'Abd al-Qays tribe and that later, on attaching himself to the Anmâr tribe, he took the name 'Alî.

   Without speaking again of his genealogy (to which we will return in detail later), we point out that he is often called by other names: cf. Appendix I.

4. Tâliqân, considered to be the largest city of Tuhâristân, has retained its name

(Tâliqân) until today. It was the third of Balkh's sixteen cities.

5. According to H. Halm, it is a typical Iranian legend.

6. "He occupied himself with astrology, witchcraft, and astrolabes," adds Ibn Abî l-Hadîd.

7. Ibn Abî l-Hadîd, who copied Tabarî's text almost to the letter, pursues his commentary in a rather disturbing way. We must question whether or not the Tabarî text he used was different from the one we know today:

> "In Samârrâ, he taught handwriting, grammar, and astronomy. Eloquent, a superior mind, and a natural poet, he had written beautiful poems. Here are the opening verses of the poem that received a great deal of attention.
>
> It is a humiliating situation (to be forced) to live in frugality, accepting it all the while . . .
>
> If the fire becomes lessened because of too many logs,
>
> its progress will depend on their separation.
>
> If a saber remains in its sheath, another
>
> saber will be victorious on the day of combat."

This author cites a few more verses. In the *Fihrist* of Ibn al-Nadîm (an Arab author who wrote in 377/987–988), we also find another verse in the funeral oration of one of his officers. Here it is:

> When one of our heroes follows his mortal destiny,
>
> we expose another to the point of the swords.

Al-Husrî (Arab author of the eleventh century) cites still more verses, and even reports Ibn Durayd's (Arab philologist and lexicographer, 873–933) claim to have written these verses for 'Alî b. Muhammad! For everything concerning the Master of the Zanj's poetry, cf. *infra*, p. 199.

8. Ibn al-Athîr gives a slightly different genealogy, just as does Nuwayrî: 'Alî b. 'Abdallâh b. Muhammad, etc.; Faysal al-Sâmir lists several suppositions that explain his departure from Samârrâ and the choice of Bahrayn: the impossibility of organizing a revolt in the capital; Bahrayn is a province remote from the central government; family ties he might have had there; a milieu long known to be ripe for all sorts of revolts.

9. Safadî adds: "The inhabitants of al-Ahsâ' respected him to the point of not allowing scraps of his food to fall to the ground; they took them and sought (to obtain) blessing through them."

10. Banû Dârim: descendants of Dârim b. Mâlik b. Hanzala, part of the Arab Banû Tamîm tribe.

11. Banû Hanzala: part of the Banû Tamîm living in Basra.

12. "Making them believe that he knew the language of the birds; he and his partisans attacked, pillaged, and destroyed a Bahrayn port," adds Safadî.

13. "Killed in the al-Kûfa region during the reign of the Caliph al-Musta' in [862–866]," adds Ibn Abî l-Hadîd.

14. H. Halm has examined the information on this period in detail and, above all, the Master of the Zanj's coalitions with the Shiites and the names of his companions. He has been able to draw important conclusions which, according to him, substantiate the Shiite nature of the revolt on one hand and the almost exclusively *mawâlî* composition of 'Alî b. Muhammad's staff on the other.

15. "Attempting to attract the weavers and the riffraff," adds Safadî.

16. Mas'ûdî: "He revolted at Bi'r Nakhl (the well of the palm tree) between Medinet el-Fath and Kerkh Basra."

17. As we have seen, *supra,* p. 24, the Zanj were employed as workers to clear away the natron.

18. *Dibs*: more precisely *rob*, a syrup made from vegetable extracts and the depurative suc of cooked fruit, thickened to the consistency of honey.

19. In al-Qayrawânî's *Kitâb al-'Uyûn* manuscript, we read "red and yellow."

20. Qur'an, IX, 112.

21. "Perhaps associated with the emerging Qarmate propaganda," writes Louis Massignon. Faysal al-Sâmir seems to be right not to accept this supposition.

22. Of the repudiation of their favorite wife.

23. Years later, he changed his filiation again, relating himself to other ancestors. For different opinions on 'Alî b. Muhammad's genealogy, see Appendix II.

CHAPTER III

The Revolt and the Beginning of the War (Spread of the Insurrection)

There were two distinct periods in the Zanj revolt. The first (255–66/869–79) was the period of success and expansion. During this time, internal and external reasons prevented the central power from effectively suppressing the revolt. The second (266–70/879–83) was the slow agony before final defeat. In this period, the Caliphate made crushing the rebellion its chief order of business.

I. RIOT AGAINST NEIGHBORING VILLAGES AND "THE PEOPLE OF BASRA" (255/869)

At the beginning, the insurrection appeared to be totally local. Masses of slaves had been stirred up against their masters, and their chief priorities were food and weapons. Confronting them were villagers trying to protect their property and the large landowners of Basra who were determined to use every means possible to regain repossession of their slaves. In the ambushes and battles between slaves and freemen that ensued, the Zanj usually got the upper hand. One after the other, successive detachments sent out by "the people of Basra" were defeated and freed slaves swelled the ranks of the insurgents. The villages either surrendered or were sacked. Confused attempts were made to form coalitions against the rebels, but finally, just when a heavy offensive against them was on the

45

verge of success, the Master of the Zanj managed to turn imminent defeat into victory. The residents of Basra were terrified by the bloody debacle, and they wrote to the Caliph to appeal for help. Meanwhile, the Zanj set up their new camp.

Tabarî gives many details of these events, and it should be possible to form a precise idea of what was a short period (about a month and a half).[1] For reasons to be mentioned later, this is not the case.[2]

The First Battles.—Rebel headquarters were set up on Maymûn Canal. On the Fast Breaking Day in 255/September 869,[3] 'Alî b. Muhammad assembled his followers, whose numbers continued to grow, under the flag for prayer. In an address to them, he spoke of their miserable condition and assured them that God had chosen him to be the instrument of their deliverance. He also told them that he, 'Alî b. Muhammad, wanted to improve their lot so that one day they, too, might have beautiful homes and slaves. After the oath, and before leaving, he asked those who had understood to translate for anyone who did not speak Arabic.

Later, the rebels won their first significant victory. They defeated al-Himyarî and his men, and their ranks were swelled by three-hundred Zanj and their leader who rallied to their cause. Their numbers grew constantly. 'Ali b. Muhammad appointed officers and promised that any man they recruited would be assigned to them. Some authors claim that he did not name leaders until a little later, after the events in Bayân.[4]

A troop of four-thousand men attacked the rebels. The Zanj "army" was poorly equipped to fend them off with only three sabers in its arsenal. One rebel was seen dashing into battle carrying only his plate as a weapon. Nevertheless, the Zanj won another victory and put the enemy to flight. One member of the attacking force was killed; others died of thirst. On orders from 'Alî b. Muhammad, prisoners were beheaded. The Zanj carried away the severed heads on their own mules.[5]

On the way back from the encounter, one of the blacks was killed by a resident of the village of al-Qâdisîya. 'Alî b. Muhammad would not give his men permission to sack the village and look for the culprit. He wanted to find out to what extent all villagers had been involved in the murder and whether or not they supported the assassin. When the rebels returned to Maymûn, they stuck the severed enemy heads on pickets and put them on display.

The next day, the Zanj headed for al-Ja'farîya, a village on al-Sîb Canal. There was no violence as they crossed the territory of al-Karkh and Jubbâ, where they found shelter. A resident of Jubbâ offered 'Alî b. Muhammad a horse. At the time, the Master of the Zanj had neither saddle nor bridle, so he improvised with a cushion of palm-tree stuffing and a cord.[6] The Zanj entered Ja'farîya. The villagers had been warned of their imminent arrival and had already fled. The rebels took their first booty: 250 dinars, 1,000 dirhams, 3 horses, and many weapons.

The following day 'Alî b. Muhammad learned that an army under the joint command of three leaders, Rumays, al-Himyarî, and 'Aqîl was on its way to attack him. He sent 500 men, under Yahyâ b. Muhammad, against them. The Zanj won another victory, and seized weapons and a small boat. The next day 'Alî b. Muhammad signed a peace agreement with the inhabitants of al-Ja'farîya and then headed for al-Madhâr. Crossing al-Sîb, he encountered Rumays and his men in the village of al-Yahûd. In the battle that ensued, Rumays suffered a new defeat and considerable loses. The Zanj sank a small boat and beheaded its rower. They moved on to Jabal al-Shayâtîn where Rumays offered 'Alî b. Muhammad five dinars for each slave returned and promised to let the Master of the Zanj leave the territory without any difficulty. 'Alî b. Muhammad violently rejected the offer.

Ibrâhîm b. Ja'far al-Hamadânî joined the insurgents. The future general explained to 'Alî b. Muhammad why he thought that instead of going toward al-Madhâr, it would be preferable to march to the south of the Ahwâz, where the people were ready to accept him and the Balâlites were even waiting for him.[7]

Both Rumays' proposal and Ibrâhîm's words caused considerable unrest among the Zanj. Disturbances erupted and some men fled. 'Alî b. Muhammad reacted immediately. That very night he assembled his men and, through an interpreter, swore that none of them would ever be returned to their former masters. "May some of you remain with me and kill me if you feel that I am betraying you." Then he called together those who spoke Arabic[8] and solemnly promised to lead them in battle personally and risk his life with them. He assured them that it was not for the wealth and honor of this world that he had rebelled. The Zanj were calmed down by his words.

The next day, there were new and bloody battles on al-Sîb Canal. When 'Alî b. Muhammad met with the inhabitants of al-Ja'farîya[9] and attempted to avoid fighting by requesting safe passage from the villagers and reminding them of their peace agreement, they responded with stones and arrows. The Zanj killed several people in retaliation. The prisoners they took were reprimanded and then released. 'Alî b. Muhammad guaranteed the village that it would be protected and told his men that any pillaging would be punished. He engaged Rumays and his allies in battles, and his Zanj forces captured four small boats and their crew. From the prisoners he learned that Rumays and the others had been promised substantial rewards by the villagers and slave owners. After inquiring about two of his own men, he ordered all the prisoners, except one, decapitated, the boats put to the torch, and the flags and severed heads removed.

The Zanj were well received by the residents of the Banû 'Ijl village and again by inhabitants of al-Karkh. 'Alî b. Muhammad spent the night in conversation with a Jew who claimed to have found a passage about him in the Torah. At the time wine was not forbidden in the army.

According to one inhabitant of al-Karkh, a large enemy army was coming their way. It would bar 'Alî b. Muhammad's path across the bridge over al-Maymûn Canal and make it impossible for him to return to his

camp. The hostile force consisted of Rumays, leading inhabitants of al-
Maftah and neighboring villages; 'Aqîl, (accompanied by people from al-
Ubulla); so-called al-Dabîlâ (a people of Dravidian origin, the original
population of India)· and al-Himyarî (one of the commanders of anti-Zanj
forces) with people from al-Furât. 'Alî b. Muhammad checked their positions and prepared an ambush in which many of the enemy were killed.
The twenty-two prisoners taken were decapitated and their heads kept, as
was the custom. With the help of a man who knew the area, the Zanj
crossed the river and returned to their camp, where they displayed the severed heads on pickets.

Rumays pursued the Zanj. Informed of the situaton by spies, 'Alî b.
Muhammad sent a thousand men against the pursuers and wrote to 'Aqîl,
reminding him of the peace agreement signed with the inhabitants of al-
Ubulla.[10] He also reminded Rumays of the agreement they had entered
into at al-Sîb Canal.

From their camp on Maymûn Canal, the Zanj headed in the direction
of their vanguard. Along the way, 'Alî b. Muhammad gave orders to sack
the villages of al-Qâdisîya and al-Shifîyâ because they had refused to
hand over the man who had previously killed one of his soldiers. The villages were sacked and the inhabitants placed in captivity.[11] The assassin
was beheaded. 'Alî b. Muhammad stopped the Zanj troops when they
began drinking the wine looted from al-Qâdisîya and reminded them that
they still had battles to fight.

Rumays' and 'Aqîl's men established a foothold on the left bank of the
Dujayl, and the Dabîlâ boats occupied the river. 'Alî b. Muhammad prepared for battle by drawing up his troops and consulting an astrolabe.
When his Zanj troops attacked, they were victorious; a great number of
their opponents were killed; others fled without looking back. Enemy
boats blown closer to the shore by the wind were seized and their occu-
pants massacred. A reward of one dinar and command of a one-hundred-
man troop of blacks was promised to any one of 'Alî b. Muhammad's men

for killing a Dabîlâ survivor who had hidden on a boat during the pillage. Two rowers from a captured boat said they had been forced to fight the Zanj; the Dabîlâ, on the other hand, were lured by 'Aqîl's promises of booty. The rebels looted and burned Rumays' abandoned boats and they set fire to the village of al-Muhallabiyya, on al-Mâdiyân Canal, as well as the large quantities of dates found in the region.

At Sûq al-Rayyân,[12] the Turk Abû Hilâl marched against the Zanj with four-thousand men,[13] preceded by a group of people with flags and drums (trumpets). Armed with clubs, the Zanj bludgeoned and chased the vanguard, then fell on Abû Hilâl's soldiers and massacred about fifteen hundred of them. Prisoners were taken and were put to death.

A certain Sayrân, one of 'Alî b. Muhammad's agents in Basra, joined him with messages from supporters there. When questioned about the situation in the city, he reported that Abû Mansûr was leading a large army against the Zanj. During the questioning, 'Alî b. Muhammad asked him to lower his voice lest his words frighten the men. He moved his forces closer to the enemy. Then he sent out a detachment that routed Abû Mansûr's army and seized one-hundred blacks found among them. The Zanj next attacked nineteen-hundred boats that were carrying pilgrims. All of the volunteer crews fled; the pilgrims and the boats were taken to 'Alî b. Muhammad. The Master of the Zanj entered into a long discussion with the pilgrims which ended when the travelers declared that they were convinced by his arguments and almost ready to join him. The next day, 'Alî b. Muhammad made them take an oath not to reveal the size of his force to anyone. The pilgrims presented him with a rug, and he offered them his in exchange. He also made them swear that they were not transporting "goods belonging to the State." A man accused of doing so swore to the contrary and was shown clemency. The pilgrims were finally released and allowed to continue on their journey.

A supporter of long-standing, Husayn al-Saydanânî, informed 'Alî b. Muhammad that serious conflict had broken out between villagers and the soldiers of a large enemy army[14] when it passed through al-Ubulla on its way to Bayan. The next day 'Alî b. Muhammad sent out a scout, posted his men, obtained information about the tide, and drew up a battle plan. At first the battle was indecisive. One Zanj officer and two enemy commanders were killed. Abû b. Abbân brought the severed heads of the foe to 'Alî b. Muhammad, claiming that he had killed the commanders with his own hands, but there are several versions of what took place. In the end, it was a complete rout for the enemy forces. The Zanj gave chase to the enemy and massacred them in the mud from the ebbing river. One of the rebels was inadvertently wounded by his fellow soldiers; 'Alî b. Muhammad gave orders to care for him. Boats laden with cargoes of cattle (beasts of burden) were seized and the rebels gave chase on both banks of the Sharîkân Canal, until they were ambushed by a thousand men lying in wait with their prisoner, Husayn al-Saydanânî, whom they beheaded as the blacks approached. Fighting raged until noon, when the Zanj finally won. More than thirty flags and a thousand severed heads were taken to 'Alî b. Muhammad. In addition, a man who was recognized as an enemy officer was beheaded.[15]

Ibn Abî 'Awn asked 'Alî b. Muhammad to cross Bayân and leave his province; for his part, he would see to it that boats in the way were removed to facilitate the operation. The Master of the Zanj ordered his men to seize boats coming from Jubbâ that would make the crossing. Two-hundred boats loaded with flour, clothing, and *brrknât* (?) were seized at Sulbân where the insurrectionists also found about ten Zanj. 'Alî b. Muhammad and his men boarded the boats, and the flow of the river helped them to reach the mouth of al-Qindal Canal. One of the boats carrying flour was blown off course by the wind. The next day Abû Dulaf,[16] who was in charge of the craft, complained to 'Alî b. Muhammad about the behavior of the people at the place where his boat ran aground. In spite of it all, fifty blacks had rallied to the Zanj.

'Alî b. Muhammad took his men to al-Mu'allâ b. Ayyûb's village. On their return from an expedition, they brought back three-hundred blacks and al-Mu'allâ b. Ayyûb's *wakîl* (steward) found in the area. Complying with a request from 'Alî b. Muhammad, the *wakîl* left the Zanj camp to find money for the rebel forces, but he never returned. When 'Alî b. Muhammad realized that the *wakîl* was not coming back, he ordered the village sacked. According to an insurgent named Rayhân, he and 'Alî b. Muhammad quarreled over a *jubba* (a man's dress) during the pillage. Zanj forces later captured al-Zaynabî's garrison, which was on the right bank of al-Qindal Canal and guarded by two-hundred men, many of whom were killed during the siege. The Zanj spent the night in the garrison.

The next day, the rebels pillaged the village of Mundhirân, where they found many Zanj. The blacks rallied to the rebel cause, and 'Alî b. Muhammad divided them among his officers. Boats headed for Dubbâ were captured next, and some claim that it was only at this point that 'Alî b. Muhammad appointed commanders of his rebel army.

A native of Basra, a certain Muhammad b. Ja'far al-Muraydî, was found in the area and taken to 'Alî b. Muhammad, who questioned him about the Balâlites. He claimed that they were interested in knowing the conditions for joining the insurgents. 'Alî b. Muhammad gave al-Muraydî assurances of goodwill and an escort as far as al-Fayyâd. After waiting four days for the Basrian to return, he inspected the region himself and noticed a group of more than six-hundred Bedouin horsemen. Muhammad b. Salm was sent out to reconnoiter the situation. He returned with his report, and 'Alî b. Muhammad, suspecting an enemy ruse, gave orders to attack the horsemen. His suspicions were justified. The Bedouins unfurled a black flag (official flag of the Abbasids); al-Zaynabî's brother Sulaymân (soon to become commander of an anti-Zanj army of Balâlites and Sa'dites from Basra) was among them.

The Zanj finally reached Dubbâ, where they slaughtered sheep and spent the night. The next day, in the al-Amîr Canal region, they attacked troops under the command of Shihâb b. al-'Alâ' al-'Anbarî, who managed to escape with a small number of men, though most were massacred. A group of six-hundred slaves (shûrjiyya) encountered by the Zanj, who killed their wakîl, rallied to 'Alî b. Muhammad. In the Basra Canal region, the Zanj stopped in the vicinity of al-Dînârî Canal. After giving his men orders not to rush to attack the big city and to wait for a signal from him, he sent them to pillage the surrounding area.

Battles in the Vicinity of Basra.—The Zanj reached al-Riyâhî Canal. Informed of the enemy's presence, 'Alî b. Muhammad dispatched 'Alî b. Abân and a detachment of three-thousand men to engage them and promised to send reinforcements if necessary. He was told that people were approaching from the direction of al-Ja'farîya, and he sent Muhammad b. Salm along that route. A member of the expediton named Rayhân left a detailed account of how it unfolded. Fighting was fierce, but the Zanj were finally victorious, and the enemy (the *jund*, or the regular army, the Bedouins, the Balâlites, and the Sa'dites) suffered five-hundred casualties. Muhammad b. Salm carried the severed heads back to 'Alî b. Muhammad. A Balâlite prisoner who was brought back was able to give information about the enemy troops and name their commanders, but as far as their exact number was concerned, he could only say that it was large.

The real battle took place the next day, 12 *Dhû' l-Qa'da* 255.[17] 'Alî b. Muhammad, who had drawn up his troops after having forbidden them, once again, to attack the city, sent reinforcements. With boats carrying his supporters' wives and loaded with beasts of burden, he himself headed for the al-Kathîr Canal bridge. After a terrible battle, the Zanj were defeated and routed. Many perished in battle; others drowned in the canal. 'Alî b. Muhammad himself narrowly escaped death after trying to organize his retreat and fighting alone while separated from his men. He returned to a place called al-Mu'allâ, on the right bank of the Shaytân Canal, with the remnants of his army. Most of his men were scattered or in flight. Attempts were made to rally the five hundred or so who remained but there was no response to the usual signal. Small groups did return during the night, and Rayhân was sent on a scouting mission to the area around the Harb Canal bridge, but he found nothing. The "people of Basra" had seized and looted Zanj boats.[18]

The next morning, 13 *Dhû'l-Qa'da* 255,[19] 'Alî b. Muhammad took a count of his men; a thousand had come back during the night. He reprimanded a certain Shibl, whose flight and return with ten deserters has been described in different versions, and questioned him about the other runaways. He sent Muhammad b. Salm to the bridge of the Kathîr Canal to speak to the "people of Basra" and explain the reasons for the revolt. Sulaymân b. Jâmî' and Yahyâ b. Muhammad accompanied the emissary as far as the river. When he was killed, they returned with the news to 'Alî b. Muhammad, who ordered them not to tell anyone. He himself told his men, after the al-'asr prayer, and promised that Muhammad b. Salm's death would be avenged the next day by the death of ten-thousand Basrians. Then he sent Zurayq to make sure that no one crossed the river.

Three boats loaded with fighters and scores of unarmed people left Basra on 14 *Dhû'l-Qa'da* 255, guided by an experienced sailor. As soon as scouts reported this activity, 'Alî b. Muhammad, who was on the Shaytân Canal, prepared his defense: two ambushes, one on each bank of the river, and a third, commanded by 'Alî b. Abân, facing the enemy. Zanj women were given the task of supplying their warriors with rocks. The Basrians suffered an overwhelming defeat. Attacked from all sides, many drowned as they tried to flee, or were killed the minute they set foot on land. 'Alî b. Muhammad said that he was aided by supernatural forces that sent great white birds to capsize the enemy boats. Many prominent Basrians lost their lives in the battle. The Zanj put some of their foes' severed heads on display and loaded the rest on boats to Basra.

The day has remained known as "Yawm al-shadhâ" (from the type of boats used) and is celebrated by poets. It was the beginning of a great deal of renewed strength for 'Alî b. Muhammad and his struggle.[20] The panic-stricken residents of Basra wrote of their defeat to the Caliph, who responded by sending the Turk, Ju'lân, to their aid. Abû l-Ahwas al-Bâhilî was named *wâlî* of al-Ubulla, and the Turk, Jurayh, was appointed his assistant.

'Ali b. Muhammad's troops were eager to attack Basra, and he had to restrain them.[21] "It is up to them to seek you out," he told them. He established a new camp on the *sabkha* (salt marsh) of Abû Qurrâ and in a friendly place, surrounded by date palm trees and prosperous villages, ordered his men to build huts. The Zanj dispersed throughout the region, killing and plundering everything in their path and seizing cattle.

II. THE ABBASID ATTEMPT TO CRUSH THE REVOLT
(256–259/870–873)

When, in answer to Basra's appeal, the Caliph sent troops commanded by the Turkish officer Ju'lân to the city (at the end of 255 and the beginning of 256/869–70), the revolt lost its local character and became "an affair of state." But disorder reigned in the capital. A few months later, however, with the assassination of al-Muhtadi and al-Mu'tamid's accession to power (*Rajab* 256/June 870), the unrest ended. Moreover, Samârrâ was probably ill-informed as to the extent of the insurrection, and its special characteristics. All of this explains the successive failures of troops sent in to crush it.

The Zanj took advantage of the situation. The rebels captured al-Ubulla and 'Abbâdân, made incursions in the Khûzistân, and seized Jubbâ and Ahwâz (*Rajab-Sha'bân* 256/June-July 870). By cutting off the principal trade route, they caused unrest in the capital and panic in Basra. The

Caliph, beset with problems, sent to Mecca for his brother, al-Muwaffaq, future master of the empire (*Dhû' l-Hijja* 256/October-November 870). During the initial period of al-Muwaffaq's command (*Safar-Ramadân* 257/January-August 871), the insurgents continued to rout the armies sent against them and succeeded in their most spectacular exploit: the temporary capture of Basra and the wholesale massacre of its inhabitants (*Shawwâl* 257/September 871). It is interesting to note that at this time 'Alî b. Muhammad was no longer found leading his men into battle. Instead of personally taking part in capturing cities, he issued orders to his army chiefs from his camp. He was kept constantly informed of battle conditions and circumstances, and no new operations were undertaken without authorization from him. In the future, however, he would no longer leave the vicinity of the capital, even when the revolt was most widespread.

Abbasid troops had little difficulty retaking the captured cities that the Zanj had pillaged and abandoned. But they were absolutely unable to suppress the revolt or win a decisive victory over an enemy, present everywhere and nowhere, who in the end always prevailed. To be finished with the rebels, once and for all, al-Muwaffaq himself marched out of Samârrâ at the head of a very large army (*Jumâdâ I* 258/March 872) to fight them. For several months, Abbasid troops and regrouped Zanj forces were engaged in ferocious battles, with each side winning from time to time. Then sickness began to decimate al-Muwaffaq's armies and he was forced to suspend the fighting. When, in addition, his camp was ravaged by fire, he abandoned the region for Wâsit, where his troops scattered (*Sha'bân* 258/June-July 872). It was both the end of the great offensive against the Zanj and of an entire period. Indeed, the failure of al-Muwaffaq's campaign marked the beginning of a new stage. Both the central government and the insurgents became conscious of the rebels' strength; but the central government, confronted with more pressing concerns, allowed the problems posed by the Zanj to recede in importance. It would not be accurate to say that the central government completely ignored the rebels; it must be emphasized, nevertheless, that its operations against them were definitely minor, not to say lacking in conviction.

The Capture of al-Ubulla and 'Abbâdân.—The Turk Ju'lân arrived in Basra and moved out to engage the Zanj.[22] He set up camp facing them, about one *farsah* away,[23] where he remained for six months without being able to do much. His troops, horsemen for the most part, were ineffective on terrain crossed by canals and waterways and covered by palm trees and other tall plants.

A Basrian army of Balâlites and Sa'dites, under the command of al-Zaynabî was defeated and routed by the rebels, and a Zanj attack on Ju'lân's camp at night left a large number of fatalities among the Turk's men. Those who survived were in such a state of panic that Ju'lân decided to withdraw to Basra. The Caliph[24] relieved him of his functions and replaced him with Sa'îd al-Hâjib, who reached his new post in the month of *Rajab* 256/June-July 870. The Zanj left their camp on the *sabkha* (salt marsh) of Abû Qurra and set up a new one on the right bank of Abû l-Khâsib Canal.[25]

With the promise of easy loot and the claim that while he was at prayer a voice from heaven had assured him of a great victory, 'Alî b. Muhammad encouraged his men to attack twenty-four ships that were sailing up the Tigris toward Basra. The rebels seized the boats, massacred their crew, took the passengers onboard as slaves that were on board, and carried away a great deal of booty. 'Alî b. Muhammad took what was left after the pillage.

There was a new Caliph in the capital. Al-Muhtadi was dismissed[26] and replaced by al-Mu'tamid, who took office on 16 *Rajab* 256/June 19, 870.

'Alî b. Muhammad sent troops to al-Ubulla,[27] once Ju'lân had fled. The Zanj launched an amphibious attack, and the city fell on 25 *Rajab* 256/June 870. The city was built of wood and when fire broke out many

people perished in the flames; others drowned. Among the victims were
the governor, Abû l-Ahwas 'Abd Allâh b. Humayd al-Tûsî, and his son.
There was the usual pillage, but most property was destroyed in the fire.

News of al-Ubulla's devastation caused great fear among the people of
'Abbâdân, who opened the gates of their city to the insurgents and presented 'Alî b. Muhammad with gifts. The rebels freed the slaves and
seized the weapons they found in the city. From there, they pushed on in
Khûzistân and captured Jubbâ, whose inhabitants had already fled. Then,
killing, burning, pillaging, and destroying everything in their wake, they
pushed on until they were just outside of Ahwâz, the provincial capital.
They had no difficulty taking the city, which had already been abandoned
by Sa'îd b. Yaksîn and his troops, as well as some residents. Among the
captives was the fiscal *wâlî*, Ibrâhîm b. Muhammad b. al-Mudabbir,[28] who
had stayed behind with his men and servants. After receiving a wound
that would leave a scar for the rest of his life, he was captured.[29] Stripped
of all his possessions, including his slaves, he was imprisoned in the
house of Yahyâ b. Muhammad al-Bahrânî. Later, with his nephew, Abû
Gâlib, and a man from Banû Hâshim, he escaped through an underground
passageway. There was nothing but bad news in Basra, and many residents fled the panic-stricken city to other localities.

'Alî b. Muhammad's army was growing stronger.[30] In *Dhû' l-Hijja*
256/October-November 870, he sent troops commanded by Yahyâ b.
Muhammad al-Bahrânî to Ahwâz against Shâhîn b. Bistâm, but they
returned having failed to achieve the victory they had expected. On the
13th of the same month, al-Muwaffaq arrived in Samârrâ from Mecca.

Fighting resumed in the month of *Rajab* 257/May–June 871.[31] Under
the joint command of the Turk Bugrâj and Sa'îd b. Sâlih al-Hâjib,
Abbasid troops defeated the Zanj at the al-Murgâb river, a tributary of the
Mâ'qil Canal. They freed a number of women and recovered some of the
property that had been looted. During the battle, Sa''îd suffered many
wounds, one in the mouth. He withdrew immediately to Furât al-Basra

with his men, both to rest and to make preparations for a new offensive. On learning of the enemy's presence in the area, he attacked and routed the hostile force,[32] which counted among its members Imrân, whose wife's grandson Ankalây was 'Alî b. Muhammad's son. Bugrâj granted Imrân's request for pardon. According to a first-hand account,[33] the women of the region flushed Zanj from their hiding places and captured them. Fighting between Sa''îd and the insurgents continued throughout the months of *Rajab* and *Sha'ban*.

On orders from 'Alî b. Muhammad, al-Bahrânî, who had a large army on the Ma'qil Canal, sent a thousand-man detachment, commanded by Sulaymân b. Jâmi' and Abû l-Layth, to attack Sa'îd's camp by surprise at night. They were successful and, during the widespread disorder that occurred with their victory, the camp was set on fire and a number of soldiers were killed. Moreover, Sa'îd and his men were short of supplies which were slow in coming from Ahwâz.[34] Sa'îd was finally removed fom his command and replaced with Mansûr b. Ja'far al-Khayyât, commander of the troops in Ahwâz at the time. Mansûr first tried to blockade the insurgents, then he attacked them by land and water; but he fell into an ambush and suffered considerable losses. A large number of his men were killed on land or perished in the river. The Zanj put five-hundred severed heads on display in Yahyâ b. Muhammad al-Bahrânî's camp.

In response to a request from al-Bahrânî, 'Alî b. Muhammad sent troops under the command of 'Alî b. Abân al-Muhallabî to Ahwâz to cut off the Qantarat Arbuk, the only bridge over the Dujayl. Ibrâhîm b. Sîmâ and his men, who were coming from Dast Arbuk, attacked the Zanj and defeated them. Many rebels were killed, and 'Alî b. Abân himself was wounded in the foot. Ibrâhîm b. Sîmâ, who was rewarded for his victory with an appointment,[35] ordered his aide-de-camp, Shâhîn b. Bistâm, to return to their camp on the Jubbâ Canal. Along the way, the aide and his men were surprised on Abû l-'Abbâs Canal by 'Alî b. Abân and his troops; Shâhîn, his cousin, and most of their soldiers were killed. In the evening of the same day, before news of Shâhîn's death had reached Ibrâhîm b. Sîmâ, 'Alî b. Abân and a small number of fighters surprised Ibrâhîm's men in their camp while they slept. 'Alî b. Abân says that, trembling with fever, he successfully fought them with only fifty men. Most of the Zanj who had accompanied him had scattered after the battle against Shâhîn. Once he had defeated Ibrâhîm b. Sîmâ, 'Alî b. Abân, ordered by 'Alî b. Muhammad to join the assault on Basra, left Jubbâ.

The Capture of Basra.—'Alî b. Muhammad launched his attack on Basra in the month of *Shawwâl* 257/August–September 871.[36] The city had already been under siege for some time. The surrounding area was controlled by the Zanj, who had destroyed villages from which Basra normally received supplies. Lacking the strength to attempt an offensive against them, Mansûr b. Ja'far al-Khayyât and his men concentrated on finding supplies for the city which the insurgents' blockade and constant harassment had weakened. Armed clashes between the two sides were almost constant.

On the 14th of the same month, there was a lunar eclipse. 'Alî b. Muhammad turned it to his advantage and solemnly declared that, when he had beseeched God to hasten the destruction of the city, a voice had promised him victory: "Basra will be a loaf of bread that you will eat from all sides; when the loaf is half eaten, Basra will be destroyed."[37] He gathered his troops and obtained the active support of some Bedouins,[38] whom he placed under Sulaymân b. Mûsâ al-Sha'rânî, with precise orders to attack the city. Another group of Bedouins was placed under 'Alî b. Abân al-Muhallabî and a third under Yahyâ b. Muhammad al-Bahrânî with the same orders.

In Basra itself the situation was hardly promising. The Turk Bugrâj and about fifty horsemen accounted for the Caliph's army. Basrians were very badly informed of the impending danger. In a meeting on Friday, 10 *Shawwâl* 257/August 31, 871,[39] Burayh[40] refused to believe that there could be an alliance between the Zanj and the Bedouins. 'Alî b. Muhammad's troops were said to be divided into nine corps (3 *Shawwâl* 257). An epidemic broke out due to the blockade,[41] and if this was not enough there was still internal conflict in the city between the Balâlites and the Sa'dites.

Basra fell on 17 *Shawwâl* 257/September 7, 871 during Friday prayer. On the morning of that day, the Zanj had launched a three-pronged attack. Rafîq led troops on the Banû Sa'd front, 'Alî b. Abân al-Muhallabî commanded troops on the al-Mirbad front, and Yahyâ b. Muhammad al-Bahrânî on that of al-Khurayba.

The first to attack was 'Alî b. Abân, whose troops were divided between Rafîq and himself. Opposing the rebel onslaught were the Turk Bugrâj's cavalrymen on the al-Mirbad and al-Khurayba fronts. Fath and the Sa'dites battled the assailants on the Banû Sa'd front. The Zanj burst into the panic-stricken city, many sections of which were already in flames. Some of the residents fled the cathedral-mosque for refuge in homes. Others, on the contrary, coming from al-Mirbad, where the home of the just defeated Burayh had been pillaged and burned, crowded into the place of worship. One individual was seen mounted on a mule, saber in hand, urging his fellow citizens to fight the enemy. It seems that Fath and a group of residents managed to defeat 'Alî b. Abân's men after they had burned the cathedral-mosque;[42] but the Zanj were victorious everywhere else. They laid the city to waste and massacred or drove out its defenders. Fearful of an ambush, the rebels withdrew from Basra in the afternoon and returned to wage new battles on Saturday and Sunday. On Sunday 19 *Shawwâl*, Yahyâ b. Muhammad al-Bahrânî was pushed back by Bugrâj and Burayh; but the next morning (Monday, 20 *Shawwâl*),[43] the Zanj entered the town with no resistance. Burayh and Bugrâj had fled with their men.

The inhabitants of the city were promised amnesty if they surrendered and were invited to assemble in front of Ibrâhîm b. Yahyâ al-Muhallabî's house. It was a trap. The Zanj occupied all the incoming streets and alley-ways. No one could escape. A few members of al-Muhallabî's family were there, and they were invited to go into the house. The door closed on them. Then, all of the people gathered outside were ruthlessly massacred; their cries filled with terror could be heard in the distance.[44] 'Alî b. Abân burned the cathedral-mosque and part of the port. The Zanj scoured the blazing city for survivors of the carnage and took them to Yahyâ b. Muhammad al-Bahrânî, who had settled in Sayhân. The rich were stripped of their possessions, then put to death. The poor were killed at once.

On Tuesday morning, 21 *Shawwâl* 257, Yahyâ b. Muhammad launched another appeal for surrender with promises of clemency, but there was no response. A delegation from the Banû Sa'd approached 'Alî b. Muhammad, but he gained nothing positive and left for 'Abbâdân. 'Alî b. Abân, who had authorized the meeting, was dismissed by the Master of the Zanj for being too lenient towards a segment of the population.[45] This left Yahyâ b. Muhammad al-Bahrânî in control, but not for long. In a let-ter 'Alî b. Muhammad ordered him to step aside for Shibl. This was done to calm the population and allow the rebels to continue plundering prop-erty of the rich who were killed only after being robbed of all they pos-sessed, while the less fortunate were killed straightaway. When there were no victims left, the Zanj abandoned the city permanently.[46]

Many of Basra's scholars were among the victims: the famous gram-marian al-'Abbâs b. al-Faraj al-Riyâshî, who was killed while at prayer in the mosque,[47] Zayd b. Akhzam Abû Tâlib al-Basrî, and Abû l-'Alâ Muhammad b. Abî Zura'a al-Bâhilî.. Another illustrious individual, Ibn Durayd, who had already left the city, escaped the massacre.

'Alî b. Muhammad's version of the capture of Basra is given by Muhammad b. al-Hasan: "After fervent prayers on the morning of the day he entered Basra, he had a strange vision: a man with the face of Ja'far Ma'lûf, the chief extortionist of the big concessionaires of the Samârrâ court, the executioner of Najâh was, standing up in the air with his left hand lowered and his right hand raised announcing that the inhabitants of Basra would ruin the city and that those attacking it would be given courage strengthened by the angels of God."[48]

It was during this period that 'Alî b. Muhammad changed his genealogy: a group of 'Alids from Basra came to him with 'Alî b. Ahmad b. 'Isâ b. Zayd and 'Abd Allâh b. 'Alî. The Master of the Zanj, who had maintained that he was a descendant of Ahmad b. 'Isâ b. Zayd, changed his genealogy saying: "I am not the son of 'Isâ, but of Yahyâ b. Zayd." That is untrue, because apart from a daughter who died when she was a small child, Yahyâ did not have any other children.[49]

Basra had certainly suffered a great deal from the Zanj forays:

> From that moment on began the decline which would continue after the death of Jâhiz, under the blows of the Zanj, then of the Qarmates. Once a renowned city, Basra would soon be no more than an obscure town.[50]
>
> This rebel,[51] whose rule had lasted fourteen years and four months, had mercilessly slaughtered young and old, men and women; he had spread arson and pillage everywhere. In the sole battle waged near Basra, he killed three hundred thousand men.

Mohallebî, one of the principal officers of 'Alî b. Muhammad, the chief of the Zanj, remained in Basra, after the battle. He had a chair set up in the section called 'cemetery of the Benou Yachkor,' where he recited the solemn prayer and delivered the Friday sermon. First, he praised the name of his master, 'Alî ben Muhammad, and invoked God's mercy for Abou Bekr and Omar, but made no mention of Othman or Alî. Then he cursed the tyrants of the Abbas family as well as Abou Mousa el-Ashâri, Amr, son of el-Ass, and Moâwiah, son of Abou Sofian. We have previously spoken of his doctrines and mentioned that he was a member of the sect of Kharedjites known as Azrakites.

Since followers of the sect who had remained in Basra continued to be strongly attached to Mohallebî's teachings and met on certain Fridays, they were declared outlaws. Some succeeded in running away, others were killed or drowned. A great number hid in houses or wells; they came out only at night to hunt dogs, rats, and cats for food; but this source was soon exhausted. When no more food was to be found, they resorted to eating the bodies of their dead companions. They watched each other closely, waiting for one another to die. The stronger killed their comrades and devoured them. Then, there was the lack of fresh water. It is said that there was a woman seated next to a companion, who was at the point of death; the dying woman's sister was there with all of the women seated in a circle waiting to gorge themselves on the other's flesh. Here is the exact account of a witness:

> She had still not breathed her last when we fell upon her, cut her into pieces, and devoured her. Her sister was with us; while we were at the crossroads called Isâ ben Abi Harb, she ran towards the river, with her sister's head in her hand, and began to cry. When asked the reason for her sorrow she replied: 'Those women gathered around my sister and, without letting her die a natural death, cut her into pieces. As for me, they robbed me, and all they left me of my sister's body was her head.' And she continued moaning over the portion that she received when he sister's body was distributed. There were many scenes of this nature and some more atrocious than the one just described.

Muhammad al-Muwallad[52] left Samârrâ to fight the Zanj on Friday, the first day of *Dhû'l-Qa'da* 257. Along the way, he stopped at al-Ubulla and from there, accompanied by Burayh, went on to reoccupy Basra, where he met no resistance. The insurgents had withdrawn, and many Basrians who had managed to escape massacre rallied around Burayh. Muhammad al-Muwallad fought Yahyâ b. Muhammad al-Bahrânî and his troops in the area around the city. The Master of the Zanj, informed of the operations, sent Abû l-Layth al-Isbahânî and his boats as reinforcements to the rebels, who attacked al-Muwallad's camp during the night. The battle lasted until noon the next day. In the end al-Muwallad was defeated and his camp captured and pillaged. Yahyâ sent a report of this new victory to 'Alî b. Muhammad, who ordered him not to stop there but to go after the enemy. Pursuing Abbasid troops, the Zanj reached al-Hawânît and wreaked havoc on the surrounding villages. After a while, Yahyâ took his men back to the Ma'qil Canal. In Samârrâ,[53] fourteen Zanj, including 'Alî b. Muhammad's *qâdî* (judge) at 'Abbâdân, were captured in the Basra area and decapitated.

Once the Zanj had definitely left Basra and its surroundings, 'Alî b. Muhammad ordered 'Alî b. Abân al-Muhallabî to Jubbâ to proceed against Mansûr b. Ja'far and his troops, who were in Ahwâz at the time. A month later, when the operation had been unable to obtain any positive results and was at a standstill, 'Alî b. Muhammad sent him twelve boats loaded with soldiers. Abû l-Layth al-Isbahânî,[54] commander of the boats, had orders to obey 'Alî b. Abân and respect his decisions, but he disobeyed instructions and acted independently; he was even at odds with 'Alî b. Abân. Mansûr took advantage of the dissension among the enemy to seriously defeat Abû l-Layth, forcing him back to 'Alî b. Muhammad. This setback obliged 'Alî b. Abân himself to beat a retreat and lose another month. When he returned to the offensive, the Zanj commander launched a night attack on a camp commanded by one of Mansûr's officers. The officer and most of his men were killed. After taking the dead enemy's horses, the rebels plundered the camp and set it ablaze. Then, following a battle on 'Amr b. Mahrân Canal, 'Alî b. Abân defeated the main body of the opponent's force. Mansûr himself and his brother, Khalaf b. Ja'far,[55] were killed in battle. Yârjûh appointed Asgajûn, another Turkish officer, to succeed him.

Al-Muwaffaq's First Campaign.—In *Safar* 257/beginning of 871, al-

Muwaffaq was named commander-in-chief of the army. On Monday, 20 *Rabî' I* 258/February 4, 872, he was given new titles and placed in charge of new imperial provinces. A few days later, al-Muwaffaq and Muflih received robes of honor and were entrusted with pursuing the war against the Zanj. The bloody events of Basra were the reason these steps were taken, and the army that went out from Samârrâ far exceeded in numbers and equipment anything that had been sent previously against 'Alî b. Muhammad and his men,[56] who were terrified by the news. Yahyâ b. Muhammad al-Bahrânî emphatically asked 'Alî b. Muhammad for permission to leave Ma'qil Canal and go to al-'Abbâs Canal. Permission was granted. This left 'Alî b. Muhammad's encampment with only a small number of Zanj men because al-Muhallabî was in Jubbâ, in Ahwâz. When Al-Muwaffaq's army arrived at Ma'qil Canal, the panic-stricken rebels fled and joined 'Alî b. Muhammad. The Zanj chief tried to find out the name of the Abbasid leader, but in vain; no one could tell him.The scouts he sent out were no more successful in identifying the enemy leader, but each one returned highly upset over what he had observed. After inspecting his army, 'Alî b. Muhammad decided to summon al-Muhallabî and his men from the Ahwâz. An officer tried to inform him of the seriousness of their own situation. 'Alî b. Muhammad called him a liar and ordered the battle to begin. When al-Muhallabî arrived the fighting was over.

The battle was fought on a Tuesday, twelve days before the end of *Jumâdâ I* 258/ April 1, 872.[57] During the conflict, many Zanj women fled with their children to the Abû l-Khasîb Canal in search of refuge, but there was no bridge and many drowned. One of the Abbasid commanders, Muflih, was gravely wounded when an arrow shot by an unknown hand wounded him in the temple. It was the telling moment that decided the outcome of the battle. The rebels were victorious. They took the severed heads of the enemy to 'Alî b. Muhammad in their teeth and divided the foe's flesh among themselves. The next day, Wednesday the 19th of the same month, Muflih died of his wound. His body was taken to Samârrâ and buried.[58] When he learned how Muflih had died and that nobody knew who had shot the fatal arrow, 'Alî b. Muhammad declared that he was responsible.[59] Prisoners had told 'Alî b. Muhammad that al-Muwaffaq was leading the enemy army in person. Fearing that such news would cause panic among his own men, the Master of the Zanj assured them that it was all a lie and that the slain Muflih had been the sole commander of the enemy troops. As for al-Muwaffaq, after Muflih's death he withdrew, first to al-Ubulla to rally his men and prepare a new offensive, and from there to the Abû l-Asad Canal.

The Zanj general Yahyâ b. Muhammad al-Bahrânî was taken prisoner and executed at Samârrâ. When 'Alî b. Muhammad had given him permission to leave Ma'qil Canal, al-Bahrânî had gone to al-'Abbâs Canal and defeated Asgajûn, prefect of the Ahwâz, in a fierce battle. After seizing boats laden with rich cargo, he had moved his Zanj troops on to al-Batîha, but not by the usual route because of the aforementioned dissension between himself and al-Muhallabî. Having been warned that there were Abbasid troops in the area by 'Alî b. Muhammad, who asked him to be careful, he immediately sent scouts to reconnoiter the situation. The Abbasid general al-Muwaffaq, whom Râfi' b. Bistâm had informed of the Zanj strategy, had already left al-Ubulla for the Abû l-Asad Canal to prevent al-Bahrânî from reaching the Tigris by boat. Al-Bahrânî's scouts returned to camp with the bad news. The Zanj went back to al-Abbâs Canal,[60] only to find the mouth of the river occupied by al-Muwaffaq's boats and Asgajûn's horsemen. They abandoned their own boats and fled to the eastern shore, seeking refuge in 'Alî b. Muhammad's camp. Al-Bahrânî, with about ten of his men, put up a fierce battle, but he was isolated from most of his troops. Wounded by three arrows, in the upper arm and the left leg, he took shelter in one of the boats. His wound was all that was needed to demoralize the Zanj, who were already in a state of panic; they abandoned the battle and fled for safety. Their boats were burned by al-Muwaffaq's soldiers, who also recovered the booty the rebels had taken. Realizing that he would be unable to reach 'Alî b. Muhammad's camp by the river, al-Bahrânî left the small boat in which he had been hiding and made his way to the right bank. He spent the night there, but the next day, betrayed by his doctor, he fell into al-Muwaffaq's hands and was ordered transported to Samârrâ. Mounted on a camel, he entered the city on Wednesday, 9 *Rajab* 258/May 21, 872. The following day, he was publicly executed in the presence of the Caliph,[61] after being given two-hundred lashes and having his hands and feet amputated. On hearing the news, 'Alî b. Muhammad was at first overcome with grief, but his attitude quickly changed. He described al-Bahrânî as an insatiable individual of whom a voice had said 'his death is a good thing for you.' 'Alî b. Muhammad declared that he rejected the *nubûwa* (prophecy), fearing that he would not be able to wear the burden of prophecy.[62]

On Abû l-Asad Canal, Abbasid troops were being decimated by numerous illnesses. Al-Muwaffaq moved them out of the area and went back to Bâdhâward,[63] where they set up camp. When his boats and weapons had been made as good as new, he moved against 'Alî b. Muhammad's encampment on Abû l-Khasîb Canal. Both sides suffered heavy losses in the battles that ensued. Abbasid troops managed to set fire to certain Zanj homes and free women and children being held, but they were forced to withdraw in the face of superior rebel numbers. During the Abbasid retreat, the Zanj surprised an isolated detachment of the enemy, and though they lost many lives in the bloody battle they were able to take 110 severed Abbasid heads to 'Alî b. Muhammad.

Once again, al-Muwaffaq took his men back to Bâdhâward, where before long a fire, aided by the wind, destroyed his encampment.[64] When he returned to Wâsit, in *Sha'bân* 258/June-July 872, almost all of his army scattered. He finally left Wâsit a few months later. On Friday, 26 *Rabî' I* 259/January 30, 873, he arrived in Samârrâ.

III. ABBASID TROOPS CONTENT WITH PREVENTING THE SPREAD OF THE REVOLT (259–266/873–879)

When al-Muwaffaq returned to Samârrâ from Wâsit, he left Muhammad al-Muwallad the responsibility of pursuing the war against the Zanj. Until seven years later, in *Rabî' II* 266/November-December 879, when he sent his son Abû l-'Abbâs on the great offensive that finally stifled the insurrection, he would direct his efforts and attention elsewhere. Al-Muwaffaq's absence and the numerous concerns facing the central government caused by local dynasties, notably the Saffarides, worked to the advantage of 'Alî b. Muhammad and his followers.

The revolt was at its height. Zanj armies, solidly installed in Lower Iraq's canal region, crisscrossed Khûzistân and part of Iraq, capturing towns and maintaining large areas under their control while trying, more or less successfully, to form alliances with other rebels. 'Alî b. Muhammad governed the territory he controlled from al-Mukhtâra, built as a capital on the Abû l-Khasîb Canal, where he struck his own money and took title of al-Mahdî. His troops, already masters of many cities of Khûzistân, took Râmhurmuz; his army in Iraq, which held Wâsit, advanced towards Baghdad and took Nu'mâniyâ and Jarjarâyâ, while another detachment, in collaboration with Bedouins, intercepted and plundered a caravan of pilgrims carrying the *kiswa* (exterior covering) for the Ka'ba. His rebels were even observed in Mecca itself, where they engaged Abû l-Sâj's son in battle. Abbasid troops and the local people fought the rebels as best they could, depending on the situation and the occasion, but at no moment was there evidence of a great campaign directed against them.

Information on this period is scarce and not uniformly important. Tabarî, who is the most complete source, abandons the Zanj for long periods, pointing out only the important events. In his *Annales,* we find the same number of lines devoted to the Zanj during these seven years as we

do for the preceding period which was twice as short. Certain facts are
reported in great detail, others by a simple phrase; there is overlapping
from one year to another, and there are two simultaneous fields of operation. As a result, it is sometimes difficult to follow the unfolding of
events.

Successive Operations.—On learning that al-Muwaffaq had left the
region, following the destruction of his camp at Bâdhâward by fire, 'Alî
b. Muhammad, driven by an extreme shortage of food for his army, sent
a large segment to Khûzistân, under 'Alî b. Abân al-Muhallabî's command. Al-Muhallabî's brother, al-Khalîl, Sulaymân b. Jâmi', the late
Yahyâ' b. Muhammad al-Bahrânî's troops, and Sulaymân b. Mûsâ al-
Sha'rânî and his men were among those who made up the expedition.

Asgajûn, the governor of Khûzistân, tried to check the Zanj advance,
but he was defeated at Dast Mârân. His aide-de-camp and a great many
of his troops were killed. He himself died of drowning, and two of his
officers were taken prisoners. 'Alî b. Abân informed 'Alî b. Muhammad
of the victory and sent him severed heads, flags, and three prisoners as
trophies.[65] The Zanj entered the city of Ahwâz for the second time and
killed a good number of its inhabitants on 6 *Rajab* 259/ May 8, 872.

On 17 *Dhû' l-Qa'da* 259/September 14, 873, the Turk Mûsâ b. Bugâ
was given command of the war against the Zanj. He sent 'Abd al-Rahmân
b. Muflih to Khûzistân, Ishâq b. Kundâj to Basra, and Ibrâhîm b. Sîmâ to
Bâdhâward. 'Abd al-Rahmân b. Muflih attacked 'Alî b. Abân al-
Muhallabî and lost the first battle. When he resumed fighting, he seriously defeated the Zanj and forced them to withdraw to Bayân. 'Alî b.
Muhammad tried to send his men back into combat but, seeing how fearful they were, he authorized them to come to the capital for rest. During
this time, Ibn Muflih, an Abbasid general, set up camp at Hisn al-Mahdî.

As for 'Alî b. Abân, who was at the rebel capital, he left al-Mukhtâra
after a while and returned to fighting the Abbasids, but he was defeated

twice by Ibrâhîm b. Sîmâ, then by one of Ibn Muflih's officers named Tâshtimur. Fearing a new attack, he wrote to 'Alî b. Muhammad for assistance and boats. He received thirteen boats and additional troops. Then, with a chosen group of his best soldiers and al-Sha'rânî, he succeeded in launching a surprise attack on the enemy camp at night. Ibn Muflih and his men fled, abandoning four of their boats to the Zanj. He and Tâshtimur took their revenge a little later when they crushed 'Alî b. Abân on the al-Sidra Canal. The rebel leader fled to 'Alî b. Muhammad, leaving ten boats behind. Ibn Muflih pitched his camp at Bayân and, with Ibrâhîm b. Sîmâ, harassed 'Alî b. Muhammad whose efforts to resupply food to his troops were being made difficult by Ishâq b. Kundâj, installed at Basra. 'Alî b. Muhammad regrouped his men, then sent a detachment to fight Ishâq in the Basra region. Ten months later, Masrûr al-Balkhî replaced Mûsâ b. Bugâ as commander of the war against the Zanj. During the year 259/872–73, a group of Zanj prisoners sent from Khûzistân, arrived in Samârrâ; residents of the city seized and killed most of them.

On 4 *Shawwâl*, 259/August 3, 873, the leader of another rebel group, Ya'qûb b. al-Layth al-Saffâr, asserted his claims and took Naysâbûr; he entered the Tabaristân in 260/873–74.[66] 'Alî b. Zayd al-'Alawî,[67] the Master of Kûfa, was killed by the Zanj in 260/873–74.[68]

In 261/874–75, 'Abd al-Rahmân b. Muflih and Tâshtimur were killed in battles against Muhammad b. Wâsil. At this juncture, Musâ b. Bugâ left Wâsit and returned to the capital. Abû l-Sâj was named governor of Khûzistân; his son-in-law, 'Abd al-Rahmân, was killed during a battle against 'Alî b. Abân al-Muhallabî in the al-Dûlâb region. Abû l-Sâj fled to 'Askar Mukram, and the city of Ahwâz fell to Zanj troops, who killed its inhabitants and pillaged and burned its houses.[69]

Abû l-Sâj was removed as governor of Khûzistân and the position was given to Ibrâhîm b. Sîmâ. In *Sha'bân* 261/May–June 875, al-Muwaffaq replaced Ibrâhîm b. Sîmâ with Masrûr al-Balkhî and gave him responsibility for carrying on the war against the Zanj.

On 12 *Shawwâl* 261/July 20, 875, the Caliph al-Mu'tamid named his son Ja'far al-Mufawwad heir to the throne and put him in charge of the western provinces, with Musâ b. Bugâ as his deputy. Al-Muwaffaq was named second in line to the throne and given control of the eastern provinces. His deputy was Masrûr al-Balkhî. Robes of honor were given to Masrûr al-Balkhî and thirty-four of his officers in Samârrâ, on 7 *Dhû' l-Hijja* 261/September 12, 875. On the 20th of the same month, they left to fight the Zanj. Meanwhile, during 261/874–75, the Zanj issued their own money.

The Spread of the Revolt to the al-Batîha and Dast Maysân Regions. —At the beginning of the year 262/875, while the Abbasids employed all their forces in their struggle against the Saffarides, the Zanj took advantage of the situation to make incursions into the al-Batîha and Dast Maysân regions. After many skirmishes against Masrûr al-Balkhî's Turkish officers, Sulaymân b. Jâmi's small units, headed by al-Jubbâ'î, harried the al-Madhâr region.

Al-Jubbâ'î informed 'Alî b. Muhammad that Abbasid troops had left the al-Batîha region as Ya'qûb b. al-Layth approached. Whereupon, 'Alî b. Muhammad ordered Sulaymân b. Jâmi' to al-Hawânît and saw to it that al-Jubbâ'î was provided with a guide[70] to the same place. On the way from al-Batîha, the Zanj troops fought Abbâ al-Turkî's men[71] (or those of Nusayr Abû Hamza); they encountered them on the Tigris with thirty boats. As for al-Jubbâ'î, he defeated Rumays, seizing twenty-four of his boats and thirty craft called "Salga." During his withdrawal, Rumays was defeated again, this time by Sulaymân b. Jâmi'. Some of his men (Balâlites) deserted him for Sulaymân. When they were interrogated about the situation, they claimed that the road was free of Abbasid troops as far as Wâsit. Sulaymân trusted the information and marched forward. He encountered Abû Ma'âdh, who defeated him and took one of his officers prisoner. Assured by the Balâlites that Abû Ma'âdh's troops were the only enemy force in the area, Sulaymân relayed the information to 'Alî b. Muhammad, then moved on to the Abân Canal region where, pillaging and burning, he put Abû Ma'âdh to flight and captured women and children. A detachment of al-Muwaffaq's forces that happened to be in the region counterattacked and forced him to flee.

From al-Hawânît, where he had settled, Sulaymân attacked and defeated Wasîf, Masrûr's envoy. Wasîf was killed, and seven of his boats were seized. To sow terror among enemy survivors, Sulaymân ordered all prisoners killed and their bodies thrown into the Tigris at al-Hawânît.

On learning that Masrûr had left Wâsit and was headed in his direction, Sulaymân went looking for a new campsite. After consulting with his officers and his allies of the moment, he chose Nahr Tahîthâ.[72] 'Alî b. Muhammad, to whom he reported his actions, approved and ordered him to send food and livestock. When Masrûr arrived in Sulaymân's former camp, the Zanj had already left and taken everything with them. There was no trace of them anywhere. Sulaymân became considerably annoyed by his fellow commander al-Jubbâ'î's practice of burning all of the provisions his troops found in the region on the grounds that they were enemy property. Sulaymân felt that it disrupted his plans, and he complained to 'Alî b. Muhamad. The Master of the Zanj ordered al-Jubbâ'î to pay attenton to Sulaymân b. Jâmi' and obey him.

Sulaymân and al-Jubbâ'î became the targets of new Abbasid forces, which included horsemen and boats and were jointly commanded by Agartmish (Agartimsh, Agartamish ?) and Khushaysh. The Zanj prevailed; Agartmish was put to flight and Khushaysh was killed. Their camp was plundered and their boats seized (Agartmish later succeeded in recovering them). Sulaymân sent word of the victory to 'Alî b. Muhammad and with it Khushaysh's seal and severed head, which was put on exhibition in the Zanj leader's camp for a day before being sent on to 'Alî b. Abân al-Muhallabî 's campsite, where it was displayed on a picket. Sulaymân b. Jâmi' and al-Jubbâ'î made an incursion into the al-

Hawânît region and carried away eleven of the twelve boats belonging to Abû Tamîm, Abû 'Awn's brother. During the engagement, Abû Tamîm was killed and his body thrown into the water. When Sulaymân returned to camp, he sent a report on the expedition to 'Alî b. Muhammad.

On 9 *Rajab* 262/April 8, 876, Ya'qûb b. Layth al-Saffâr and his independent group marched on Baghdad, but they were trounced at Dayr al-'Aqûl and forced to withdraw. On 11 *Rajab* 262, while the retreating Ya'qûb was at Jundaysâbûr, 'Alî b. Muhammad offered him an alliance and urged him to return to Baghdad. Ya'qûb refused categorically, replying with a passage from the Qu'ran: 1. "Say, O infidels, I will not worship what you worship. 2. You do not worship what I worship . . . To you, your religion. To me, my religion."[73]

Ahmad b. Laythawayh, whom Masrûr al-Balkhî dispatched to Ahwâz Province to fight the Zanj, arrived in the city of Sûs. Previously, the Kurd Muhammad b. 'Ubâyd Allâh b. Azârmard had been appointed governor by Ya'qûb the Saffarid. Ahmad wrote to 'Alî b. Muhammad, offering to defect to the Zanj chief's side. 'Alî b. Muhammad replied that he had only to place himself under the authority of 'Alî b. Abân al-Muhallabî, the Zanj governor in Khûzistân. The Kurd accepted, and 'Alî b. Abân's brother, Khalîl, was sent to him with troops. The Kurd joined Abû Dâwûd al-Su'lûk and together with Khalîl and Ya'qûb moved on Sûs, where they were routed by Ibn Laythawayh, who pushed on to Jundaysâbûr. 'Alî b. Abân left the city of Ahwâz for the 'Askar Mukram region and made plans with Muhammad b. 'Ubayd Allâh for a joint attack on the troops under Ibn Laythawayh's command. Meanwhile, in the province of Ahwâz, the Kurd, who had come over to the Zanj side, entered the city of Tustar. To his surprise, his *khâtib* said the Friday prayer in the name of al-Mu'tamid, al-Saffâr, and Muhammad b. 'Ubayd Allâh. On learning of this, 'Alî b. Abân left at once for Ahwâz and along the way saw to it that the bridges over which he had traveled were rendered unusable to pursuers. En route, his own men plundered 'Askar Mukram, and he could not prevent it because he was too far in the rear. At news of the Zanj's departure, Ahmad b. Laythawayh attacked and captured Tustar. He drove out the Kurd, and sent Abû Dâwud al-Su'lûk to Caliph al-Mu'tamid as a prisoner. Ahmad settled in Tustar and was attacked in turn by 'Alî b. Abân al-Muhallabî. During the battle, a group of Bedouins who had been fighting with the Zanj asked for pardon and went over to Ahmad, whose army of 400 horsemen succeeded in routing 'Alî b. Abân's forces. The Zanj officer managed to escape despite being wounded in the leg.

Al-Muwaffaq tried to force Ahmad b. Tûlûn (Abbasid governor of Egypt) to send him taxes from Egypt, but Ahmad, supported by Caliph Mu'tamid's attitude and aware of the situation in Iraq, refused to obey. All al-Muwaffaq could do was to send Mûsâ b. Bugâ to Syria to take whatever he could. After six months at al-Raqqa, Mûsâ returned with no great results. He died in Iraq in 263 or 264/876–78.

Following his dispute with the Kurd Muhammad b. 'Ubayd Allâh and his defeat of Ahmad b. Laythawayh in 262/876, 'Alî b. Abân left Ahwâz and went to 'Alî b. Muhammad's headquarters in al-Mukhtâra, the capital city, to seek care for his wound. He returned to Ahwâz, on recovering, and sent troops, commanded by his brother Khalîl against Ibn Laythawayh, who was at 'Askar Mukram.[74] The Zanj suffered a new defeat when they fell into an ambush about a *farsakh* from the city. The Abbasid commander of the victorous forces returned to Tustar with the severed heads of Zanj killed in battle as trophies. 'Alî b. Abân sent a detachment to al-Masruqân; Ahmad b. Laythawayh dispatched thirty of his best horsemen to engage them in battle. Informed of the enemy's movement against his brother, Khalîl b. Abân killed Ibn Laytawah's thirty men in an ambush and sent their severed heads to 'Alî b. Abân, who passed them on to 'Alî b. Muhammad.

Battles between the Zanj and the Saffarid Troops.—In 263/876–77, Ya'qûb b. al-Layth al-Saffâr entered Khûzistân with his Saffarid troops

and went as far as Jundaysâbûr, forcing the Abbasid troops and their com-
mander to draw back and quit the region. When Ya'qûb sent his officer
Hisn b. al-'Anbar against Ahwâz, 'Ali b. Abân al-Muhallabî withdrew to
al-Sidra Canal and the city was occupied by the Saffarids. An attack by
'Alî b. Abân shortly afterwards inflicted heavy losses on Hisn's troops and
forced the Saffarids to seek refuge in 'Askar Mukram. After retaking
Ahwâz and sowing panic in the city, 'Alî b. Abân returned to the al-Sidra
Canal, where he ordered Bahbûdh to attack Ya'qûb's Kurdish ally at
Dawraq. Bahbûdh's expedition was successful and 'Alî b. Abân expected
a Saffarid counterattack, but Ya'qûb ordered his men to cease fighting and
wrote to 'Alî b. Abân proposing peace, conditional on his recognition of
Saffarids' right to reside in Ahwâz.[75] 'Alî b. Abân rejected the proposal
because it made no arrangement for the transport of foodstuffs. Ya'qûb's
assurances that there would indeed be such deliveries finally put an end
to the hostilities.

Sulayman b. Jâmi' and al-Jubbâ'î[76] continued fighting Abbasid forces
in the al-Hawânît region. At the beginning of the year 264/878, they
fought Takîn[77] al-Bukhârî and his men. As al-Jubbâ'î had planned successfully, Takîn fell into a trap set by Sulaymân and suffered a serious
defeat. Then Zanj troops plundered and burned his camp. When
Sulaymân b. Jâmi''s previous request to visit 'Alî b. Muhammad was
finally granted, he turned over his command to al-Jubbâ'î and set out for
al-Mukhtâra. He arrived in the rebels' capital in Jumâdâ I 264/January-
February 878, with flags seized from Takîn's camp and boats seized from
Abû Tamîm, Khushaysh, and Takîn. After Sulaymân b. Jâmi''s departure
for al-Mukhtâra, al-Jubbâ'î left their installation in search of provisions,
but his troops were driven back by Ju'lân. Villagers in Tahîthâ told al-
Jubbâ'î that the Abbasid troops had felt free to wreak havoc on their village when they learned that Sulaymân had gone to visit the Master of the
Zanj. Al-Jubbâ'î immediately conveyed this information and news of his
defeat by Ju'lân to Sulaymân, who returned to Tahîthâ and rallied his

men. Then he and al-Jubbâ'î, with his fleet, set out for the Ahwâr region where they decimated Muhammad b. 'Alî b. Habîb's forces, seized his horses and cattle, and killed his brother. On the way back, Sulaymân encountered four-hundred Banû Shaybân horsemen, whose chief had been killed in the preceding battle and whose son had been taken prisoner. Bent on avenging their leader's death, they massacred 'Umayr b. 'Ammâr and his men, allies whom Sulaymân, like a coward, left with the responsibility of battling the avengers. At the end of the month of *Rajab* 264/beginning of April 878, Sulaymân took the spoils from the Ahwâr expedition to 'Alî b. Muhammad.

The following month (*Sha'bân* 264) Sulaymân defeated the Abbasid commander, Jaysh b. Hamartakîn, whose camp at the time happened to be in a village called Hassân. The Zanj seized the cattle they found there and burned the village. In the al-Hawânît region, on 10 *Sha'bân* 264,[78] al-Jubbâ'î attacked boats carrying Ju'lân's horses; his men killed the crew and took twelve horses. There was a new foray on the 27th of the same month.[79]

Sulaymân asked 'Alî b. Muhammad for ten boats, and when they arrived he used them immediately to attack Abbâ (one of Ju'lân's officers ?). He seized a few of the enemy's boats, burned the rest, and carried away horses and weapons (10 *Ramadân* 264).[80] A joint attack on Ju'lân by Sulaymân, al-Jubbâ'î, and Ja'far b. Ahmad yielded twenty-seven horses, two foals, and three male mules, without mentioning arms and other effects. Sulaymân reported on his latest expedition to 'Alî b. Muhammad and sent him the captured flags and weapons. In *Dhû'l-Qa'da* 264/July-August 878, Sulaymân defeated Matar b. Jâmi' at al-Rusâfa. After pillaging and setting fire to the city, he took his plunder of cattle and enemy flags to 'Alî b. Muhammad.[81]

The following month (*Dhû'l-Hijja* 264/August-September 878), Sulaymân went to al-Mukhtâra where he attended a celebration, and Matar b. Jâmi' took advantage of his absence to attack the village of al-

Hajjâjiya. Many inhabitants who had collaborated with the Zanj were taken into captivity.[82] When al-Jubbâ'î sent him a message with news of what had taken place, Sulaymân returned on the 28th of the month.[83]

Ju'lân was replaced as prefect of Wâsit by Ahmad b. Laythawayh, one of whose officers, Turnâj, was killed in the battle against Sulaymân on the Abân Canal.[84] Ahmad fought a series of battles against Sulaymân's troops at al-Shadîdiyya; but in the end the Zanj would carry off seventeen enemy camels. Ahmad was removed from his post and in his place Muhammad al-Muwallad was named prefect of Wâsit.

The Capture of Wâsit.—Sulaymân b. Jâmi' asked for reinforcements. 'Alî b. Muhammad sent him Khalîl b. Abân, 'Abdallâh al-Mudhawwab, and fifteen-hundred horsemen. The Zanj routed Muhammad al-Muwallad and killed the residents of Wâsit. Then they plundered and burned the city.[85]

Sulaymân and his troops prepared to destroy Junbulâ. Khalîl b. Abân, following a disagreement with Sulaymân, wrote to his brother, 'Alî b. Abân al-Muhallabî,[86] and received authorization from 'Alî b. Muhammad to go to al-Mukhtâra.

In 264/877–78, the Zanj were still striking their own coins.

Authorized by 'Alî b. Muhammad, Sulaymân b. Jâmi' advanced towards Sawâd al-Kûfa with the intention of digging a canal to facilitate the transport of supplies, but Ibn Laythawayh attacked him and he lost fourteen officers.[87] Muhammad b. al-Hasan, who reports the defeat in detail, claims in addition to the ordinary soldiers who lost their lives, forty-seven officers were killed. At any rate, Sulaymân's forces were destroyed. His boats were set ablaze and he fled to Tahîthâ, where he remained until al-Muwaffaq arrived. An Abbasid officer named Nusayr also defeated a Zanj officer and seized some of his boats.

In *Muharram* 265/September-October 878, Ibn Tûlûn captured Syrian cities and killed Sîmâ al-Tawîl. In the same period Muhammad al-

Muwallad rejoined Ya'qûb b. Layth, whereupon the Caliph ordered all his property seized. In that year also Ya'qûb b. al-Layth al-Saffâr died in Khûzistân.[88]

With thirty-three boats, the Zanj attacked Jabbul and seized the four vessels with heavy cargoes of food they found in the port. Then they captured al-Nu'maniyya, burning the city and taking some of its residents prisoner in the process, before moving on to seize Jarjarâyâ. The frightened population of Sawâd fled to Baghdad.[89]

The city of Tustar was so completely surrounded by Zanj forces that its residents were on the verge of surrender. Masrûr al-Balkhî who, as already mentioned, had been given the responsibility of directing the war against the Zanj, sent Takîn al-Bukhârî to Ahwâz. He arrived just in time to save its inhabitants, and after defeating and routing 'Alî b. Abân al-Muhallabî, set up camp at Tustar. The Zanj regrouped, but a deserter named Wasîf al-Rûmî warned Takîn. He also reported that Zanj troops had scoured the region in search of food and that wine flowed like water in their camp.[90] Takîn attacked at night and again routed the Zanj, killing several of their officers. After defeating 'Alî b. Abân and taking his aide-de-camp, Ja'farawayh, prisoner in yet another successful battle, Takîn returned to Tustar, while 'Alî b. Abân and his brother beat a retreat to the city of Ahwâz. From there, 'Alî b. Abân sent a letter to Takîn, asking him to spare Ja'farawayh. Takîn responded by putting the aide-de-camp in prison, but the two adversaries began a correspondence.[91] When news of this strange situation reached him, Masrûr decided to investigate personally. Pretending to be pleased with Takîn, he headed for Tustar. Takîn learned of Masrûr's imminent arrival and let the governor of Khûzistân know that he had confidence in him and submitted to his judgment. Masrûr relieved him of his sword. On seeing this, Takîn's troops dispersed, with some going over to the Zanj and some joining the Kurd Muhammad b. 'Ubayd Allâh. Thereupon, Masrûr immediately announced pardon for the rest of the troops. As for Takîn, he was confined as a prisoner in Ibrâhîm b. Ju'lân (?), where he remained until his death. These events occurred in 265 and 266/878–80.

A Zanj detachment under the command of Abû l-Mugîra b. 'Isâ b. Muhammad al-Makhzûmî attacked Mecca. The following year Abû l-Sâj's son, Muhammad (Afshîn) Abû 'Ubayd Allâh,[92] fought the Zanj.

In Khûzistân,[93] Masrûr al-Balkhî sent Agartmish to replace Takîn al-Bukhârî in the war against the Zanj.[94] When Agartmish and Matar b. Jami' arrived in Tustar, they killed the Zanj prisoners they found there, including Ja'farawayh. Then they moved south to 'Askar Mukram where they engaged 'Alî b. Abân and Khalîl b. Abân in an indecisive battle. 'Alî moved on to the city of al-Ahwâz, while Khalîl returned to al-Masruqân. Pursued by Abbasid officers, Khalîl immediately informed his brother, who returned with his troops. After several skirmishes, combat began. At first the advantage went to Agartmish, but the Zanj counterattacked and were victorious. Matar b. Jâmi' was taken prisoner and decapitated; other officers died in battle. When Matar asked that his life be spared, 'Alî reminded him of Ja'farawayh's death and, with his own hand, severed his enemy's head. Agartmish fled back to Tustar. 'Alî b. Abân al-Muhallabî returned to the city of Ahwâz and from there sent severed heads as trophies to 'Alî b. Muhammad, who had them planted on the walls of his city. The battles between the two armies continued with varying fortunes. Then there was a truce. 'Alî b. Muhammad took advantage of the suspension of hostilities to plunder cattle from the surroundings and send it to al-Mukhtâra. The Bedouins, some of whom rallied to the Zanj army, intercepted and carried off the kiswa destined for the Ka'ba; it was a violent year for the Hajj.

Relations between 'Alî b. Abân al-Muhallabî and the Kurd Muhammad b. 'Ubayd Allâh were still very tense, and if 'Alî was on the lookout for the right moment to rid himself of Muhammad, the Kurd thought of nothing less. So it was that in 266/879–80, Muhammad sent gifts to 'Alî b. Muhammad's son Ankalay[95] and asked him to influence his father to declare Kurd territory henceforth subjected to Ankalay, "and that the hand of 'Alî b. Abân be lifted from him." This maneuver angered al-Muhallabî, and he asked his master for permission to punish the Kurd and force him to pay the tax he owed. His request was granted; al-Muhallabî wrote to the Kurd demanding the unpaid tax, but Muhammad b. 'Ubayd Allâh turned a deaf ear. 'Alî b. Abân moved his troops forward and took the city of Râmhurmuz,[96] forcing the Kurd to flee. The city was pillaged and devastated.[97] After a few long discussions, the Kurd asked for peace and brought 200,000 *dirhams* to 'Alî b. Abân, who sent them to 'Alî b. Muhammad.

Relations between the two parties soon took a turn for the worse again. Together, the Zanj and Muhammad's men attacked the Kurds of al-Dâribân to steal cattle. Just when victory seemed won, Muhammad's men stopped fighting. The Zanj were beaten and pursued in their retreat by their former allies! When 'Alî b. Abân reported what had occurred in a letter to 'Alî b. Muhammad, the Master of the Zanj responded with a letter full of reproach, then wrote to the Kurd demanding immediate compensation for what he had done. In an effort to exonerate himself, the frightened Kurd replied with a humble letter and returned the horses that his men had stolen from 'Alî b. Abân. When more gifts and correspondence had been exchanged, the affair finally came to an end.

After a while 'Alî b. Abân tried to take al-Mattûth, but without success. He was attacked and routed by Masrûr al-Balkhî, whose troops seized all the matériel the Zanj had collected to lay siege to the city.

Hamdân Qarmat's Meeting with the Master of the Zanj.—It is most probably at this period (259–266) that we should place Hamdân Qarmat's famous proposal[98] to the Master of the Zanj for an alliance between them:

> One day, I sought out the Prince of the blacks, Carmath said. When I was ushered into his presence, I told him that I professed a certain doctrine and had one-hundred-thousand swords behind me.

'Let us compare our beliefs. If we agree, my men and I will join you, if not we will go away. Give me your word of honor that you will not detain me.' When he had promised that I would be permitted to leave safe and sound, we began discussions that lasted until noon. I realized then that he and I could never agree. He rose for prayer and I took advantage of the occasion to leave the city secretly and go to the land of Kûfa.[99]

As for the supposed discussion between the famous mu'tazilite Abû Ya'qûb al-Shahhâm and 'Alî b. Muhammad,[100] for which we have no date, it perhaps has another meaning under its moralizing aspect. I confess it escapes me.

NOTES

1. From the end of the month of *Ramadân* to the middle of *Dhû' l-Qa'da* 255/September-October 869.
2. Let us say, without delay, that the information provided by Tabarî (as far as this period is concerned) cannot be read without some difficulty. It contains a great many details without continuity.
3. *'Id al-fitr* gives 1 *Shawwâl* (and the days that followed) as the date of the celebration.
4. Village on a stop of the trip from Hisn Mahdî, in the direction of Basra on the Tigris.
5. They would walk around with them to intimidate their enemies.
6. Heinz Halm comments at length on this passage from Tabarî. He thinks that, according to Ibn Abî l-Hadîd, the passage has an eschatological meaning (the horse without a saddle is that of the Mahdî).
7. Tabarî's passage is not explicit enough here. Was it one of 'Alî b. Muhammad's agents who came to give him a report? Tabarî speaks of writings that he brought. What was the nature of these writings? Why has Tabarî never introduced these personages to us as he usually does? Should this be taken as proof that the *Annales* have really been abridged?
8. It is a question of the Furatîiya, Qarmâtiyûn, and Nûba principally.
9. Here the text is not very clear.
10. We have no knowledge of this. Is it a question of cuts in Tabarî's text, or should we believe, on the contrary, that it is an allusion to the meeting on al-Sîb Canal?
11. Tabarî emphasizes that this was the first time it happened.

12. al-Rayyân: large city on the al-Rayyân Canal of the al-Ahwâz region.

13. We read "ashâb al-Sultân" for the first time. It most certainly designates a local garrison and not yet troops sent by Baghdad.

14. Of about 4,400 men.

15. Again we can wonder about cuts in Tabarî's text. He speaks to us of this Zuhayr as though we have known him for a long time.

16. Probably a Banû 'Ijl man, for this is the name the 'Ijlites bear.

17. October 22, 869.

18. The beasts, the goods, the books, and the astrolabes.

19. October 23, 869.

20. Whom Tabarî calls for the first time "enemy of God."

21. For the first time, Tabarî calls him "wicked," "base."

22. In *Muharram* 256/end of 869–beginning of 870 at the latest.

23. About 6 km.

24. It is difficult to say which, al-Mu'tamid's accession having taken place on the 16th of the same month.

25. From the moment they arrived in this place, they built their capital, al-Mukhtâra, which in the early days was called "Mu'askar al-Imâm" (the Imâm's Camp).

26. He was put to death on 18 *Rajab* 256/June 21, 870.

27. Tabari cites 'Alî b. Muhammad, who explains his hesitation between al-Ubbulla and 'Abbâdân and the reasons for his choice.

28. It is a question of the brother of the famous Ahmad b. al-Mudabbir who exercised the same functions in Egypt and whose quarrels with Ahmad b. Tûlûn occupy much space in the history of the Tulunids.

29. His captivity and escape are well-known facts. Al-Buhturî (famous Arab poet, 821–897 and therefore a contemporary of the revolt) devotes a long poem of 35 verses to them. Ibn al-Rûmî (also a great Arab poet, 836–896, a contemporary of the revolt) also celebrates them in a shorter poem of 5 verses.

30. 'Aynî and Makîn speak of eighty-thousand men. We find the same figure in the Anonymous Manuscript and in Flügel's work. I do not know where they found it.

31. Al-Muwaffaq had been commander in chief of the Caliph's army since the month of *Safar* 257.

32. Probably a detachment.

33. The famous Muhammad b. al-Hasan Shaylama, to be mentioned again on many occasions.

34. Tabarî tells us that Mansûr b. Ja'far al-Khayyât left Sa'îd voluntarily.

35. Probably to fight the Zanj.

36. For historians, it is the most outstanding event of this whole period if not of the entire

revolt. The abundance of information forces me to intervene more often than I would like in presenting it. Tabarî, as is his wont, gives us several versions, reported by eye-witnesses.

37. Allusion to a lunar eclipse.

38. Banû Tamîm and Banû Asad.

39. One week before the city was captured.

40. One of the personalities in the city who was supposed to look after its defense.

41. I do not believe it was the plague. If so we would have many more details.

42. It is difficult to know whether the event occurred Friday the 17th or Monday the 20th *Shawwâl.*

43. Another witness claims that it was on a Sunday that 'Alî b. Abân returned to the city unopposed.

44. It seems that the great massacre was the work of Yahyâ b. Muhammad al-Bahrânî.

45. Ibn Abî l-Hadîd points out that when the city fell, Ibrâhîm b. Muhammad al-Muhallabî, his cousin, came to him asking that mercy be shown the inhabitants of Basra.

46. Historians suggest several figures for the number of victims who perished during the capture of Basra. The one most often given is 300,000 put forward by Mas'ûdî. It seems far in excess of what might be true. Other historians cite numbers such as 20,000, 12,000, or 10,000.

47. Completely surprised by being told to hand over his money, his dying words were: "but what money?"

48. Louis Massignon in keeping with Tabarî's text which, moreover, definitely does not indicate that 'Alî b. Muhammad was in Basra during those days. Quite the contrary, Tabarî makes it clear that the Zanj leader issued his orders by letter.

49. In Tabarî's work and above all, in detail in Ibn Hazm's work. Cf. also R. Strothmann's article, in which he writes, in particular: "The leader of the Zanj claimed to be a great-grandson of this Yahyâ. In fact Yahyâ's posterity was already extinct at the time and the true descendants of Zaid came from Zaid's half brothers."

50. Charles Pellat, who then cites at length the sad description of a copyist in the employ of Ibn Hawqal, who visited Basra in 537/1142–43. This description is, therefore, almost three centuries later than the capture of Basra by the Zanj and, of course, cannot be considered for the period that interests us, no more than the description given by the famous Ibn al-Rûmî who, contrary to Ibn Hawqal, was a contemporary of the revolt. His long poem, devoted entirely to retracing this event, paints a very sugges-tive and poetic picture of the situation and atmosphere of the city in flames. In fact: "The revolts of the years . . . 255–270h. are not easily pinpointed" (Massignon). Adamov (*Irak,* p. 291) speaks of 15,000 houses and 200 mosques destroyed. I have

found no trace of such information anywhere.

51. This well-known passage from Mas'ûdî must be accepted with many reservations. It will obviously come up again in later chapters.

52. I do not dare confirm R. Levy's supposition (*The Social Structure of Islam*, pp. 421–22), who writes: "If it was necessary to fight a rebel or a heretic nearer home, the Caliph or the officer charged by him with the command of a punitive force could often rely upon local aid as when the Caliph Mu'tamid in 257/871, after a regular force under his chamberlain had been defeated (Ibn al-Athîr, VII, 166), sent Ahmad al-Muwallid to Basra against the Zanj. There a great number of men 'gathered about him' (*Ibid.*, VII, 170), presumably volunteers, whose lack of training and skill led to their being easily routed by a determined force more accustomed to fighting."

If the fact is confirmed more than once, I strongly doubt that the "information" furnished by Ibn al-Athîr is more than a turn of phrase in the specific case. At this place in the text (as almost everywhere else in what concerns the Zanj) Ibn al-Athîr only abridges Tabarî's text. Tabarî makes no mention of al-Muwallad's troops and even less of the quality of these troops. Obviously, Ibn al-Athîr can provide information independently of Tabarî, but in the rare cases where this occurs it is a question of complete information taken from elsewhere and not a complementary detail for a fact already mentioned by Tabarî.

53. At the beginning (?) of the year 258/end of 871.

54. It was practically always he who filled the role of "admiral" of the Zanj fleet.

55. Separated from his men, Mansûr fought valiantly until his spears were broken and his supply of arrows exhausted. He then plunged into the river with his horse so as not to fall into the hands of the Zanj. After swimming in pursuit of him, one of them cut his head off.

56. Tabarî says he personally saw this expedition in Baghdad and reports the impressions of citizens who claim never to have seen anything similar.

57. Tabarî agrees with Mas'ûdî: "Mouflih the Turk, fought this chief on Tuesday, the twelfth day before the end of djemadi I of the same year. Struck in the temple by an arrow Mouflih died the next day, Wednesday. His body was taken to Samârrâ where it was buried. Mouwaffak then interrupted his struggle against the Zanj."

58. We have two anecdotes concerning this person before he left Baghdad for his last battle. If Shâbushtî's anecdote has practically no interest for us (it is about a homosexual affair) it is not the same for the one given us by Ibn al-Mu'tazz: en route to fight the Zanj, Muflih had a poet accused of Shiite tendencies decapitated. On hearing of this, 'Alî b. Muhammad exclaimed: "If he killed for love of 'Alî and the people of his house, he will no longer be successful, Muflih!" (Play of words on Muflih's name). One does not have to dwell on this to show the degree to which it appears suspect and

in the tradition of fabricating a maxim after an event. I will speak of this passage again.

59. It is again Muhammad b. al-Hasan who reports this anecdote, saying that it is untrue. He assures us that he was at ʿAlî b. Muhammad's side during the battle and that the Zanj leader did not get off his horse.

60. Disease was rampant in the swamps.

61. On the hippodrome where a platform had been erected for the occasion.

62. A new quote from Shaylama (Muhammad b. al-Hasan) absolutely irrelevant to the context.

63. Between Basra and Wâsit.

64. Yaʿqûbî gives another version. According to him the fire destroyed al-Muwaffaq's fleet, which was transporting the entire expedition (soldiers with their matériel and weapons).

65. Nöldeke says, in *Sketches*, p. 161: "The prince of the blacks spared several noble persons who fell into his hands probably so that he could obtain a high ransom for them."

66. Beginning of Saffarid indirect aid to the Zanj.

67. On the subject of this person, cf. A. K. Khalifa's note: "'ʿAlî Ibn Zayd the ʿAlid, is ʿAlî b. Zayd b. al-Husayn b. ʿIsâ b. Zayd b. ʿAlî b. al-Husayn b. ʿAlî b. Abî Tâlib; emerged at Kûfa, at the head of a section of the common people and Bedouins, under Caliph al-Muhtadi's regime. In spite of the small numbers of his followers, he succeeded in routing the force, under the command of al-Shâh b. Mikâl, the Caliph had sent against him. Shortly afterwards, in the Bassora region, the leader of the Zanj rebelled, whereupon ʿAlî b. Zayd and a group of Tâlibites joined his ranks. ʿAlî b. Zayd then conspired against the Zanj leader, trying to alienate his officers by claiming that he had deceived them about his origins. The very same officers denounced ʿAlî b. Zayd, who along with his accomplices, also Tâlibites, was ordered executed by the Zanj chief." From the same A. K. Khalifa: "The failure of this ʿAlid's attempt and the fact that he himself and his accomplices were the only ones executed without causing any visible discontent on the part of the rebels shows both an important aspect of the Zanj revolt and their relations with the Shiites. On the other hand, the situation of the Shiites is altogether in keeping with the Carmathian position regarding this revolt."

68. In the same year the Zanj are said to have destroyed a convent of ʿAbbâdân (see, *supra*, Chapter I, note 22).

69. The Zanj seized Ahwâz for the third time. Some authors cite 50,000 as the number of dead.

70. It was a Bâhilite guide. On this subject, A.K. Khalifa writes: "The Bâhilites (Bâhila), an Arab tribe living in the swamp region of al-Batâ'ih. They tried to help themselves to the materials of the worksite abandoned by the Zanj at the beginning of their revolt.

But the central government succeeded in capturing the leader of the Bâhilites, Sa'îd b. Ahmad b. Sa'îd b. Salm al-Bâhilî, who was taken to Baghdad in 258 (871–872) where he died a victim of torture in the month of *Rabi' II* (February-March 872). After this the Bâhilites joined the the Zanj."

71. The latter, passing through a village already pacified by the leader of the Zanj, devastated and burned it.

72. Ibn Rustah, "At Qatr, the Tigris divides into three branches. One goes in the direction of Tahitha, a large city with a cathedral-mosque. It is in this place that Abû Zakariya Bahrânî secured himself until he was expelled."

73. Chapter 109 ("The Infidels"), trans. Blachère. Tabarî does not tell us about this famous proposal for an alliance. It is Ibn al-Athîr who reports it, but without specifying his source. Therefore it is difficult to assess. Cf. *infra,* p. 152 (in the Conclusion, " 'Alî b. Muhammad's Doctrine").

74. This occurred in 263/876–77.

75. Here it is difficult to understand Tabarî's text.

76. Who are not mentioned since their victory over Agartmish and Khushaysh in 262/875–876.

77. The Turkish officer was probably named Tegîn.

78. April 17, 878.

79. May 4, 878.

80. May 16, 878.

81. Tabarî, III, p. 1924, then on the following page (after the events of the end of the year 264): "Sulaymân captured al-Rusâfa, Matar b. Jâmi''s camp, took seven boats and burned two others, *in Rabî' II* 264." Just as the events concerning a victory by Takîn al-Bukhârî, reported later, must certainly be placed well before.

82. We are told twice about the collaboration between the Zanj and the inhabitants of the region.

83. August 31, 878.

84. But there is another version in Tabarî.

85. Tabarî does not give us the date, which is strange.

86. Probably to exonerate himself.

87. According to Ibn al-Athîr, forty officers were killed.

88. This is a key date for the Zanj revolt. Actually, his brother 'Amr, satisfied with the fiefs he had received from al-Muwaffaq, gave him (al-Muwaffaq) a free hand against the Zanj.

89. It is the high point of the revolt's expansion toward the north and the northwest.

90. "This story (and the one that follows) that people told is false, a complete fabrication: 'The chief of the Zanj had conquered (the Sawâd) the vicinity of Baghdad and lived

at al-Madâ'in. From Baghdad, al-Muwaffaq (Abû Ahmad) sent against him an expedition that was transporting, among other things, jars of wine and must have beat a retreat from its very first engagement with the Zanj, abandoning tents and other materials. This action was carried out by the government army. The Zanj seized the jars (of wine). That night they drank and got drunk. Then a great number of them were massacred by Abû Ahmad, in a surprise attack.' It was really Tikkyn al-Bukhary, then governor of the Ahwâz, who attacked them the night they got drunk." See Ibn Abî l-Hadîd, p. 361.

91. Al-Tabarî's text causes Nöldeke to suppose that there were suspect negotiations, which led him to say: "These affairs throw a strange light on the loyalty and discipline of the government army."

92. Tabarî mentions their presence in 265, without giving a precise date, then also in 266. On this topic: Defrémery writes: "He left two children, Mohammad, also called Afshin and nicknamed Abou-Obayd-Allah, and Youssef. The first was given authority over the road to Mecca and the two holy cities. He went to Mecca where he had to fight a person named Abou l-Moghayrah 'Isa, son of Mohammad, al-Makhzoumi who had come to this city, the year before, in the name of the prince of the Zanj (Ibn al-Athîr, f. 107 v.). He put him to flight, and seized his possessions, the 8 of dhou 'l-hiddjeh (July 20, 880), (Ibn al-Athîr f.110 v; Beybars. f. 50 v.)." F. Wustenfeld also has a passage on the subject: "In folge eines Schreibens von dem Mitregenten el-Muwaffac, welches Abul-Mugira am 20 Dhul-Higga in dem Commandantenhause vorlas, wurden die Umhänge der Ka'ba abgenommen. Das wechselnde Glück, womit um diese Zeit der Krieg in el-Ahwâz gegen die Zing geführt wurde, brachte den Abul-Mugira sogar in die Lage, deren Oberhaupte 'Ali ben Muhammad in J. 265 huldigen zu müssen. Vielleicht aber stand er mit ihm im Einvernehmen, sodass dies der Grund war, wesshalb er gleich darauf abgesetzt wurde; denn sonst wäre es den Beduînen Arabern wohl nicht so leicht gelungen, Mekka zu überrumpeln und die Umhänge der Ka'ba wegzuholen, von denen sie enen Theil dem Oberhaupte der Zing Zusandten."

C. Huart provides another detail: "His son Muhammad Afshîn Abû 'Ubayd took Mecca from the Zanj leader's lieutenant, Abû l-Mughîra 'Isâ b. Muhammad al-Makhzûmî, in 266 (880; three years later he marched on Djidda and captured two ships full of silver and weapons from al-Makhzûmî."

93. The events that are going to follow should be placed after the next first sub-chapter because Abû l-'Abbâs's campaign began in *Rabî' II* 266/end of 879. However, (as Tabarî himself certainly knew very well) the events that occurred in Khûzistân during the entire year 266/879–80 are *logically* related to the preceding period because the beginnings of Abû l-'Abbâs's expedition represent practically no change for the Zanj troops of Khûzistân.

94. *Ramadân* 266/April-May 880.
95. Heinz Halm emphasizes that it is a Persian name. He sees this as a further indication of the Master of the Zanj's Persian origin.
96. High point of the revolt's expansion towards the east and the southeast.
97. In the Anonymous: "They reduced the mosque to ashes, massacred many people, took away many captives, and made off with rich booty"; without doubt following a remark by Ibn al-Jawzî. Tabarî does not mention the fire at the cathedral-mosque.
98. Cf. *infra,* p.153.
99. De Goeje. Before the translation of Tabarî's text, De Goeje wrote: "Among the causes that most favored the development of Carmathe domination we must place the civil war that devastated the territory of Basra for fifteen years. Thanks to the disorder prevalent in southern Iraq, the mission was able to become organized everywhere. For a moment, there was even seriously question of an alliance with the prince of slaves. Tabarî reports an account given by the brother-in-law of Zikrwayh that the latter had personally received from Carmath, great *dâ'î* (propaganda agent, recruiter) of the land of Kûfa."
100. Cf. 'Abd al-Jabbâr, *Tathbît,* II, p. 341–42.

CHAPTER IV

Continuation of the War and the End of the Revolt (The Zanj, the Caliphate's Chief Concern)

I. OFFENSIVE UNDERTAKEN BY ABÛ L-ʿABBÂS (RABÎʿ II 266-SAFAR 267/ NOVEMBER– DECEMBER 879–SEPTEMBER 880)

Al-Muwaffaq was finally free to act; the Saffarids were calm, the Tulunids had been abandoned, and the Qarmats had not yet been heard of publicly. Moreover, the Zanj, who were becoming more oppressive than ever, posed a direct threat to the capital. During the ten years that they had occupied or controlled extensive regions, the economy of the central provinces had been ruined. Having learned from successive failures and his own campaign, al-Muwaffaq prepared his army and put together matériel for a special type of war. Boats and small craft of different types would allow his soldiers to attack and pursue the enemy to their camps in hitherto inaccessible areas. At the head of an army of ten-thousand men, he placed his son, Abû l-ʿAbbâs, who methodically cleared everything in his path, leaving the Zanj to take refuge in their cities. The surroundings of Wâsit were liberated, and Sulaymân b. Jâmiʿʾs troops were defeated on several occasions. It was not long before the Zanj realized their error in underestimating Abû l-ʿAbbâs. Such was the situation for about a year. No important city was captured, no spectacular victory was won, but during that time the ground was already being laid for future exploits that would be associated with al-Muwaffaq, who would join his son at the head of a new army in *Safar* 267/September-October 880. It was not long before the Zanj understood that to have underestimated Abû l-'Abbâs was a mistake.

Once again, it is to Tabarî that we owe the information concerning this period. This information was repeated by many other historians without adding anything new to the subject.

Abû l-'Abbâs's Campaign.— In the month of *Rabî' II* 266 (November-December 879), a year before assuming joint command with his son, al-Muwaffaq sent a new army[1] against the Zanj. The ten-thousand troops under the command of his son, Abû l-'Abbâs, were well-armed and supported by a fleet of different types of boats.[2] They passed through Bustân Mûsâ al-Hâdî, al-Firk, and al-Madâ', before stopping at Dayr al-'Aqûl. There, briefed by his fleet commander, Nusayr Abû Hamza, who had been sent ahead, Abû l-'Abbâs studied the Zanj position. Sulaymân b. Jâmi' and al-Jubbâ'î were in the Bardûdâ area with their men, and Sulaymân b. Mûsâ al-Sha'rânî was on the Abân Canal. Abû l-'Abbâs proceeded through Jarjarâyâ to al-Silh where, in a village called 'Abd Allâh, he won his first victory. Some of the rebels surrendered and asked for clemency; others were taken prisoner. Captured boats were sunk.

Abû l-'Abbâs entered Wâsit[3] and attended Friday prayer. A number of his officers wanted to set up camp north of there, but he chose instead al-'Umr, one *farsakh* down-river from the city. He put his men through training in warfare and saw to it that new boats were built. To the overconfident Zanj, all of this was a performance put on by an inexperienced young man. Abû l-'Abbâs was twenty-three years old. They decided that a three-pronged attack would teach him a lesson and rid them of him once and for all.

Sulaymân b. Jâmi' divided his Zanj fighting men into three groups. Each one was to attack Abû l-'Abbâs from a different direction.[4] Warned by spies that the Zanj were approaching and had made preparations to ambush him, Abû l-'Abbâs deployed his men and planned for battle. He himself embarked on one of the boats after carefully selecting its crew. The battle was fought on terrain between the villages of al-Raml and al-Rusâfa. The rebels were defeated, and the government troops seized four-teen boats. Sulaymân and al-Jubbâ'î fled to Tahîthâ. Abû l-'Abbâs returned with his men to al-'Umr and assigned crews to the captured boats once they were refurbished.

The Zanj did not reappear for the next twenty days, though al-Jubbâ'î left his camp every three days to dig traps for Abû l-'Abbâs's horsemen. When an Abbasid horseman was caught in one of the traps, the govern-ment army changed its route. Before long, the Zanj began harassing Abû l-'Abbâs's troops on a daily basis but when their provocation proved to be ineffective, they suspended raids for a month. Sulaymân b. Jâmi' weighed Abbasid strength and wrote to 'Alî b. Muhammad asking for additional small boats. Twenty days later he received forty craft. Al-Jubbâ'î began daily raids on Abû l-'Abbâs's camp. His tactic was to attack and then fall back so as to draw pursuing enemy boats into an ambush.[5]

Abû l-'Abbâs organized an expedition that included a large fleet with small boats in the vanguard. Some of the boats were captured by the Zanj who, nevertheless, were unable to withstand the onslaught from the fleet. The Abbasids seized thirty-one Zanj boats, in addition to those they had just lost. Abû l-'Abbâs, who took part in the fighting personally, distin-guished himself by his energy and courage.[6] Once back in his camp, he ordered gifts distributed to the elite soldiers he had chosen especially for the operation. Then he gave instructions to outfit the boats seized from the Zanj.

A reconnaissance mission that Abû l-'Abbâs led to the al-Amîr Canal to examine the routes by which Zanj boats arrived almost ended in tragedy. Separated from his fleet commmander, Nusayr, who had gone to another canal, Abû l-'Abbâs was at first successful, but then found himself attacked by a very strong force under the command of Muntâb. In spite of finding himself in a serious situation, he managed to return to his camp, where he ordered that three rowers who had abandoned their posts to steal cattle be decapitated, rewarded the men who had remained faithful, and ordered all the others not to leave their craft during battle under pain of death.

Zanj forces were concentrated in three places: in Tahîthâ under the authority of Sulaymân b. Jâmi'; in Sûq al-Khamîs under al-Sha'rânî; in al-Sîniyya under the command of Nasr al-Sindî. From these three centers, they wreaked havoc all over the region, looting and destroying everything in their path.

Abû l-'Abbâs led a large expedition of horsemen, small craft, and boats against Nasr al-Sindî. When the Zanj saw the cavalry springing towards them, they tried to take refuge in their vessels, but the Abbasid fleet entered into action and slaughtered them. Many Zanj were killed, others were taken prisoner. Small boats belonging to their commander, Nasr al-Sindî, were seized, as were boats loaded with rice. Some of the Zanj forces fled to Tahîthâ, others escaped to Sûq al-Khamîs. The insurgents had been ousted from al-Sîniyya once and for all. One witness speaks of the terror that gripped the Zanj when they learned of Abû l-'Abbâs's presence.

Informed that there was a large Zanj force at 'Abdasî, commanded by Thâbit b. Abî Dulaf and Lu'lu', Abû l-'Abbâs launched an attack with a detachment chosen from some of his very best men and defeated the rebels. Lu'lu' was killed in battle, and Thâbit was taken prisoner. Abû l-'Abbâs pardoned him, spared his life, and enlisted him in a troop commanded by one of his officers.[7] A large number of women prisoners held by the Zanj were freed and returned to their families.

Back in his camp, Abû l-'Abbâs ordered his men to rest while he began preparations for an attack on Sûq al-Khamîs. He discussed the difficulties of the operation, especially the narrowness of the Sûq al-Khamîs river, with his officers, then ordered his troops to move forward. Nusayr went ahead towards al-Manî'a (in Sûq al-Khamîs), Sulaymân b. Mûsâ al-Sha'rânî's city. Two *farsakh* away Abû l-'Abbâs was attacked by a large number of insurgents and cut off from his vanguard. During the fighting the Zanj circulated the rumor that Nusayr had fallen into their hands; Muhammad b. Shu'ayb embarked on a small boat[8] to verify the truth of the news and found Nusayr in the process of recapturing the boats the Zanj had taken from him and setting fire to the enemy's city. Nusayr took many prisoners before rejoining Abû l-'Abbâs, who courageously engaged in yet another battle, exposing himself to insurgent arrows.[9] He was victorious again and took six Zanj small boats. When he returned to his camp at al-'Umr, he distributed robes of honor to his sailors. He remained at the camp until his father, al-Muwaffaq, arrived.

II. AL-MUWAFFAQ'S RETURN AND THE CLEANSING OF IRAQ AND OF THE AHWÂZ (*SAFAR–RAJAB* 267/SEPTEMBER 880–FEBRUARY 881)

A little less than a year after sending his son, Abû l-'Abbâs, against the Zanj, al-Muwaffaq personally led a new army against the insurgents (*Safar* 267/September 880). The united Abbasid forces went from one victory to another. They razed al-Manî'a and al-Mansûra, strongholds of Sulaymân b. Mûsâ al-Sha'rânî and of Sulaymân b. Jâmi', and freed thousands of women and children held as slaves by the Zanj. Then, after giving two officers responsibility for pursuing fugitives and mopping up the area of Lower Iraq between Wâsit and Basra, al-Muwaffaq and his son, Abû l-'Abbâs, pushed forward in the province of Khûzistân. Already greatly upset by the events in Iraq, 'Alî b. Muhammad decided to withdraw his troops from the canal region around his capital. He ordered his generals to abandon all matériel and food and join him as soon as possible. The Abbasids reoccupied the province with no resistance; the whole expedition lasted only six weeks. Increasingly, there was evidence of the famous " policy of amnesty" which would cause the Master of the Zanj great losses in years to come. In the middle of the month of *Rajab* 267/February 881, all the Abbasid troops came together on al-Mubârak Canal, ready for the final stage of the campaign, the siege of al-Mukhtâra, the Zanj's last refuge. The provinces were now reoccupied for good. The insurgents, who had reassembled on the Abû l-Khasîb Canal, were surrounded by the Abbasid army and would be unable to leave before their final defeat.

All we know of this six-month period comes from about twenty pages of Tabarî's work.

Having learned that the Master of the Zanj had asked 'Alî b. Abân al-Muhallabî to return to Iraq with his men and join Sulaymân b. Jâmi' against Abû l-'Abbâs, al-Muwaffaq assembled a new army on 11 *Safar* 267/September 21, 880, and joined his son to take personal command of combined operations against the insurgents.[10] On 2 *Rabî' I* 267, when the army had been mustered and the various craft of the fleet had been prepared, al-Muwaffaq left al-Firk.[11] Passing through Rumiyya al-Madâ'in, al-Sîb, Dayr al-'Aqûl, Jarjarâyâ, Qunna, Jabbul, and al-Silh, he arrived near Wâsit where he met with Abû l-'Abbâs.[12] After the meeting, al-Muwaffaq offered robes of honor to his son and his son's officers, who then returned to their camp at al-'Umr.

The combined forces advanced towards the Zanj. On 28 *Rabî' I* 267,[13] al-Muwaffaq was on the Sindâd Canal and Abû l-'Abbâs on the left bank of the Tigris. Each of the two men led a detachment of selected fighters to the Bar Musâwar Canal, leaving most of the troop behind. On the way, Abû l-'Abbâs encountered and defeated a group of Zanj (from al-Sha'rânî's forces); he carried off the severed heads and the corpses. On al-Muwaffaq's orders, prisoners taken were decapitated.

The Capture of al-Manî'a.—On 8 *Rabî' II* 267[14] the Abbasids launched a joint attack, by land and water, on "al-Manî'a," Sulaymân b. Mûsâ al-Sha'rânî's city in Sûq a-Khamîs on the Barâtiq Canal. They stormed the city and large numbers of Zanj were killed or captured; others, including al-Sha'rânî, fled. Abbasid soldiers pursued them as far as Batâ'ih, where many of them drowned. Five-thousand Muslim women[15] held as slaves in Sûq al-Khamîs were set free and taken back to Wâsit to be reunited with their families. Al-Muwaffaq ordered his soldiers to leave the city and return to camp before sunset. The next day, when al-Manî'a had been completely plundered, the walls of the city were razed, the ditches were filled in, and the Zanj boats burned. Wheat, barley, and rice belonging to al-Sha'rânî were confiscated and sold. The money from the sale was distributed to the troops.

From al-Madhâr, where he had fled with his two brothers, al-Sha'rânî, who now found himself devoid of his possessions and separated from his family, wrote to 'Alî b. Muhammad, informing him of the events that had just taken place. The Master of the Zanj was dismayed at the news[16] and immediately wrote to Sulaymân b. Jâmi' to warn him.

Once al-Manî'a had fallen, al-Muwaffaq began to look for Sulaymân b. Jâmi'. False information led him to believe that the Zanj officer was at al-Hawânît. Al-Muwaffaq sent his son there,[17] but Abû l-'Abbâs found only two of Sulaymân's officers and their men; they had been left behind to guard the food. Fighting broke out, and the Zanj suffered serious losses before night separated the two adversaries.[18] One of the insurgents surrendered, asking for clemency, and informed Abû l-'Abbâs that Sulaymân b. Jâmi' was in al-Mansûra, his fortified city in Tahîthâ. This information was passed on to al-Muwaffaq, who immediately gave orders to set out for Bardûdâ which he designated as the place where his troops should gather because of its position. He arrived in Bardûdâ on 18 *Rabî' II* 267[19] and ordered the completion of preparations of matériel, particularly boats which would be used as bridges. He also asked for a large number of

workers and equipment to fill in the canals and make roads for the cavalry. A misunderstanding created panic in the camp, but it was quickly
cleared up and calm was restored.

The Capture of al-Mansûra.—Al-Muwaffaq left his Bardûdâ encampment on 20 *Rabî' II* 267 and led his troops against Tahîthâ. Boats of different types facilitated the transport men and matériel, and he had a temporary bridge built to enable his men to cross the Mahrûdh Canal. When
the Abbasid army reached the vicinity of Sulaymân b. Jâmi''s city, al-
Muwaffaq chose what he considered to be a good place to set up camp.
They stayed there two days, until 22 *Rabî' II* 267, but the rain and cold
weather prevented them from attempting any military action. On 26 *Rabî'
II* 267,[20] while al-Muwaffaq and a small party of officers were inspecting
the future battleground, they were attacked by a large group of Zanj.
Several of his officers, including Wasîf, were captured, but, during the
skirmish, an arrow shot by Abû l-'Abbâs struck and mortally wounded
Ahmad b. Mahdî al-Jubbâ'î. The fatally wounded Zanj leader was immediately transported to 'Alî b. Muhammad's location[21] where, despite all
the care given him and to the chagrin of the Master of the Zanj, he died
two days later. 'Alî b. Muhammad followed the preparations for the man's
burial closely and was present at his funeral. He declared that through
supernatural gifts he already knew his officer had died when news of it
arrived.[22]

Al-Muwaffaq returned to his camp on the evening of 26 *Rabî' II*
267/December 4, 880. He put his men on alert and ordered them to prepare for combat. The next morning, 27 *Rabî' II* 267/December 5, 880,
after deploying his foot soldiers, his horsemen, and his boats, he prayed
for the success of the operation, then ordered Abû l-'Abbâs to rouse the
men to battle. Mansûra was surrounded by a ditch and five enclosures, but
the Abbasids stormed the city and sank Zanj boats found there. Sulaymân
and a small party managed to escape, though his women and children

were taken prisoner; other Zanj sought refuge nearby. Ten-thousand[23] women and children from Wâsit, Kûfa, and other places were freed and sent to Wâsit to be reunited with their families. Wasîf and the other Abbasid officers were also liberated. The city was pillaged completely and part of the booty was sold; the money it brought was distributed to the soldiers. Al-Muwaffaq remained in Tahîthâ seventeen days, then he ordered the ramparts razed and the ditches filled in. His men continued to pursue the fleeing enemy and received a reward for each fugitive they brought back. Al-Muwaffaq treated the captives well; he pardoned them and integrated them into his army. Nusayr Abû Hamza was given responsibility for finding the fugitive Sulaymân b. Jâmî' and his group and for cleaning up the reed-filled area between the Abû l-Khasîb Canal and the Tigris. Al-Muwaffaq ordered an officer named Zirâk to remain in Tahîthâ. His assignment was to continue pursuing the remnants of the enemy still hiding in the vicinity and to induce residents chased out by the Zanj to return. The Abbasid leader then returned to his camp at Bardûdâ to make preparations to liberate Khûzistân, to which he had already dispatched his son Abû l-'Abbâs. Al-Muwaffaq was joined by Zîrak, who now had carried out his assignment. He made him and Nusayr Abû Hamza reponsible for purging the region of the "One-eyed Tiger," pursuing the insurgents to the Abû l-Khasîb Canal, and keeping him informed of the situation. Then, leaving part of his army in Wâsit, under the command of his son Hârûn, he set out for Khûzistân.

Al-Muwaffaq's Recapture of Khûzistân.—Al-Muwaffaq left on 1 *Jumâdâ II* 267.[24] He passed through Bâdhbîn, Jûkhâ, al-Tîb, Qûrqûb, Darastân, and Wâdî al-Sûs (where he had to build a bridge) and arrived in the city of al-Sûs, where he remained three days. During that time, he met his governor of the province, Masrûr al-Balkhî, and his troops, to whom he gave robes of honor.

A Zanj commander who had been taken prisoner at Tahîthâ died from wounds he had received in battle. Al-Muwaffaq had him decapitated and ordered his head displayed on the bridge at Wâsit. News of this led 'Alî b. Muhammad to change his tactics. He wrote to 'Alî b. Abân al-Muhallabî, who was in Ahwâz with an army of thirty-thousand men, to evacuate the region and join him, abandoning food and matériel on the spot. 'Alî b. Abân al-Muhallabî obeyed, but left someone behind who saw to it that everything was abandoned and, in turn, to join 'Ali b. Muhammad. Bahbûdh b. 'Abd al-Wahhâb, who was in the al-Fandam and al-Bâsiyân region, received the same order as 'Alî b. Abân. He, too, left a large quantity of food on the spot and went to rejoin 'Alî b. Muhammad. This explains how all the provisions in Khûzistân fell into al-Muwaffaq's hands and the shortages felt by the insurgents. On their way to join 'Alî b. Muhammad, al-Muhallabî's troops pillaged villages, even though they were held by the Zanj. Some of his men even deserted and remained in the vicinity. Aware of the clemency al-Muwaffaq had shown after the capture of al-Mansûra, they wrote to him, asking for pardon.

From Sûs, al-Muwaffaq pushed on to Jundaysâbûr, remaining there three days, then to Tustar, where he appointed tax collectors for the province. He sent one of his men to the Kurd Muhammad b. 'Ubayd Allâh to let him know that he had only good intentions toward him and that he was ready to forgive and forget his past misdeeds. He also gave orders to provide for the needs of Masrûr al-Balkhî's troops, who had joined him in the fight the Zanj. From Tustar, he went to 'Askar Mukram, and from there to the city of Ahwâz, where he thought he would find food for his army. His hopes were dashed; the city was experiencing a shortage of food and its residents were in a state of agitation. After waiting three days, during which the situation grew increasingly worse, the causes of the shortage became clear. Caravans were unable to cross the bridge linking Ahwâz to Râmhurmuz because it had been destroyed by the Zanj.[25] Al-Muwaffaq used the blacks in his army[26] to make quick repairs; food began to flow in as before, and everything returned to normal. Plans were made to use boats to build another bridge on the Dujayl. The Abbasid army took advantage of their stay to repair their matériel and rest their animals who now had enough barley. Al-Muwaffaq promised pardon to the Zanj who had refused to follow al-Muhallabî and those who had written him from Sûq al-Ahwâz; about a thousand men who were given clemency joined his army. Once the bridge on the Dujayl was finished, al-Muwaffaq left Ahwâz and went to the west bank of the river. He set up camp at Qasr al-Ma'mûn, where there was an earthquake during his stay. From there, he sent Abû l-'Abbâs to one of the tributaries of the Tigris, called Nahr al-Mubârak, to which he also summoned Hârûn with the troops that had been left at Wâsit. He headed there himself and, on the way, was joined by the messenger he had dispatched to the Kurd Muhammad b. 'Ubayd Allâh. The messenger was returning loaded with gifts from the Kurd as tokens of reconciliation. Concerned with making sure that his men would always have water, he finally joined his two sons at Nahr al-Mubârâk in the middle of the month of *Rajab* 267/February 19, 881.

Al-Muwaffaq's officers, Zîrak and Nusayr, won important victories during the expedition in Khûzistân. Warned that a large Zanj fleet, commanded by Abû 'Isâ (former secretary to al-Jubbâ'î) occupied the Tigris and was blocking passage and threatening Nusayr's camp, the two men attacked and dispersed it on the Yazîd Canal. The Zanj lost many men, and thirty of their boats were seized. Zîrak returned to Wâsit with his trophies and from there informed al-Muwaffaq of his victory. Nusayr wrote to al-Muwaffaq for advice about two-thousand insurgents who asked for pardon. The reply was an order to grant it, to see that they had what they needed, and to make them part of his own troops. Finally, Zîrak and Hârûn, together with Nusayr, obeyed the command to rally at Nahr al-Mubârak.

As for Abû l-'Abbâs, who arrived at Nahr al-Mubârak before any of the others, he had already used boats to attack 'Alî b. Muhammad's city on the Abû l-Khasîb Canal. During the battle one of Sulaymân b. Jâmi''s officers, named Muntâb, and a group of Zanj surrendered and received first from Abû l-'Abbâs, then from al-Muwaffaq, robes of honor. Muntâb was the first of the Master of the Zanj's officers to betray him.

III. THE SIEGE OF AL-MUKHTÂRA AND THE END OF THE REVOLT (*RAJAB* 267–*SAFAR* 270/ FEBRUARY 881–AUGUST 883)

The last phase of the Zanj revolt began in the middle of the month of *Rajab* 267. Driven out of all the areas they had conquered, the insurgents regrouped in their capital on the Abû l-Khasîb Canal, ready to sustain a long siege. It has been said that they numbered three-hundred-thousand, and though this figure is probably inflated, we must not forget that, in spite of a complete blockade, they repelled the 50,000 Abbasid troops for two and a half years! Al-Muwaffaq was perfectly aware of the forces at 'Alî b. Muhammad's disposal. He began by preparing the siege in minute detail. He cut off the enemy's food and ammunition while facilitating supply for his own troops, built a new city, continued the policy of winning over enemy troops with promises of amnesty, attacked often, and returned before nightfall. Both sides were well supplied with weapons and equipment for construction and demolition. During each truce (caused by al-Muwaffaq's wounds, the Caliph al-Mu'tamid's attempt to escape in Egypt) the Zanj repaired the breaches in their defense and again rendered the canals impassable for boats. But little by little they ended up capitulating. Al-Mukhtâra was taken section by section; its buildings and markets were burned, one after another. The last battle took place Saturday, 2 *Safar* 270/August 1, 883. 'Alî b. Muhammad was killed. His closest companions and officers were captured and sent to Baghdad where, two years later, they were decapitated. Some members of his family ended their days in prisons. His soldiers experienced varying fortunes, but the Zanj revolt was definitely over. The inhabitants of the region returned to the villages they had abandoned for several years, while, in Baghdad, a great public celebration greeted Abû l-'Abbâs, who returned carrying the Master of the Zanj's severed head.

Tabarî provides us with a great deal of information on this period. His data have been copied and summarized by later historians. Here and there we found a few supplementary details, which are not in Tabarî's report, but are in the works of other authors.

Al-Muwaffaq's Offer of Pardon to 'Alî b. Muhammad.—On arriving at Nahr al-Mubârak (Saturday, 15 *Rajab* 267/February 19, 881), where all the Abbasid forces had gathered, al-Muwaffaq sent 'Alî b. Muhammad a very formal invitation to surrender, with the promise of absolute pardon and great rewards. He waited five days for a reply,[27] making use of the time to inspect troops and matériel; then, on Thursday, 20 *Rajab* 267/February 24, 881, he moved out to the vicinty of al-Mukhtâra for closer scrutiny of the city's defenses and the state of its access routes. Once satisfied with his appraisal of how solid the installations were and the number of the insurgents in the city, he ordered his own men back to their camp. As for the Zanj, they were deeply impressed by Abû l-'Abbâs's bravery in bringing his boat up to the very wall of the city to test its defenses.

Increasing numbers of rebels took advantage of the Abbasid policy of amnesty. They deserted 'Alî b. Muhammad for al-Muwaffaq, who received them with open arms, showering them with gifts and honor garments. He also saw to it that the deserters were put on display where they could be seen from al-Mukhtâra. This drew new deserters who became very useful, once enrolled in the Abbasid army, because of their knowledge of the area. Two of the deserters were commanders of Zanj boats; because of this the Master of the Zanj ordered his boats on the Tigris to leave and return to the Abû l-Khasîb Canal. Then he sent Bahbûdh b. 'Abd al-Wahhâb to the mouth of the canal to defend the passageway. In battles with Zîrak and Abû l-'Abbâs, the Zanj officer was wounded and defeated. This led to new desertions.

Al-Muwaffaq wanted to get closer to al-Mukhtâra, the Zanj capital. On Monday, 24 *Rajab* 267,[28] accompanied by his officers, he went out in search of a new campsite and chose Nahr Jattâ, at an eastern tributary of the Tigris. The next morning, men and matériel were ordered to the new camp. Three weeks passed before he undertook any action against the Zanj.

He advanced his men[29] to al-Mukhtâra on Saturday, 14 *Sha'bân* 267,[30] and once again, promising amnesty, invited the rebels to surrender. There were new cases of desertion; and the same day, two Abbasid officers, clients of his, arrived with reinforcements.

The Construction of al-Muwaffaqiyya.—The next day, Sunday, 15 *Sha'bân* 267[31] the Abbasid troops left their camp at Nahr Jattâ for Furât al-Basra. There, facing al-Mukhtâra, 'Alî b. Muhammad's city, they built al-Muwaffaqiyya, on terrain prepared in advance, which would rapidly take on the appearance of a large city. To ensure provisions for his troops, al-Muwaffaq quickly brought in and installed merchants while cutting off supplies to the Zanj. He ordered that taxes be brought there, sent for craftsmen, opened offices and exchange bureaus as well as markets, had a cathedral-mosque built, organized commerce, and directed that provisions be brought in by sea-going boats. He minted coins,[32] and al-Muwaffaqiyya quickly became like all the other large Muslim cities. Abbasid troops took up positions in the neighboring area.

In a surprise attack, on 17 *Rajab* 267/February 21, 881, Bahbûdh b. 'Abd al-Wahhâb set fire to Abû Hamza's camp and killed or captured the soldiers he found there. Abû l-'Abbâs counterattacked and defeated a troop of four-thousand Zanj commanded by al-Hamadânî. New deserters were welcomed, showered with gifts, and put on exhibit for the insurgents to see. Bahbûdh b. 'Abd al-Wahhâb intercepted a caravan transporting supplies from Khûzistân. He massacred the members of the caravan and looted its cargo. Al-Muwaffaq responded by ordering compensation for the victims, doubling the number of horsemen accompanying the caravans, and placing boats where necessary. Abû l-'Abbâs further assured the safety of the caravan routes by positioning boats as strong points from al-Muwaffaqiyya to the Persian Gulf.

The Abbasids Nusayr and Zîrak were attacked in their camp on 2 *Ramadân* 267/April 6, 881, but warned in time, they routed the group of Zanj, captured their chief, Sandal al-Zanjî, and put him to death. In the same month, five-thousand Zanj surrendered to al-Muwaffaq.

In *Shawwâl* 267/May–June 881, 'Alî b. Muhammad sent two-hundred officers and five-thousand men to attack al-Muwaffaq's camp by surprise, but one of his rowers surrendered to the enemy and betrayed the plan. Abbasid reaction inflicted a terrible defeat on the rebels, and a good number of Zanj were massacred. Abû l-'Abbâs paraded the severed heads and prisoners on boats to demoralize the Zanj. 'Alî b. Muhammad claimed that news of Abû l-'Abbâs's victory was all a hoax. When al-Muwaffaq learned of this, he ordered the severed heads of rebels catapulted into the Zanj capital. In *Dhû' l-Qa'da* 267/June–July, 881, 'Alî b. Muhammad, taking advantage of the fact that al-Muwaffaq's fleet was scattered, sent fifty boats to attack Abbasid craft. They were divided into three groups, and the plan was to attack the enemy vessels one after the other. Nusayr Abû Hamza avoided combat with them because of their superiority. That caused panic among government troops. However, it was not long before long boats from Sîrâf and Jannâbâ that al-Muwaffaq had ordered built came to his aid. Abû l-'Abbâs defeated the insurgents, sank three of their boats, seized two others, and had their crews decapitated. Informed of this, 'Alî b. Muhammad restricted his fleet to al-Mukhtâra. There were new desertions, and 'Alî b. Muhammad ordered a turncoat officer's wife, who had been unable to follow her husband when he defected to al-

Muwaffaq, sold as a slave.

Supplies were becoming increasingly scarce among the Zanj. 'Alî b. Muhammad sent ten-thousand men, commanded by two of his best officers, to pillage the al-Batîha region and bring back as much food and ammunition as possible. Al-Muwaffaq dispatched Zîrak and a large army to attack them. The Abbasid forces cut them to pieces on the Ibn 'Umar Canal and seized four hundred of their boats.

Officers deserted the Zanj ranks with increasing frequency, forcing 'Alî b. Muhammad to place guards at likely escape routes. A group of insurgents who wanted to join al-Muwaffaq asked him to send troops to create an opportunity for them to defect. He sent Abû l-'Abbâs, whose defeat of al-Muhallabî and Sulaymân b. Jâmi''s troops on the al-Garbî Canal enabled those who wanted to leave their camp to do so. Most of the Abbasid troops had already headed back to al-Muwaffaqiyya when a detachment attacked a small number of Zanj on the Atrâk Canal, not far from al-Mukhtâra. When he knew that the Zanj had received reinforcements, Abû l-'Abbâs turned back to aid his men. He defeated the Zanj but was in turn over powered by Sulaymân b. Jâmi', whose forces outnumbered his.

The First Attack on al-Mukhtâra.—Al-Muwaffaq had made preparations to cross the river and attack the city. A violent wind forced him to delay putting his plan in action. It was on Wednesday, 24 *Dhû' l-Hijja* 267/ July 26, 881 that he assaulted al-Mukhtâra from several directions so that its defense forces would have to spread out. Abbasid soldiers entered al-Mukhtâra by the Atrâk Canal after swimming across it and successfully scaling the ramparts of the city. Losses were heavy on both sides. Abû l-'Abbâs made a breach in the wall and, after routing al-Muhallabî and his men, clashed with the powerful army commanded by Sulaymân b. Jâmi'. Abbasid soldiers entering the city destroyed Ibn Sam'ân's house, which they burned, pursued the fleeing Zanj, and pushed on as far as the racecourse in front of 'Alî b. Muhammad's palace. The Master of the Zanj took part in the battle personally, and his horse was wounded when struck by a shield. As the sun began to set, al-Muwaffaq ordered his soldiers to return to their boats; they took their loot and severed insurgent heads with them, burning houses and markets on their way. The return was difficult. Boats overloaded with large numbers of deserters were caught in the mud created by the ebbing river. A violent wind blew in from the north, and night fell. Emboldened by the enemy's adversities, the Zanj attacked.

They recovered part of what they had lost and killed many Abbasid soldiers. On the same day, Rashîq defeated the Zanj fleet on the Tigris, forcing it to turn back and take refuge on the Abû l-Khasîb Canal.

Following the Abbasid incursion into al-Mukhtâra and the panic it caused, there were many reports of desertion among rebel forces. Muhammad and 'Isâ, al-Sha'rânî's two brothers, fled, but returned when they learned that al-Muwaffaq's soldiers had abandoned the city. A group of Bedouin allies who also fled were given amnesty and showered with gifts by their erstwhile adversaries. On Sunday, 29 *Dhû' l-Hijja,*[33] Rayhân b. Sâlih, chamberlain to Ankalây ('Alî b. Muhammad's son), and his men defected, aided by Zîrak and his large fleet. This led to new desertions.

The Zanj presence in Mecca was reported once again.

On Tuesday, 1 *Muharram* 268[34] one of 'Alî b. Muhammad's confidants, Ja'far b. Ibrâhîm al-Sajjân, went over to al-Muwaffaq. Showered with gifts and paraded in front of the embattled city, he harangued the rebels inside, exhorting them to desert. New flights were the result.

The Second Attack on al-Mukhtâra.—Al-Muwaffaq stormed al-Mukhtâra again on 16 *Rabî' II* 268/November 13, 881. His troops were arranged in groups so that they could attack several targets; and since his main objective was to smash the city walls, he included a demolition specialist in each group. Rashly, his soldiers went beyond the plan as ordered. Bursting into the city, they scattered and set about killing, burning, and plundering. Eventually they were surprised and defeated by the rebels, who had recovered after their initial panic. The Zanj recaptured the booty they had lost and massacred, to the last man, the thirty Daylamites guarding the enemy retreat. Abbasid losses in both men and weapons were heavy. Back in their camp, al-Muwaffaq called his men together to express his displeasure at the turn of events and warn them of promised serious punishments if his orders were disobeyed in the future. Then he gave orders to provide for the families of soldiers who had fallen during the attack.

Keeping al-Mukhtâra in supplies became increasingly difficult in spite of all the attention 'Alî b. Muhammad devoted to the problem. After the fall of Basra, a certain Ahmad b. Mûsâ b. Sa'îd al-Qalûs, one of his closest companions, regularly supplied the capital with provisions bought from the Bedouins and merchants in the region until he fell into al-Muwaffaq's hands. Mâlik b. Bishrân, whom 'Alî b. Muhammad appointed to fill his position, continued al-Qalûs' work first in the same region, then on the al-Dînârî Canal. He supplied al-Mukhtâra with fish from al-Batîha on the one hand and produce from the Bedouins on the other. In time, he was attacked and defeated by the Abbasid fleet under the command of Zîrak; his men were scattered and he himself was forced to flee to 'Alî b. Muhammad, who sent him to the al-Yahûdî Canal to do the same job. Frightened by the implacability Abû l-'Abbâs had shown recently in exterminating a group of Bedouins, he asked for and was granted pardon by al-Muwaffaq. 'Alî b. Muhammad replaced him with one Ahmad b. Junayd, whose functions were reduced to nil because Abbasid troops cut off his supply routes. To divert the Bedouins from al-Mukhtâra, al-Muwaffaq had safe and convenient markets opened for them in Basra. For lack of any other resources, the Zanj tried to fulfill their needs with saltwater fish, which was brought in with difficulty by canals and dry land. Even this solution became impossible when al-Muwaffaq dispatched Rashîq with five-thousand men and thirty boats to the region.

On the al-Ishâqî Canal, Rashîq and his men surprised the Banû Tamîm Bedouins, already allies of the Zanj at the time the rebels captured and burned Basra, as they were taking food to besieged al-Mukhtâra. Some of the Bedouins were killed; the rest were captured. The severed heads of the dead were put on display as a warning, then the survivors were decapitated but not before one was horribly mutilated. Their possessions were given to al-Muwaffaq's soldiers as booty and badges of honor were bestowed on Rashîq. That provoked new desertions. Great hardship was being caused by the blockade. Prisoners reported that it had been a year or two since they had seen bread. Large numbers of rebels spread out through the area, scavenging for food; they were pursued by Abbasid troops with orders to pardon those who surrendered and kill those who refused. When there was a sizable number of deserters, al-Muwaffaq divided them into two groups. Those capable of bearing arms were inserted into the ranks of his own troops, where they were found to be useful chiefly because they knew the terrain. The others were presented with gifts and sent to sow discord among the rebels by telling them of what they would gain if they deserted. During all this, there was no interrupton in the fighting. Abû l-'Abbâs was wounded by an arrow, but he recovered quickly.

The Death of Bahbûdh b. 'Abd al-Wahhâb.—Bahbûdh b. 'Abd al-Wahhâb was a true pirate of the Tigris and nearby canals. He made it a practice to attack al-Muwaffaq's boats, draw them into the side canals (where he had set up traps), and then plunder them. At the first signs that his ploy had been detected, he lost no time making changes in his boats and flying the Abbasid flag; by the time trap was discovered it was too late to escape. Al-Muwaffaq stationed boats in different places to guard the passages. Bahbûdh waited for the right moment to act. Passing himself off as one of theirs, he attacked the Abbasid boats and seized six of them with all the matériel they were transporting. Then he returned to the

Abû l-Khasîb Canal. Al-Muwaffaq sent his son, Abû l-'Abbâs, against him. The young Abbasid laid a trap for Bahbûdh and severely defeated him. The pirate was forced to flee. Most of his men were killed, others surrendered or were captured.

The lack of provisions continued to place the rebels in dire straits. Faced with famine, many of them were forced to leave their camp in search of food. Abû l-'Abbâs kept them under constant surveillance as they scoured the region and knew just where they went. Bahbûdh was sent against him on orders from 'Alî b. Muhammad, and in the battle that ensued was wounded in the stomach. He died during the return to al-Mukhtâra (*Rajab* 268/January–February 882). Al-Muwaffaq rewarded the soldiers who had fought him from their boat.

Other events in that year included: Abû Ahmad's capture of al-Dhuwâ'ibî, a town friendly to 'Alî b. Muhammad; the assassination of the king of the Zanj's son, on orders from 'Alî b. Muhammad, when he learned he was going to defect to al-Muwaffaq;[35] trouble in Mecca, in 268/881–882, stirred up by Abû l-Mugîra al-Makhzûmî, a Zanj "lieutenant"; *Muharram* 269/July-August 882 saw Hârûn the 'Alid[36] defect to al-Muwaffaq's camp and displayed to the insurgents. Abû l-Sâj's son defeated al-Makhzûmî (in 269/882–83) and seized two boats loaded with goods and weapons. Lu'lu', Ahmad b. Tûlûn's prefect in Syria, deserted and went over to al-Muwaffaq's side.[37]

Bahbûdh had stored up great treasure, and, after the pirate's death, 'Alî b. Muhammad resolved to find it. Persons who had been close to Bahbûdh were imprisoned and scourged in an effort to make them reveal where the treasure was hidden. This created an atmosphere of extreme nervousness among the rebels, and al-Muwaffaq took advantage of the situation to appeal to Bahbûdh's soldiers to surrender and offer them amnesty. Many joined him.

Al-Muwaffaq thought that a full-scale assault on al-Mukhtâra would be more difficult than necessary because of the huge waves the wind whipped up on the Tigris, so he decided to build a camp on the west bank of the river, from where it would be clearly easier to attack the already besieged city. 'Alî b. Muhammad was aware of the danger and he threw all of his troops into action to thwart the realization of any such plan. The day the Zanj succeeded in cutting to pieces an Abbasid detachment that was isolated on the west bank and beyond any assistance because of the violent wind, al-Muwaffaq abandoned his project. From then on, improving the roads leading to al-Mukhtâra and opening large breaches in the wall around the city were his main objectives.

The Wounding of al-Muwaffaq.—As the result of fierce battles, the Abbasid troops managed to open the road to al-Mukhtâra, after having destroyed two bridges blocking their way. After demolishing part of the wall, they burst into the city. Houses belonging to Ibn Sam'ân and Sulaymân b. Jâmi' were pillaged and destroyed. Al-Jubbâ'î's home, 'Ali b. Muhammad's treasury depot which was connected to his house, and one of the city's markets, al-Maymûna, were also devastated. A long, bloody battle was fought around the cathedral-mosque, which the insurgents defended furiously. The Abbasids finally captured its *minbar* and carried it off to al-Muwaffaqiyya as a trophy. They destroyed part of the city's ramparts and plundered and burned offices and treasuries in a thick fog that shrouded the city. Just when victory seemed near, a Byzantine slave named Qirtâs shot an arrow (Monday, 25 *Jumâdâ I* 269/December 10, 882)[38] that struck al-Muwaffaq in the chest. The Abbasid tried to hide his injury. After having it cared for overnight at al-Muwaffaqiyya, he returned to battle; but the wound grew worse and he was forced to give it more serious attention.[39] As news of this spread throughout al-Muwaffaqiyya, many residents began to panic; some even left the city.

Meanwhile, on Saturday, 15 *Jumâdâ I* 269/ November 30, 882, Caliph al-Mu'tamid, took advantage of his brother al-Muwaffaq's preoccupation with the war against the Zanj, to leave his residence in an attempt to flee

to Ahmad b. Tûlûn in Egypt. In view of Mu'tamid's action it was suggested to al-Muwaffaq that he return to Baghdad, but he refused, fearing
the effects his absence might have on his troops and on the residents of
al-Muwaffaqiyya, so he remained there, under treatment, for the next
three months. The Zanj made use of the lull in the fighting to repair the
breaches in their wall and other damage to their fortifications. The Caliph
was joined by Ishâq b. Kundâj, governor of al-Jazîra and al-Mawsil, who
took him back to Samârrâ on 4 *Sha'bân* 269/February 16, 883. Four days
later, he was honored and showered with gifts by al-Muwaffaq's envoys.

In the month of *Sha'bân* 269/February–March 883, al-Muwaffaq, who
had recovered from his wound, gave orders to assault the rebels and
destroy everything they had managed to repair. To brace the rebels'
courage, Alî b. Muhammad told them that reports that al-Muwaffaq was
back in action were just lies. Nonetheless, Abbasid troops attacked, and
in one engagement burned and pillaged several of al-Mukhtâra's palaces.
Any women found in them were released and taken back to the west bank
of the Tigris. Many horses seized were taken there as well, in large numbers. The house belonging to 'Alî b. Muhammad's son, Ankalây, was also
destroyed. Fighting increased and became more and more deadly. The
rebels tried new defense measures: they flooded the passages and dug
new canals to block any enemy advance. The Abbasids, on the other hand,
attempted to open up a path for themselves. The number of dead and
wounded rose steadily on both sides.

Al-Muwaffaq attempted to burn 'Alî b. Muhammad's palace and attack
him on the Tigris; The rebels defended themselves against his fleet not
only with various machines of war but also with melted lead. This caused
the Abbasids to take time out to equip each of their boats with a beamed
roof, which was then covered with buffalo hides and wrapped in material
coated with special products that prevented fire from spreading. Fighting
resumed when this operation was completed.

On Friday, 18 *Sha'bân* 269/March 2, 883, Muhammad b. Sam'ân, who had been 'Alî b. Muhammad's secretary and *wazîr*, surrendered to the Abbasids.[40] The next day, Saturday, 19 *Sha'bân* 269, there was a new attack on al-Mukhtâra. Abû l-'Abbâs and the Abbasid fleet succeeded in burning 'Alî b. Muhammad's palace and the surrounding buildings. 'Alî b. Muhammad fled, leaving behind all his furniture, his personal effects, and his treasury. The Abbasid soldiers plundered what they could snatch from the flames and freed many Muslim women who had become 'Alî b. Muhammad's slaves. Then they seized and burned the outbuildings of the palaces that belonged to 'Alî b. Muhammad and his son, Ankalây. Fighting continued on the racecourse in front of 'Alî b. Muhammad's palace; other buildings, al-Karnabâ'î's house, for example, were also destroyed by fire. Abû l-'Abbâs cut the great iron chain that prevented boats from entering the Abû l-Khasîb Canal and took it to al-Muwaffaqiyya. 'Alî b. Muhammad's son was wounded in the stomach and barely escaped death.

On Sunday, 20 *Sha'bân* 269/ March 4, 883, one of al-Muwaffaq's officers, Nusayr Abû Hamza, drowned while trying to escape the rebels. Fighting continued unabated, and Sulaymân b. Jâmi' was wounded in the leg and narrowly avoided being burned alive. The siege was interrupted once more, during the rest of *Sha'bân, Ramadân,* and part of *Shawwâl* because al-Muwaffaq became ill.[41] The insurgents made use of the time to recover and took advantage of it to fortify their city as well as could be expected.

Al-Muwaffaq resumed his offensive in the month of *Shawwâl* 269. His target was the first of the two stone bridges and the dam in front of it, on the Abû l-Khasîb Canal, which the insurgents had just reinforced and which barred the passage of his boats. He sent four-thousand soldiers along the two banks of the river and led the others by boat to the place where the canal and the Tigris came together. Once the Zanj were driven away from the bridge, the demolition "specialists" entered into action. Aided by the flood tide, boats filled with naphta-saturated reeds were launched against the bridge to burn it. Most of the troops landed and the fierce battle that followed ended in an Abbasid victory, despite the rebels' valor. They were pushed back to the first of the two bridges (of boats ?) that blocked the passage of small craft. The Zanj suffered heavy losses; and there were numerous desertions among them, which al-Muwaffaq immediately turned to his advantage. Seeing that night was approaching and fearful of ambushes, he ordered his troops to return to camp. At his request, descriptions of the events praising his soldiers' bravery were written down and read in the mosques throughout the empire. Then, in spite of the fortitude shown by the Zanj, Abbasid soldiers destroyed the two stone dams built at the entrance of the canal to block navigation.

Capture of the Western Section of al-Mukhtâra.—With his palace burned, 'Alî b. Muhammad and his family took refuge in Ahmad b. Mûsâ al-Qalûs's home. The nearest market was al-Husayn. It became the principal market, but there was no food left in the city. Corpses were disinterred so that their flesh could be eaten and their shrouds sold. People killed each other to eat human flesh. 'Alî b. Muhammad was powerless against these actions. All he could do was to punish those guilty of such behavior with a few days in prison. A loaf of bread was worth ten *dirhams.*

When the Zanj abandoned the western part of al-Mukhtâra and took up positions in the eastern section (in relation to the Abû l-Khasîb Canal), al-Muwaffaq immediately gave orders to attack that corner of the city and sent Abû l-'Abbâs with the fleet to the area around al-Karnabâ'î's house, with orders to destroy everything they could. As his own target, he chose al-Hamadânî's palace, which was extremely well protected by high walls and a large contingent of well-armed and well-equipped soldiers. After bloody battles with the Zanj, the two Abbasid forces met outside the walls of the al-Hamadânî's palace. They proved to be too high for the ladders al-Muwaffaq had brought, but, eventually, the troops managed to tear

down the white flags[42] inscribed with 'Alî b. Muhammad's name, drive
out the rebels, wreck the palace, and set fire to it. The many Muslim
women who were freed were taken to al-Muwaffaqiyya. Rebels surrendered in large numbers, asking for pardon. A new battle broke out, this
time in al-Mubâraka, the market place behind al-Hamadânî's palace, with
al-Muwaffaq's soldiers attacking from three sides. Merchants fled, asking
for mercy. Combatants on both sides were caught by the flames of spreading fire and burned alive. At nightfall, the soldiers returned to their camps.

While the Zanj continued to fortify eastern al-Mukhtâra, Abbasid
troops razed the walls of the western section amid constant battles. There
were heavy casualties, and al-Muwaffaq took great interest in his wounded. Serious defeat during one attack caused him to realize that the rebels
should be engaged on several fronts so they would have to spread out their
men. He decided to act on this and won a new victory. Again, many
women were freed and returned to al-Muwaffaqiyya.

Preparations to attack eastern al-Mukhtâra got underway. Al-
Muwaffaq's first step was to order that routes on both sides of the canal
be put in better condition and that the portal of 'Alî b. Muhammad's cas-
tle be removed to make easier passage for his troops. (The portal, which
'Alî b. Muhammad had taken from a fortress in Basra, was sent to
Baghdad). Then, with a boat of naphta-saturated reeds, he launched an
attack on one of the city's two bridges (*jisr*), but the Zanj dove into the
water and sank the boat before fire from it could burn the bridge completely. On Saturday, 14 *Shawwâl* 269/April 26, 883, al-Muwaffaq sent
along both banks of the canal a well-equipped contingent of reliable
troops who, despite strong enemy resistance, succeeded in cutting off and
burning the bridge. Then they raided the places where the rebels built
their boats. Many craft were seized; others were destroyed by fire.
Inmates of prison on the right bank were released, but the soldiers captured the family of one of the most experienced Zanj officers and demol-
ished their house after it was sacked. When they had destroyed what

remained of the bridge, the Abbasid fleet set fires on both banks of the canal; the Zanj, abandoning their positions, fell back to al-Mukhtâra's eastern section. Many rebels asked for and were granted amnesty in the panic following the devastations. Among those who surrendered were one of 'Alî b. Muhammad's *qâdîs* and a man carrying the *minbar* (pulpit in a mosque from which the sermon and solemn announcements to the Muslim community are made), from a mosque in the right-hand section of the city. The rebels concentrated all their remaining boats in front of the second bridge. It was attacked by the Abbasids who also regrouped, burning everything they could in the western part of al-Mukhtâra. On 22 *Shawwâl* 269/May 4, 883 al-Muwaffaq deployed his troops and put his battle plan into action. When the fighting ended, he was victorious and severed rebel heads were floating in the canal. The second bridge was burned by the Abbasid fleet, forcing Ankalây and Sulaymân, both of whom had been wounded, to seek refuge in the eastern part of the city. Many of their soldiers drowned. The Abbasids burned houses, palaces, and markets and freed women and children prisoners. 'Alî b. Muhammad's new residence was also put to the torch, after being plundered, and some 'Alid women were freed. Inmates of a prison captured in eastern al-Mukhtâra were released from their irons and sent to al-Muwaffaqiyya. All of the Zanj craft retrieved from the Abû l-Khasîb Canal were brought to the Tigris and offered as loot to al-Muwaffaq's soldiers. Ankalây, 'Alî b. Muhammad's son, asked al-Muwaffaq for amnesty and stated his conditions for passing over to his side. Al-Muwaffaq responded favorably, but when 'Alî b. Muhammad learned of his son's intentions, he succeeded in dissuading him from defecting.

Another important figure of the revolt, Sulaymân b. Mûsâ al-Sha'rânî, made overtures to join al-Muwaffaq. At first, the Abbasid leader denied him pardon because of his crimes, but then, realizing that there might be bad consequences to his refusal, he granted clemency to Sulaymân, his brother, and a number of their followers. He saw that they were richly rewarded and had them displayed in a boat to encourage hesitant rebels to surrender. Immediately, there were new defections. 'Alî b. Muhammad gave Sulaymân's post to Shibl, another of his long-standing companions, who lost no time asking al-Muwaffaq for a boat to facilitate his defection. A boat was sent to the place agreed upon, but the deserters could not embark without first doing battle with the troops 'Alî b. Muhammad had sent to prevent their escape. When the deserters finally arrived in al-Muwaffaqiyya, they, too, were showered with gifts and then exhibited to the insurgents. Shibl showed a great deal of zeal, and al-Muwaffaq tried to take advantage of the defector's knowledge of the terrain to launch a night attack on the place where 'Alî b. Muhammad could be found in person. The surprise attack was a success; with other deserters, Shibl massacred a number of Zanj soldiers, captured some of their officers, and seized many weapons. Alarmed by the raid, the rebels intensified their vigilance; their sentinels' cries could be heard as far as al-Muwaffaqiyya. Abbasid troops continued to harass the Zanj day and night, obliging them to be on constant alert and pursuing them the moment they came out to search for food.

Attack on the Eastern Section of al-Mukhtâra.—Satisfied that his soldiers had familiarized themselves enough with the terrain, al-Muwaffaq decided to attack eastern al-Mukhtâra. He called a general meeting to which he invited the rebels who had defected to his side. He reminded them of their past mistakes and of his largesse towards them, asking them to show that they were ready to help him in this final attack with their knowledge of the terrain. They responded with great enthusiasm and solemnly committed themselves to serving him bravely and with complete obedience.

He then collected all the boats from the Tigris, al-Batîha, and the vicinity and made them part of his fleet. He now had at his disposal ten-thousand rowers (paid monthly from state funds), without counting the "official sailors" or the crews of boats used to transport men and food. After deploying his forces and assigning them tasks, he formed his plan of attack: Abû l-ʿAbbâs and eight-thousand men were assigned a position to the west of the Abû l-Khasîb Canal, in the direction of al-Muhallabî's palace (the rebels had erected very solid fortifications there); Rashîd was given twenty-thousand horsemen and foot soldiers and sent to the east of the canal (part of them in the direction of the al-Karnabâ'î's palace, at the eastern corner of the canal, and from there, along the canal, to Abû ʿIsâ's house, where ʿAlî b. Muhammad was then in residence; the two other parties on two other canals, with ʿAlî b. Muhammad's house as their objective). If all went well they would meet up with Abû l-ʿAbbâs in front of al-Muhallabî's palace.

On Monday, 7 *Dhû' l-Qaʿda* 269/May 18, 883, the Abbasid troops began to take up their positions in the space prepared for them in advance behind ʿAlî b. Muhammad's palace where they spent the night. Their forces were estimated at fifty-thousand "perfect" horsemen and foot soldiers. They spent the night praying and reading the Qur'an; the sight of the huge number of fires lit by the Abbasids impressed the rebels. As for al-Muwaffaq, he installed his fleet of one-hundred-fifty boats on the canal, escorted on both banks by ten-thousand horsemen and foot soldiers under his direct orders. Fighting began according to plan the next day, Tuesday, 8 *Dhû' l-Qaʿda* 269. Zanj resistance was fierce. Both sides suffered large numbers of wounded and dead, but the government troops clearly had the advantage. Al-Muwaffaq ordered the prisoners that were captured brought to him, and then he had them decapitated. ʿAlî b. Muhammad's residence was sacked and burned. His harem and his children (more than one-hundred persons in all) were seized and carefully transferred to al-Muwaffaqiyya. ʿAlî b. Muhammad escaped to al-Muhallabî's palace. Although al-Muwaffaq's plan called for all his troops to come together in front of al-Muhallabî's palace after their missions, an impatient group of Abû l-ʿAbbâs's soldiers decided not to wait for the others to arrive and began taking their loot to the boats. The Zanj saw in this an opportunity to pull themselves together and come out of hiding. They killed a certain number of horsemen and foot soldiers and retrieved the women and loot they had just lost. They were in turn, attacked by another Abbasid detachment and fighting raged until al-Muwaffaq ordered his men to return to their camp. Women freed by the Abbasids were sent to al-Muwaffaqiyya. On the same day, one of Abû l-'Abbâs's officers managed to set fire to the rebel area, thus depriving them of their last reserves of food. Al-Muwaffaq ordered written descriptions of these events and had them read throughout the country.

On Wednesday, 2 *Dhû' l-Hijja*/June 12, 883, al-Muwaffaq's secretary and *wazîr,* Sâ'id b. Makhlad, arrived from Samârrâ to join him with an army of ten-thousand men. Lu'lu', Ahmad b. Tûlûn's former prefect in Syria, wrote to al-Muwaffaq for permission to join him with his troops. Al-Muwaffaq responded favorably and decided not to order the final assault until he arrived.

'Alî b. Muhammad's family were transferred from al-Muwaffaqiyya to Baghdad in *Dhû' l-Hijja* 269/May–June 883.

Lu'lu' left al-Raqqa with a very large army of "Farganians, Turks, Rûmîs, Berbers, blacks and others," made a stop in Baghdad and, on Thursday, 2 *Muharram* 270/July 12, 883, reached the camp that Abû l-'Abbâs had ordered prepared for him. The next day, Friday, 3 *Muharram* 270/ July 13, 883, he and one hundred and fifty of his officers were received by al-Muwaffaq, who showered them with luxurious gifts and generously provided Lu'lu''s troops with anything they might need.

Taking advantage of a truce, the rebels again made the Abû l-Khasîb Canal difficult for navigation. But after several days of fighting, one of Lu'lu''s detachments destroyed the insurgents' installations. Lu'lu''s men proved to al-Muwaffaq that they were great fighters, and he decided to handle them with care.[43] Attacks, burnings, and desertions continued on both sides. On the al-Garbî Canal, Abû l-'Abbâs and his troops routed the rebels posted at the two bridges protecting Zanj fields and orchards. Many of the enemy were killed, and the two bridges were destroyed.

The struggle against the rebels was becoming almost a "holy war," and more and more volunteers swelled Abbasid ranks. Such was the case with, among others, Ahmad b. Dînâr who rallied to al-Muwaffaq with a large force from Khûzistân, with a member of the 'Abd al-Qays tribe,[44] who brought over two-thousand men from Bahrayn under his command, and with a thousand fighters from Fârs headed by Abû Salma, and others. They were, of course, well received and showered with gifts.

Al-Muwaffaq ordered all weapons and his fleet of different types of vessels put in a state of readiness for the general offensive against eastern al-Mukhtâra. From an army of two-thousand horsemen and fifty-thousand foot soldiers, apart from the volunteers (not registered in the records) and the soldiers who remained in al-Muwaffaqiyya, he chose his bravest soldiers. He deployed his men and asked them not to begin fighting until he gave the signal. The moment came on Monday, 27 *Muharram* 270/ August 6, 883. The horn was sounded and the black flag raised over al-Karnabâ'î's house. A group of soldiers had disobeyed al-Muwaffaq's order to wait and had already attacked al-Muhallabî's palace; the Zanj retaliated and massacred many of them. The rebels had been alerted by the impatient action of the disobedient Abbasids, but the superiority of al-Muwaffaq's army was such that the fighting became a slaughter. Abbassid troops captured the city, seized al-Muhallabî's palace, and freed a number of prisoners. 'Alî b. Muhammad, al-Muhallabî, Ankalây, and Sulaymân b. Jâmi' fled with the remainder of their forces to the al-Sufyânî Canal, a tributary of the Abû l-Khasîb Canal. Zanj chiefs' families were transferred to al-Muwaffaqiyya. Al-Muwaffaq's soldiers plundered al-Muhallabî's palace, where all that remained of Zanj wealth was stored. Rebels fleeing the city were pursued by Lu'lu' and his men but to no avail, despite their courage, because of the difficult terrain. Seething with rage, al-Muwaffaq had to accept the situation and ordered them to return. In al-

Muwaffaqiyya, where people believed that a decisive victory had already been won, he assembled all his generals and reprimanded them. They responded with excuses and tried to explain their actions. They promised that there would be evidence of their dedication in the next battle. To prove it, they asked him to order that, as soon as the troops disembarked, the boats come back to al-Muwaffaqiyya in order to prevent them from returning before the final victory. Al-Muwaffaq pardoned them, promised them rewards, and ordered that preparations for the final attack begin.

The Last Battle, Death of 'Alî b. Muhammad.—At the end of four days of preparations, al-Muwaffaq deployed his men for the final assault. It was launched on Saturday, 2 *Safar* 270/ (Sunday ?) August 11, 883. The Zanj, who had reassembled in the city after Monday's battle, were completely defeated. 'Alî b. Muhammad, al-Muhallabî, and a group of rebels were cut off from the troops commanded by Ankalây and from Sulaymân b Jâmi'. Abbasid soldiers pursued them. They captured Sulaymân b. Jâmi'; then Ibrâhîm b. Ja'far al-Hamadânî and Nâdir al-Aswad were captured and seized under guard to Abû l-'Abbâs. The rebels' resistance dissolved. Al-Muwaffaq received reports of 'Alî b. Muhammad's death and was presented a human hand, said to be that of the Master of the Zanj. Immediately afterwards, one of Lu'lu''s men galloped up, holding the Master of the Zanj's severed head.[45] The rebel leader's former comrades confirmed that it was indeed 'Alî b. Muhammad's head. Al-Muwaffaq prostrated himself in thanksgiving to God; Abû l-'Abbâs and his officers did likewise. Al-Muwaffaq then ordered the head impaled on a lance and paraded in front of him. While al-Muhallabî and Ankalây were trying to flee, al-Muwaffaq's boat returned to al-Muwaffaqiyya, bearing 'Alî b. Muhammad's severed head and the two crucified prisoners: Sulaymân b. Jâmi' and al-Hamadânî. There, al-Muwaffaq entrusted his son, Abû l-'Abbâs, with taking them to the Abbasids' first camp on the Nahr Jattâ, displaying them all along the route. A thousand Zanj surrendered, and al-

Muwaffaq granted them amnesty. He thought it would be counterproductive and dangerous to plunge the surviving rebels into a state of raging despair. In the three days that followed, five-thousand more Zanj surrendered. Countless numbers of rebels were dead. A thousand Zanj fled to the desert, where most of them died of thirst; the rest were enslaved by the Bedouins. On realizing that there was no possibility of escape, Ankalây and ʿAlî b. Abân Muhallabî gave themselves up as prisoners.

Qirtâs, who had wounded al-Muwaffaq with an arrow on 25 *Jumâdâ I* 269, did not wait to be pardoned; he fled to Khûzistân. In Râmhurmuz, a man who had seen him before in al-Mukhtâra recognized him and denounced him to the governor of the city. Captured and put in irons, he was handed over to al-Muwaffaq. Abû l-ʿAbbas asked for and was given the right to punish him with his own hand.

A Zanj leader named Darmawayh, who had been sent to the Basra region, on the west bank of the Tigris and the border of al-Batîha, where he had attacked and plundered Abbasid boats and villages in the area, was totally unaware of ʿAlî b. Muhammad's death and the end of the revolt. On hearing the news, he asked for pardon. Once it was granted, he tried to atone for his acts by returning his plunder to its rightful owners. Compared to other rebels who had surrendered, he and his men looked well when they joined al-Muwaffaq's camp.

Al-Muwaffaq ordered the country informed of ʿAlî b. Muhammad's death, and he invited the population that had fled Zanj devastation to return. He also appointed a governor and a *qâdî* for the province.

On 18 *Jumâdâ I* 270/ May 23, 883, Abû l-ʿAbbâs made his triumphal entry into Baghdad, preceded by ʿAlî b. Muhammad's severed head. The city was jubilant.[46] Several poets have celebrated the event.

The Torment of the Leaders of the Revolt.—In 272/885–86, the Zanj rioted in Wâsit, crying: Ankalây, O Mansûr! Al-Muwaffaq responded by writing Baghdad, ordering Fath al-Saʿîdî (who was holding the rebel leaders imprisoned in Muhammad b. Abdallâh b. Tâhir's house)[47] to decapitate them and send him their severed heads. One by one, their throats were cut and their heads sent to al-Muwaffaq.[48] The riot was quelled immediately. That occurred in the month of *Shawwâl* 272/ March–April, 886. In obedience to al-Muwaffaq's orders, Muhammad b. 'Abdallâh had the severed heads of prisoners impaled on staves in Wâsit; he commanded that their bodies be crucified near the Baghdad bridge. Two were crucified on the eastern side of the bridge and three others on the western side. That occurred on 23 *Shawwâl* 272/April 2, 886.[49]

'Alî b. Muhammad had four sons: Muhammad (Ankalây), born before the revolt; Yahyâ, Sulaymân, and al-Fadl (all three born after the revolt had begun). Muhammad was killed two years after his father. The three others spent their lives in prison. They were children when they entered and adults when they died. He also had two daughters. One was married to 'Alî b. Abân al-Muhallabî and had a son (whom al-Muwaffaq took as a slave. He gave him the name Nasîf and eventually appointed him governor of different provinces). He was killed in Basra, on the night the Qarmates took the city. His conduct was laudable. The other was married to Sulaymân b. Jâmi', a black slave, who was measurer of grain in Hajar.[50]

On 7 *Muharram* 280/March 29, 893, Muhammad b. al-Hasan b. Sahl Shaylama died.[51] Al-Mas'ûdî writes about him:[52] "In 280, a certain Muhammad, son of el-Hasan, son of Sehl, nephew of Dou'l-riaseteyn Fadl, son of Sehl, was arrested in Baghdad. This Mohammad, known by his nickname Chemilah [Shaylama], was arrested with Obeyd Allah,[53] son of the Caliph Mouhtadi. This same Mohammad, grandson of Sehl, is the author of several reports on the Mobaydites and of a work devoted to the history of 'Alî ben Mohammad, appointed leader of the Zanj as we have already mentioned. Several of the Zanj chief's soldiers, who had obtained the *aman* (grace), lodged complaints against Muhammad; papers with the names of persons to whom he had administered an oath in favor of a descendant of 'Alî, son of Abou Talib, were found in his possession. The conspirators planned to revolt on a certain day in Baghdad and attack Caliph Moutaded. They were led into the presence of this prince; the accomplices of Mohammad, son of el-Hasan, made no confession and simply said: 'As for Abou Talib's descendant, we do not know him; the oath was administered to us without showing him to us, and here,' they added designating Mohammad, son of el-Hasan, 'is the intermediary between him and us.' The Caliph ordered them tortured; but he spared Chemilah (Mohammad) in the hope that he would put him back on the track of the Talibite. He released Obeyd Allah, son of Mouhtadi, whose innocence had been admitted. Moutaded did all he could to bring Mohammad to denounce the Talibite in whose favor he had administered the oath, but he was not successful. He had a long interview with the prisoner and in the course of a discussion, let slip these words: 'Even if you have my flesh roasted, I would add nothing to the words you have just heard. I will never reveal the name of the person in favor of whom I administered the oath and whom I recognize as an *imam*. Do what you will with me.'—'We will inflict on you no torture other than the very one you have just designated,' replied the Caliph. It is said that the poor wretch was skewered on a long iron rod which penetrated him from his anus to his mouth; he was kept like this over a huge fire until he died, heaping invective and curses on the Caliph, who attended his torture. But the most widespread version is that he was tied between three spears, bound together at the end, and thus restrained was placed above the fire, without being put in contact with the flames and, fully alive, turned and roasted like a chicken, until his skin began to crackle. Then he was removed from the fire and tied to the gallows, between the two bridges in the eastern quarter of Baghdad."

NOTES

1. Tabarî speaks of fifty-thousand men, and Makîn claims to know the number of Zanj: "He set out with ten-thousand men both cavalry and infantry, and went to join them, though there were more than one-hundred-thousand . . . "

2. We read in Nöldeke: "The fleet which was propelled exclusively by oars consisted of all types of boats. The larger vessels were used for transport on the one hand and as floating fortresses on the other. The smaller ones (we are speaking of boats of forty and twenty rowers) were used mostly for attack."

3. "A great number asked him for pardon," Tabarî. Were they members of the population who were collaborators of the Zanj or were they Zanj themselves? We know that the city was captured in 264/878, but no information has come to us since.

4. For two of these groups, Tabarî gives the number of combatants as ten thousand.

5. These operations were repeated for two months.

6. "He shot arrows until his thumb was bloody."

7. Nöldeke sees there already the first example of the "pardon" which was so well utilized later: "One of their leaders was taken prisoner and granted amnesty. This was the first example of a new policy aimed at winning over the officers of the rebel troops. The policy, more intelligent than heroic or noble, had great success."

8. "Of twenty rowers."

9. "Twenty-five arrows were taken out of the clothing he wore over his armor."

10. Tanûkhî reports the eyewitness account of the preparations. An astrologer was consulted before the departure, in order to determine the opportune moment. Rampoldi speaks of 40,000 Abbasid solders and 80,000 Zanj, without naming his source. Yâfi'î gives the number as 300,000 Zanj and 50,000 Abbasid soldiers, following an estimate in Tabarî.

11. October 11, 880.

12. "At one *farsakh* from Wâsit," Tabarî. Ibn Kathîr, on the other hand, claims that it is in Wâsit proper.

13. November 6, 880.

14. November 16, 880.

15. "Without speaking of the Zanj women," Ibn al-Jawzî. Ibn al-'Imâd, and Ibn Khaldûn give the number as 15,000 evidently because they include released women from al-Manî'a and al-Mansûra.

16. As usual, it is through Muhammad b. al-Hasan that we learn about 'Alî b. Muhammad's attitude in detail.

17. "With ten-thousand men," adds Ibn Abî l-Hadîd.

18. Muhammad b. Hammâd claims that it was on this occasion that the anecdote of Abû

l-'Abbâs with the crane originated. Muhammad b. Shu'ayb places the anecdote during the battle of al-Sîniyya.

19. November 26, 880.

20. December 4, 880.

21. "At his request," adds Ibn Abî l-Hadîd.

22. It is again Muhammad b. al-Hasan who casts doubt on 'Alî b. Muhammad's words.

23. Thus in Tabarî. Ibn al-Athîr gives, on the contrary, the figure of 20,000.

24. Saturday, January 7, 881.

25. So states Ibn Abî l-Hadîd; Tabarî, on the other hand, says that it was a question of the *jund,* therefore, of its own soldiers.

26. Were they rebels who had been pardoned?

27. Nöldeke supposes that the Master of the Zanj could hope for various types of trouble to break out, thus obliging al-Muwaffaq to abandon the siege.

28. On February 28, 881.

29. According to Tabarî's estimate that the Abbasids numbered 50,000 men and the Zanj 300,000. On this subject Muir writes: "With all allowance for the masses of slaves that flocked to the Reprobate, such numbers are clearly fabulous." Nöldeke is of the same opinion: " . . . even though the number of 300,00 men ascribed to the prince of the Negroes seems strongly exaggerated."

30. On March 20, 881.

31. On March 21, 881.

32. We have a coin that was struck in this city. This *dinar* was struck in 270.

33. On July 31, 881.

34. On August 1, 881.

35. I do not know this "king of the Zanj," nor his son, any more than does Nöldeke. Is it once more a matter of cuts in Tabarî's text ?

36. This is al-Husayn b. Muhammad b. Hamza b. 'Abd Allâh b. 'Alî b. al-Husayn b. 'Alî b. 'Abû Tâlib, known by the name al-Harûn.

37. See more details on this subject a little farther on, at the moment when Lu'lu' actually joined al-Muwaffaq's camp.

38. Tanûkhî gives a great many details on the wounding of al-Muwaffaq, on the means employed to heal him, and on Qirtâs's execution (in 270). He mentions that when Abû Ahmad was shot by an arrow, he refrained from fighting " . . . then the Zanj cried 'Salt him, salt him,' that is-to-say: he is dead and you are hiding him, then keep him as preserved meat."

39. Speaking of al-Muwaffaq's doctor, the celebrated Yûhannâ b. Bukhtîshû, Ibn Abî Usaybî'a, writes: "He cured al-Muwaffaq of a wound by an arrow that struck him in the chest"; but we do not know whether it was the wound in question.

40. Muhammad b. al-Hasan, who wanted to flee with him, gives us a detailed account of the event.

41. March-April, 883.

42. For Heinz Halm, it is one more proof that 'Alî b. Muhammad was a Shî'ite.

43. Al-Qayrawânî claims that it is about something completely different. In his view, al-Muwaffaq prevented Lu'lu''s troops from continuing the fight out of fear of being done out of the glory of the final victory. There must be some truth to this supposition. We will see indications of it later (cf. *infra*, Appendix III).

44. The tribe that was 'Alî b. Muhammad's ally and perhaps also his tribe of origin.

45. There are several hypotheses concerning 'Alî b. Muhammad's death. It is evidently impossible to make a definite pronouncement on the subject (cf. Appendix III).

46. See the anecdote, cited by Ibn Abî l-Hadîd, of what happened in a section of Baghdad, called Bâb al-Tâq, at the time of Abû l-'Abbâs' arrival: ". . . when he reached the Bâb al-Tâq quarter, the people greeted him with hostility, and that caused him to want to burn the entire quarter, but his adviser succeeded in dissuading him." We are obviously confused by this phrase, which permits several suppositions.

47. *Emir* of Baghdad.

48. Tabarî speaks of six chiefs but names only five: Ankalây, al-Muhallabî, Sulaymân b. Jâmi', al-Sha'rânî, and al-Hamadânî: "That year, Muhammad Ibn Tâhir (*sic*) received a letter from Abû Ahmad ordering him to crucify the bodies of the six tortured victims on the square at the bridge. The disinterred corpses were swollen, smelly and in a state of decomposition. They were transported on stretchers, each carried by two men. Three of these cadavers were crucified in the east and three in the west. This occurred on 23 *Shawwâl* of that year (April 2, 886). Muhammad Ibn Tâhir (*sic*) attended this crucifixion on horseback."

49. This is the continuation of the text given by Ibn Abî l-Hadîd, who speaks of only five chiefs and does not name al-Sha'rânî but adds Nâdir al-Aswad. We find the same account, very much abbreviated and in bad condition, in Abû l-Mahâsin b. Tagrîbirdî. It also figures in the manuscript of Sibt b. al-Jawzî. According to him, as in Tabarî's work, there were six corpses, since he emphasizes that there were three on each side of the bridge.

50. This absolutely unique piece of information was passed on to us by Ibn Hazm. To my knowledge it has not been reported until now. I do not know its origin and I found it through Ibn Khaldûn. Commenting on it, Heinz Halm wondered whether Ibn Hazm might have been familiar with a copy of Shaylama's book (cf. *infra*, note 51). He asks himself the same question, but in a more positive way, about the unique information passed on to us by Safadî.

51. One of 'Alî b. Muhammad's former partisans and among those who wrote a book

about the revolt. The work has since been lost but Tabarî made wide use of it. For details on this person, see *infra*: Final Remarks.

52. Al-Mas'ûdî, *Murûj*, VIII, p. 140 (in the French translation).

53. In Tabarî, we read 'Abdallâh.

CHAPTER V

Internal and External Organization
of the New State

I. INTERNAL ORGANIZATION

The study of the organization of the "Zanj State" is an extremely delicate and difficult, not to say impossible, undertaking. The difficulties it presents can be understood better if it is emphasized right from the outset that all we have for such a study is the same information that served to trace the factual history of the revolt. There are two reasons for this. On the one hand, historians of the time were interested, above all, in the details of the war between the Abbasid troops and the Zanj; on the other hand, they considered the rebels "enemies of God," people without religion and without laws.

We may well ask to what extent our lack of information about the new state is due to the simple reason that there was nothing special to report, in other words whether the organization of 'Alî b. Muhammad's State was so simple and "ordinary" that nothing about it attracted the attention of contemporary authors. Three totally unconfirmed assertions on the subject need to be corrected. Louis Massignon asserts, "Our sources unfortunately give few details about its communist-type system of government"; M. Gaudefroy-Demombynes writes, "But the principles that could best assure its authority over the black masses are those that we have seen repeated by all the Iranian agitators since Mazdak: wives and property in

129

common"; and finally, in G. Wiet's work, we find: "Their chief, who declared himself a descendant of 'Alî, disciplined these Zanj, Negroes originally from Zanguebar, as best he could, and created a communist-type government."

Since there is nothing like this in any of our sources, we can suppose that Massignon and Wiet's error comes from Gaudefroy-Demombynes' passage, the origins of which I do not know.[1]

Indeed, most Orientalists[2] agree that we are ignorant of the Zanj system of government. Nevertheless, if the meager information that has come down to us is grouped into categories, we can discern certain aspects of the workings of the Zanj state.[3] Needless to say, the choice of categories was dictated by these bits of information rather than by any definite plan.

Political, Religious, and Social Organization.—There is not much to say about the political organization of the Zanj State. 'Ali b. Muhammad, who took the title Mahdî,[4] was the absolute ruler, and he governed from the capital through orders issued to his "generals" who, for the most part, had been loyal supporters since the beginning of the revolt. *'Amils* (government tax collectors, administrators, agents) and *qâdîs* (judges) are also mentioned, but we have no information about them.

The state's religious structure is also rather obscure. The Master of the Zanj professed a religion that seems to have been a curious mixture of Shiism and Kharijism.[5]

As for the social structure, it was obviously a stratified society:
• 'Alî b. Muhammad and his family,
• his close companions,
• the revolutionary masses (Zanj for the most part),
• the subject population or people (not reduced to slavery) living in an occupied region,
• the slaves (the Zanj in turn became owners of slaves).

There is a very revealing passage on this subject in Safadî's work: "Al-Khabîth obtained property and riches, seized them (to the detriment of the others) and gave them to his wives and children. (When) a group of them (his companions) disapproved, he replied: 'My wives are not to be compared to your wives. They have been put to the test (living) in company with me[6] and are forbidden to (other) men after me. In that I am equal to the Prophet, may God bless him and grant him salvation, and to the Imâms of the right path after him . . . . '" And a little further on: "When his followers became numerous, he moved the Zanj away from the palm trees and lands under cultivation, and forced them to pay a tax, which he distributed to his kin. (Then) the Zanj became cold-hearted towards him, their situation worsened and they considered revolting." It should be noted in passing that there were no Zanj among 'Alî b. Muhammad's high officials.[7]

We know nothing about the status of the population of subject or occupied regions who were not reduced to slavery, except that such a category did exist. On several occasions, there are references to peasants of certain villages, not to mention the Bedouins, who brought supplies to al-Mukhtâra to sell.

As for the Zanj slaves, we have an anecdotal passage in al-Mas'ûdî's work:

> The insolence of the Zanj army was such that they auctioned off the women of the Hasan, the Husayn and the Abbâs families, descendants of Hâshem, of Quraysh and of the most noble Arab families. A young girl would be sold for two to three dirhams; the crier would announce her genealogy in these terms: 'Such-and-such, daughter of so-and-so, from such-and-such family!' Each black owned ten, twenty and even thirty of these women, who served them as concubines and performed humble tasks for their wives. One of these captive women who, through Hasan, descended from 'Alî, son of Abû Tâlib, and belonged to a black, begged 'Alî b. Muhammad, leader of the Zanj, to give her another master and free

her from the one who owned her. 'No,' replied the leader, 'he is your master and suits you better than any other.'

Various Buildings.—Tabarî mentions the different buildings erected by the Zanj rather often, and even gives some details.

We have scant information about the rebels' first encampments, and we know absolutely nothing about the one at Furât al-Basra in the place called Bi'r Nakhl. We know nothing either about the next one, the one on Maymûn Canal, except that it was strewn with pickets on which were impaled the heads of adversaries killed in battles. As for the camp located between the Abû Qurrâ Canal and the al-Hâjir Canal, 'Alî b. Muhammad had ordered his partisans to build huts there. It was later that the rebels built their three main cities: al-Manî'a, al-Mansûra, and al-Mukhtâra.

Al-Manî'a, Sulaymân b. Mûsâ al-Sha'rânî's city, was in Sûq al-Khamîs on the Barâtiq Canal and was fortified by walls and ditches. It seems that it was rather important since Tabarî emphasizes that five-thousand Muslim women were found there and set free. Al-Mansûra, Sulaymân b. Jâmi''s city, was in Tahîthâ. It, too, was fortified (by five enclosures and as many ditches) and must have been even larger than al-Manî'a because ten-thousand women and children prisoners were found there. If there is reason to wonder whether al-Manî'a and al-Mansûra were not simply fortresses built alongside existing cities, such is not at all the case as far as al-Mukhtâra, the Zanj capital, is concerned. Al-Mukhtâra was truly a very large city that the insurgents had built completely in a place chosen for its inaccessibility. Tabarî gives us a great deal of information on the subject; but unfortunately, he is more concerned with providing a better understanding of how the battles for the city unfolded than with the city itself.

Al-Mukhtâra was located[8] on both banks of the Abû l-Khasîb Canal, a western tributary of the Tigris, and was interspersed by several other canals. A large iron chain and two huge stone barriers closed the entrance to the main canal which was divided by two bridges. Two other bridges on the Abû l-Khasîb Canal linked both parts of the city, and there is mention of still two more on the Mankâ Canal. Walls, fitted out with different types of war machines, surrounded the city. Most of the houses must have been built of dried bricks and palm leaves, but several chiefs' palaces, including that of 'Alî b. Muhammad, had been built with bricks of baked clay; the portal of his palace had been brought from Basra. The palace was in the western part of al-Mukhtâra (in the corner formed by the Tigris and the Abû l-Khasîb Canal) overlooking the racecourse. The houses of Ibn Sam'ân, of Sulaymân b. Jâmi', of Ankalây, of al-Qalûs, and of al-Jubbâ'î, the cathedral-mosque, a prison, and the al-Maymûna and al-Husayn markets were in this part of the city. Eastern al-Mukhtâra contained the houses of al-Karnabâ'î, Muslih al-Zanjî, and Abû 'Isâ; the palaces of al-Hamadânî, of Bahbûdh b. 'Abd al-Wahhâb, and of al-Muhallabî; the al-Mubâraka market and the cattle market, as well as another prison. There were also other buildings and mosques in the city.

Al-Mukhtâra was the Zanj state's true capital, the center of its political, administrative, and economic activities.

The Administration.—Even though it is presumptuous, given the information available to us, to speak of the administrative organization of 'Alî b. Muhammad's state, it should be pointed out that we do have a little information on the subject.

The existence of *dîwâns* (offices) in al-Mukhtâra is mentioned on several occasions by Tabarî, and we can suppose that these *dîwân*-s were in charge of taxes for the Treasury, the Army, the Judicial, and other departments.

The Master of the Zanj, who resided in the capital, constantly informed of conditions by his troop commanders, sent them messages containing his orders. We know that there were persons close to the Zanj generals who functioned as their secretaries. Al-Karnabâ'î was secretary to 'Alî b. Abân al-Muhallabî; Muhammad b. Ibrâhîm Abû 'Isâ served Ahmad b. Mahdî al-Jubbâ'î in that capacity; and Muhammad b. Sam'ân was 'Alî b. Muhammad's personal secretary and *wazîr (wizir*, minister).

Coins prove that mints existed as early as the year 258/871–72, which certainly facilitated and improved trade.

Whether or not there were hospitals in al-Mukhtâra is not known, but on two occasions Tabarî notes that wounded officers were taken to that city for care.

The Economy.—The little information that has come down to us about the Zanj state's economy concentrates, for the most part, on the problem of getting supplies to al-Mukhtâra. This is altogether understandable since the Zanj state's two main sources of revenue must have been taxes and the spoils of war. The army found what it needed on the spot; therefore, it was important to supply the markets of the cities, with the first priority given to those of the capital. On several occasions, Tabarî tells us about this and, most of all, about the means the Abbasids employed to cut off all supplies to the rebels. The supplies consisted of agricultural produce (which is probably the explanation of a certain tolerance shown the region's villagers), fruit (most of all dates), cattle, and fish. They were routed to the markets through Bedouin merchants or sent by the troops after successful raids. Whatever stocks of food the Abbasid army found in al-Manî'a and al-Mansûra were sold and the money from the sales was distributed to its soldiers; on the other hand, they burned the reserves they found in al-Mukhtâra. There were orchards and vegetable gardens in the area surrounding the capital, which was itself situated in a place covered with date-palm trees. Naturally, as we have already noted in previous chapters, 'Alî b. Muhammad placed great importance on providing his capital city with food.

If we consider the manufacture and repair of weapons, war matériel, boats, and other sorts of craft, clothing, and various other objects, and the minting of currency, it would be logical to believe that the Zanj had "industries" and an artisan class. Unfortunately, the only information we have on the subject is the following: "Abbasid troops reached the sites where the rebels' *shadhâ* (types of boats), the *sumayriyya* (also types of boats), and the war matériel they used were made."

The Army.—As is true of all rebel armies, there were obviously profound modifications in the "Zanj army" over the years, most noticeably in its armament. Originally, it must have been organized very simply. As Gaudefroy-Demombynes notes:

> "Arab historians give us a few characteristics of the strange crowd that made up this Negro army: the great majority did not understand a word of Arabic, and during the great harangues, the chief had the rare individuals capable of understanding his words placed around him: the others would faithfully shout their approval. Its first actions were those of a crow that abandoned the farms and spread out through the country to pillage; soon the inhabitants fled them leaving their possessions behind. That is how the Zanj 'army' collected a few weapons, horses, clothing, and ordinary utensils. At the beginning of their engagements with the Caliph's troops the Zanj had a few weapons for their front lines; the rest were clubs, bludgeons and pieces of wood which they used to kill and wound. Nevertheless, in 870, they captured Ubulla, 'Abbâdân and the Khûzistân, including Ahwâz; in 871, they pillaged Basra. They became a little more organized, but it was still a gang of 'drunken slaves,' good only for pillaging, killing and raping."

Despite this extremely unfavorable opinion and the fact that it concerns the beginnings of the revolt rather than the rest of it, there are a few details in Tabarî that deserve attention:

The Zanj army was composed (roughly) of three corps: the navy, the infantry, and the cavalry, but it is likely that only the cavalry (a Bedouin prerogative) was aware of being a unit. In truth, the Zanj army consisted mostly of troops commanded by 'Alî b. Muhammad's 'generals,' each of whom must have had a certain number of horsemen and a certain number of boats and other craft. It seems that these troops could be identified by the color of their flags; Abân al-Muhallabî's men flew the yellow flag, 'Alî b. Muhammad's flag was white and inscribed with his name.

The troops included scouts and spies. Signals were given by horns and drums. From time to time, commanders were authorized to bring their troops to the capital for rest. As has already been mentioned, wounded officers were also transported to the capital to be given care. The weapons at the rebels' disposal must have been the same, more or less, as those employed by the Abbasid soldiers.

As far as the composition of the army is concerned, it was undoubtedly heterogeneous: "Even though the events are known in Muslim history as the 'Zanj revolt,' and the leader is referred to as 'Sâhib (Master) of the Zanj,' it is not difficult to believe that actual Zanj were only part of the rebel army. Besides whites, there were many Negroes who most certainly were not from the east coast of Africa. As we have said before, the term Zanj has been wrongly applied to blacks regardless of their origin."[9]

It is very difficult to express an opinion on the numbers of the Zanj troops, even the estimates. Those given by the sources are unfounded and remain impossible to verify.[10]

II. EXTERNAL ORGANIZATION

The "external" relations of the Zanj state can be divided into two categories: relations with the population and relations with other contemporary movements.

Relations with the Population.— "Success brought success, and there is no doubt that the blacks were quickly aided by poor peasants, Bedouins always eager to pillage or to profit from others' pillage, and finally, even black deserters from the Caliph's army."

Nöldeke suggests quite rightly that alliances between peasants and the Zanj were more frequent than the sources lead us to believe. In fact, apart from rare exceptions, they are divined rather than clearly mentioned. This explains Bernard Lewis's reservation: "Peasants of the region seem also to side with the leader of the Zanj, probably through solidarity in the struggle against the owners," and that of Claude Cahen: "In any case, in the slave revolt . . . there seems to have been also the adherence of many peasant neighbors."

The few passages in Tabarî referred to in preceding chapters are about all we can say on the subject. Mention is made of the hospitality offered by the villages of al-Karkh and Jubbâ, the peace treaty with the inhabitants of al-Ja'fariyya, the signs of friendship shown by the Banû 'Ijl and again the peasants of al-Karkh. In 264/877–78, villagers in the vicinity of Tahîthâ warned al-Jubbâ'î of the government army's advance. During the same year, Abbasid troops captured al-Hajjâjiyya and imprisoned many of its inhabitants for having collaborated with the rebels. Finally, we are told that in 267/880–81, before leaving Khûzistân, al-Muhallabî's soldiers plundered villages inhabited by populations with whom they had lived in peace until then.[11]

Although we may assume a certain feeling of class solidarity in the peasants' support for the Zanj revolt, it would be difficult to contradict Bernard Lewis as far as the Bedouins are concerned: "The prospect of substantial spoils brought them the support of Bedouin tribes in the vicinity."[12]

Tabarî often mentions the presence of Bedouins among the rebels, alliances with Bedouin tribes, and the role they played in supplying the markets of al-Mukhtâra. Already in Bahrayn, in 255/868–69, certain

Bedouin tribes rallied to 'Alî b. Muhammad, only to abandon him after his defeat. Banû Tamîm and Banû Asad Bedouins were part of 'Alî b. Muhammad's forces when Basra was captured; they had submitted to training by Zanj generals before the attack.

In 262/875–76, a group of Bedouins who had been fighting on the side of 'Alî b. Abân al-Muhallabî asked for pardon and rejoined Ahmad b. Laythawayh's troops. Other Bedouins are mentioned as being among the insurgents in 264/877–78. In the same year, Bedouins, some of whom were members of the Zanj army, intercepted and carried off the *kiswa* (fabric cover which is changed every year) for the Ka'ba (the most famous sanctuary of Islam, called the "Temple" or the "House of God," *Bayt Allâh*, located in about the middle of the Grand Mosque of Mecca).

However, it is above all in speaking of supplying al-Mukhtâra that Tabarî records Bedouin participation. He relates in detail the flight of a group of Bedouins from the capital during the battle in *Dhû' l-Hijja* 267/July 881 and the operations of Abbasid troops against other Bedouin "suppliers," particularly the Banû Tamîm.[13]

Notice should also be taken of the relations between the Zanj and the blacks who deserted the caliphal army to join them. However, for under-standable reasons our sources are rather discreet on the subject. Cases of desertion are mentioned above all at the beginning of the revolt, that is, before the real Abbasid forces entered into action.

As for the relations between Takîn al-Bukhârî and 'Alî b. Abân al-Muhallabî in 265/878–79, al-Masrûr al-Balkhî's officer does not seem to have been compromised by the contact. The situation was evidently dif-ferent as far as other fugitive slaves were concerned, and Tabarî frequent-ly mentions the affiliation of new groups.

Zanj relations with city dwellers do not really come to light, except in the names and professions of some supporters.[14] It should not be forgot-ten, however, that during his first stay in Basra, in 254/868, 'Alî b.

Muhammad lived with the Banû Dubay'a and that some of them rallied to his cause. As already mentioned, he also sought (and obtained ?) support from the weavers in Baghdad.[15] The events that occurred in one section of Baghdad during Abû l-'Abbâs's triumphal return to the city were perhaps related to this.[16] We do not know.

Would research on the names of his supporters advance the study of relations between the Zanj movement and residents of the cities? On this point, I remain skeptical.

Relations with Other Contemporary Movements.—We have already seen that there was no alliance between the Zanj and the Qarmats.[17] The well-known passage in Tabarî's work is the only information we have on contacts between these two movements.

There was no agreement between the Zanj and the Saffarids either because, as we have already mentioned, Ya'qûb violently rejected the treaty of alliance that the Master of the Zanj proposed.[18] Nevertheless, Tabarî mentions several times tacit, less important agreements between detachments of the two groups in Khûzistân. On this subject, we should recall the ambiguous game played by the Saffarid governor in Khûzistân, the Kurd Muhammad b. 'Ubayd Allâh b. Azarmard, who changed his position vis-à-vis the insurgents several times during the years 262/875–76 and 266/879–80. It is the same for the correspondence and arrangements between Ya'qûb b. al-Layth and 'Alî b. Abân al-Muhallabî that followed battles between their troops in 263/876–77.

Several indications clearly prove that there were indeed relations between the Zanj and the Shiites. Unfortunately, they are inadequate to enable us to form a definite judgment. Were they individual cases or groups of people? Were these individual cases "liaison officers" to the Shiite community? We do not know.

All that we know for certain is that some Shiites were members or sympathizers of the rebel movement: al-Dhuwâ'ibî, Hârûn the 'Alid, the famous Muhammad b. al-Hasan b. Sahl Shaylama, and 'Alî b. Zayd al-'Alawî.

Speaking of the latter, A. K. Khalifa says: "The failure of this Alid's attempt and the fact that he himself and his accomplice were the only ones executed without causing any visible discontent among the rebel insurgents also reveals an important aspect of the Zanj revolt and their relations with the Shiites. On the other hand, the situation of these Shiites was entirely in keeping with the position of the Qarmats regarding this revolt."

If I have understood the last sentence correctly, it means that there was no alliance between the Shiites and the rebels. I fail to see what permits us to make such a statement unless it is al-Mas'ûdî's two passages, which should be taken with many reservations. Without claiming that the Zanj revolt was principally Shiite in nature, as Heinz Halm assumes, we must underline the *definite* existence of relations between the Shiites and the Master of the Zanj; but the importance and true circumstances of these relations are unknown to us.

NOTES

1. I do not believe that he could have been influenced by the passage in *Siyaset Name* of Nizâm al-Mulk, who writes: "Thus this is the period when Mouqanna, a native of Merv, made his appearance in the Maverra ann-nehr. He began by turning his partisans away from the path of observance of religious law, and professed Bathinian principles. Bou Saïd Djennaby Maghreby and Muhammad Alewy Bourqouy (that is to say 'Muhammad the 'Alide,' 'the veiled,' therefore our 'Master of the Zanj'), as well as Mouqanna and their missionaries held the same opinions and lived in the same period. They were united by bonds of friendship and corresponded with one another."

2. Theodor Nöldeke, Claude Cahen, and Bernard Lewis, for example.

3. The only attempt in this area was made by Faysal al-Sâmir.

4. It is his official title that we find on the coins. Faysal al-Sâmir errs (twice) when he maintains that he ['Alî b. Muhammad] thought of himself as caliph, which is absolutely false. Indeed, according to these coins, the "Commander of the Faithfuls" would be his grandfather, Muhammad's father. Heinz Halm writes along the same lines, listing

various clues that would prove that the Master of the Zanj truly thought of himself as caliph (with the right to impose taxes, the right to appoint *qâdî*-s, the right to have his name mentioned in the Friday *khutba* (sermon), and the right to strike money). According to him, the famous inscription on the Master of the Zanj's coins, "Muhammad ibn . . . amîr al-mu'minîn," can only be attributed to 'Ali b. Muhammad, which seems to me most unlikely. For me, this (lacunar) inscription remains inexplicable.

5. Cf. the expressions on the Zanj coins, and *infra,* p. 152 (in the Conclusion: 'Alî b. Muhammad's Doctrine).

6. Allusion to the Qur'an, LX/10.

7. It is mostly, but not totally, a question of *mawâlî,* as Heinz Halm, for whom this is the basis for his entire thesis, underlines so well. Indeed, pursuing an idea dear to Ignaz Goldziher, Halm tends to show that the revolt was above all a revolt of *mawâlî,* who used the Zanj to carry it out. It is an interesting and very important opinion because it could drastically change the way we look at the problem. Once more we must add that the present state of our knowledge does not allow us either to accept this totally, nor to reject it. Be that as it may, it tremendously broadens the field of future research.

8. Obviously, we have only vague knowledge of its location. On some maps where it was indicated, al-Mukhtâra was southeast of Basra.

9. "Furâtîya, Qurmâtîya, Nûba, and the others speaking Arabic."

10. In any case, tens of thousands of men.

11. For a general view of the relations between the Zanj and the peasants, cf. relevant remarks by Heinz Halm, who attempts to discover the origins and tendencies of the populations of these villages.

12. We have seen that Claude Cahen (among many others) shares this opinion. Typical, because of its position on the subject, is the following passage from Faysal al-Sâmir: "Some claim that the Zanj revolt was a war between two races (*jins*), between blacks and whites. As for me, I do not share this opinion, and I am convinced that it was a war between the slave class (*tabaqa*), half-slaves, *fellâh,* and Bedouins exasperated (*sâkhitîn*) with the existing order, on the one hand, and the landowners, slave masters, and the caliphate, on the other."

13. For a general view of the relations between the Zanj and the Bedouins, cf. H. Halm, *Die Traditionen,* pp. 61–62.

14. But if Theodor Nöldeke and Bernard Lewis are of the same opinion, the authors of Soviet collective works (*Istorija stran . . .* and *Sovjetskaja Enciklopedija*) see the movement as one supported by peasants, by Bedouins, and by the poor elements (and workers, *sic!*) of the cities. We should point out in this connection a passage from Dhahabî, who, in speaking of the Master of the Zanj, writes: "It was at Basra that he

first launched his appeal to revolt; he succeeded in misleading the garbage collectors (*zabbâl*) and the blacks."

15. Cf. *supra*, Chapter II: The Sojourn in Baghdad.

16. Cf. *supra,* Chapter IV, note 46. Bâb al-Tâq was a Shiite quarter.

17. Cf. s*upra,* p. 28, 81.

18. Cf. s*upra*, p. 135 according to Ibn al-Athir. As for Claude Cahen (speaking of Ya'qûb b. al-Layth), he writes on this subject: "He was less fortunate in his thrust, by way of southern Iran, toward Iraq where, unwilling to combine his operations with the contemporary, but very different, Zanj movement, he ended up being defeated by the caliphal armies. . . . "

Final Remarks

When we think of discoveries that could complete our present knowledge of the Zanj revolt, two possible fields come to mind: epigraphy, numismatics, and archaeology on one hand and manuscripts on the other.

I have found nothing on the Zanj in the field of epigraphy.

As far as numismatics is concerned, G. Miles's discovery of new pieces of 'Alî b. Muhammad's money shows the possibilities this field offers. We should add, however, that, except for the words *Mu'askar al-Imâm* (the *Imâm*'s military camp), the inscriptions are practically always the same.

There is little information to hope for from archaeology because the topography of the terrain has changed a great deal, and the riverbeds and waterways have constantly shifted. Building materials were, for the most part, flimsy, and the conquerors' main concern was to carry off whatever was worth the effort. and to burn and demolish the rest, filling in the canals and ditches. Therefore, it is quite difficult to expect discoveries in this area. We read: "The revolts of the years . . . 255–270 h. are not easily tracked."[1]

Nevertheless, we also read: "In such a long lapse of time, the Zanj had built cities for themselves in the theater of war and Muwaffaq, too, had built some. Later these cities fell in ruins and traces of them still remain."[2] But should we really take seriously this author who is "more harmful than useful" and who wrote these lines in the thirteenth century, while we know that the city of al-Muwaffaqiyya very quickly disappeared.[3]

As far as al-Mukhtâra is concerned, Nöldeke thinks that it will probably never be possible to find its exact location due to the total change in the waterway's bed. Nevertheless, Maximilian Streck is definite about the canal on which the city was built. He says, "Its bed still exists." The obvious question is the bed of what period. Even if al-Mukhtâra's exact location were found, it is hardly likely that excavations could yield great results. This is true, above all, when we reread Tabarî's passage on the capture and destruction of the city and when we realize where we are in regard to knowledge of cities as important as Wâsit and Basra were in the same period.

New information that could change or complete our present knowledge of the Zanj revolt will probably come one day from manuscripts. Tabarî, who had the tremendous advantage of being contemporary with the events, has left (in spite of all of the imperfections of the *Annals* system) about three-hundred pages on the question. To have more details than he gives, there are then two solutions: either find a "universal history" even more voluminous than Tabarî's for the period that interests us, and we do not know of any such work; or find works on the revolt written by contemporaries. We know the titles and even the names of the authors of such volumes, but the works have long been lost.

In manuscripts that have already been recorded and catalogued and are more or less known, it is unlikely that anything truly important will be discovered, except in the details, but there are certainly other names to be added to the bibliography. Given the slight importance of these sketchy compilations, I do not believe that much can be expected, above all from historians. I am thinking of the numerous historians later than Tabarî (Arabs, Persians, and Turks) who preceded the actual story of their period with a more or less broad picture of "universal history."

The manuscripts that have not come down to us can be divided into three categories, according to their degree of interest: works devoted to the Zanj revolt, books with sections devoted to the Zanj revolt, and finally those that must have at least mentioned the revolt.

The first category is obviously the most important. In fact we know of two persons who wrote works on the revolt:

a) First of all, the famous Muhammad b. al-Hasan b. Sahl, nicknamed Shaylama, who wrote the *Kitâb Akhbâr Sâhîb al-Zanj*. His work has been lost, but Tabarî made extensive use of it for the *Annals*. For one thing, almost all the information we have on 'Alî b. Muhammad comes from him. Mas'ûdî cites him:

> The first author who wrote the history of this rebel, the origins of his protest, his expedition against Bahrayn and his problems with the Arabs, was Muhammad son of el-Hasan, son of Sehl, nephew of Fadl, son of Sehl, vizir of Mamoun and nicknamed Dou-l-riâseteyn; it was the same Muhammad, whose relations with the Caliph Moutaded Billah were known; we have spoken about it elsewhere and we have told how, finally, this prince ordered him placed on a burning fire where his skin swelled up and crackled like that of a roasting chicken.

Ibn al-Nadîm has a note on him under his nickname, "Shaylama," and cites his work. Ibn al-Jâwzî mentions him in abridging Mas'ûdî, and Yâqût also mentions him briefly.

Speaking of the family of Banû Nawbakht, Louis Massignon writes:

> The same year another Nawbakhtî, Aboû al-Hasan Muhammad Ibn al-Hasan Ibn Sahl Shaylamah . . . former partisan of the 'Alid chief of the Zinj, and who had organized a conspiracy against the Caliph in Baghdad by having an unknown 'Alid swear an oath, was discovered and executed . . . Who was he? Was he a son of al-Wâthiq?, the son of Saqîl?[4]

Heinz Halm devoted long pages to Shaylama and his work. He is too inclined to consider all information later than Tabarî as coming from Shaylama's lost work, which, naturally, is far from being proven.

In spite of the great interest this work might hold for a better understanding of the Zanj revolt, we must point that the author is one of 'Alî b. Muhammad's former supporters who, like so many others, was granted amnesty after the revolt had been crushed. That is why we find that it con-

tains, most of the time, only invective against his former master and anecdotes accusing him of every possible sin, while the author is at pains to
exonerate himself. Obviously, we do not know whether the entire book
was written in the same style or whether Tabarî chose the most unfavorable passages to support his own attacks on the Master of the Zanj.
Personally, I rather believe the first hypothesis. For this reason I believe
that, although this book could shed light on the unfolding of the events, it
would be unsatisfactory as far as the core of the problem is concerned.

b) Ahmad b. Ibrâhîm b. al-Mu'allâ b. Asad al-'Ammî (whose grandfather al-Mu'allâ b. Asad had joined the insurgents in the Zanj revolt) also
wrote a *Kitâb Akhbâr Sâhib al-Zanj,* which is, unfortunately, lost. If we
were able to form impressions of the first work, we can say practically
nothing about this one. In al-Astarâbâdhî's lithographed edition, we find
hardly more than has been indicated above. Dissatisfied with both the
lithographed edition of Teheran and this seventeenth-century writer's text
and intrigued by the origin of his source, I went back in time, questioning
Shiite authors. It was in al-Tûsî's (d. 458/1066) *Fihrist Kutub al-shî'a* that
I found the same report. If al-Tûsî's printed text is read more easily than
the Teheran lithograph, this one provides no more information on the
work that interests us. Al-Astarâbâdhî refers to al-Tala'bakrî,[5] and al-
Tûsî's edition of Baghdad to Ibn al-Nadîm and al-Najâshî. Al-Tala'bakrî
is unknown to me, and I found no trace of our author in Ibn al-Nadîm's
work. As for al-Najâshî,[6] his note on this person does not differ from those
of authors already cited.

It is obvious that none of this tells us anything about what chiefly interests us, namely, the contents of this lost book.

We know of a few works (long lost) that give less extensive coverage
of the Zanj revolt in certain sections. Mas'ûdî writes: "We also find information about the leader of the Zendj in the history of the Mobaydites and

in the books of this sect; everything concerning this rebel, as well as the origin of the Bellalites and of the Saadites in Basra, is in our 'Intermediate History,' which dispenses us from going back to that here." There is no doubt that the disappearance of his *Kitâb al-awsat* is an irreparable loss for us; as for the Mobaydite sect's book, I cannot see what it is about.

Finally, there is a series of titles of works that have not come down to our time and which, though there is no indication of it, must at least mention the Zanj revolt.

I am thinking of authors such as:

Abû Sa'îd b. al-'Arabî (d. 340/951–52), *Ta'rîkh al-Basra*, a lost work, passages in Daylâmî and Dhahâbî. His other work, *Tabaqat al-nussâk* has been found.

Ibn Abî Tâhir Tayfûr, *Ta'rîkh Baghdad.*

Al-Khotabî, Abû Muhammad Isma'îl b. 'Alî (d. 350/961), *Ta'rîkh Baghdad.*

Niftawayh, Abû 'Abdallâh Ibrâhîm b. 'Arafah (d. 322/935), *Ta'rîkh.*

'Umar b. Shabba (d. 262/876), *Kitâb Akhbâr al-Basra.*

NOTES

1. Louis Massignon, "Explication du plan de Basra," p. 157.
2. Ibn al-Tiqtaqâ, trad. Amar, p. 50.
3. Nöldeke, "Sketches . . . ," p. 174: "Already in the following century it was no longer mentioned by geographers."
4. All of my efforts to study the Nawbakht family were in vain. I was unable to find out on what basis Massignon connected Shaylama to this family. This sheds light, however, on his expression, "the bias of their historians. . . ."
5. Professor Wilfred Madelung kindly informs me that here it is certainly a question of the celebrated Shiite traditionalist Abû Muhammad Hârûn b. Mûsâ b. Ahmad b. Sa'îd al-Talla'ukbarî (or al-Tal'ukbarî), who died in Baghdad in 385/995–96, and who is

mentioned in all the Shiite works since al-Najâshî.

6. On this subject, I refer to Sprenger's report in al-Tûsî's edition of the *Fihrist*: " . . . The second is the *Ismâ' al-rijâl* of Ahmad b. 'Alyy Najaschy, who was born in 372 and died in 450. It professes to be an independent work, but on comparing it with the *Fihrist* of Tusy we find that a new edition of it is more complete and generally more correct."

Conclusion

As we have already noted in the preceding chapters, opinions on the Zanj revolt and the personality of its leader, 'Alî b. Muhammad, are extremely divided. Obviously this is due to various authors' positions and differences in their interpretation of the facts, or rather in their choice of what facts to interpret. We must not forget that there are a great many hasty, secondhand judgments, formed not from sources but from the opinion found in the work of one of the great masters one has perused. Let us add also that these sources are not easily read and even less easily compared, without speaking of the bad faith of some and the incompetence of others. For manifold reasons then I prefer to group my personal opinions in a separate chapter, with the understanding that my aim is not only to present my point of view but, above all, to reexamine all the information available. It is true that on more than one occasion I have not been very strict and that, in certain cases, not to take a position is the equivalent of taking one all the same. Now that the moment has come to draw certain seemingly imperative conclusions, I want to emphasize that many questions remain unanswered or have several answers and that we are far from being able to form a definitive judgment for most of the problems concerning the Zanj revolt. This is easily explained by the two remarks that follow.

First: almost all of the information comes to us from sources which, without being truly official are so, more or less. It is difficult to see how a "pro Zanj" text could have survived the suppression of the revolt, if indeed such texts ever existed. Sources that are not of this category are also very biased.

Second: our conclusions are based on a certain number of more or less incomplete facts. They represent only a small part of what must have existed on the subject and has not come down to us. How can we be sure that a certain number of these lost pieces of information would not change totally, or partially at least, conclusions that seem logical today?

'Alî b. Muhammad's Personality. —If, as I have suggested in Chapter II, I do not believe that the Master of the Zanj was of Persian origin,[1] it is nevertheless impossible for me to decide in favor of Tabarî's rather than Safadî's account of 'Alî b. Muhammad's parents. Too little is known about the subject for me to take a definite position.

I do not believe that he was an 'Alid either because, apart from several doubtful or definitely false genealogies and a few details that can be interpreted in support of his ties to 'Alî's lineage, we have nothing to indicate that he was truly descended from the Prophet's son-in-law.

For reasons already mentioned, it is not at all easy to judge 'Alî b. Muhammad's personality. He was certainly an outstanding person who was cunning and persuasive. Besides those traits, he was intelligent, eloquent, educated, versed in poetry, astronomy, and psychology. Able to organize and command men (who under the circumstances must not have been easy to control), he possessed indisputable military and revolutionary talents. Two techniques, one as imperfect as the other, are available to us to judge his character. We can analyze the little information we have about his life and we can analyze his poetry.

Unfortunately, I am unable to speak of 'Alî b. Muhammad's poetry at the moment because to do so would require an analytical study of his verses and comparison with poetry of his times prior to the third century of the *hijra*. Such a delicate task requires, as I have already written, a special study and I intend to undertake it later.

The number of poems that 'Alî b. Muhammad is supposed to have written and that I know of is not very great. To be precise, there are one-hundred-ninety verses,[2] but when repetitions and variants are taken into account, the number must be in the area of about a hundred if all are accepted as truly 'Alî b. Muhammad's works. Our first impression of them is that they are samples of poetry from various periods of the Master of the Zanj's life, poems written during his sojourns in Samârrâ, poems written following events that occurred in Bahrayn, and finally poems written much later, during the revolt.

In the poems of the Samârrâ period, 'Alî b. Muhammad claims to be an 'Alid, revolted by the miserable condition of the caliphate which was in the hands of Turks. He swears to take his horses to Baghdad, where people are living in sin and where wine flows like a river. In other works of the same period, he either complains about his own situation and that of the destitute, or indulges in self-glorification.

Poems written after the events that dictated his return to Bahrayn promise the 'Abd al-Qays tribe vengeance.

The verses that came later are even more personal. They express his moods and anxieties, give his reasons for the revolt, repeat his love for 'Alî, and extol his own person.

To attempt to draw conclusions from the few poems, rightly or wrongly, attributed to the Master of the Zanj would be extremely precarious no matter how much interest they hold for us.

It is no easier to form an opinion of 'Alî b. Muhammad from the information available to us. Not only is the material inadequate, it is always suspect or difficult to interpret. Deciding whether he was a sincere man, deeply convinced of his mission and ready to risk his life for social reform, or on the contrary an ambitious, power-hungry person with no scruples[3] is obviously the chief problem.

When all is considered in the light of what we know about him, I believe it would be difficult to see in 'Alî b. Muhammad anything more than an ambitious, totally unprincipled man. A few verses attributed to him justify this view but, be that as it may, 'Alî b. Muhammad was a typical revolutionary: a person of humble descent, an educated man, and one versed in the occult sciences. Having had contact with the greats of his time, he embraced different doctrines and attempted several uprisings before kindling the great Zanj revolt.

It must be quickly added, however, that this judgment is not made without some reservations. How can we understand, for example, his refusal of five *dînâr*-s for each slave returned or forget that, having fought to the end, he died rejecting al-Muwaffaq's offer of pardon and promises of rewards.[4] There is apparently no answer to the question for all discussion based on the meager information we have is futile.

Alî b. Muhammad's Doctrine.—As we have seen, this is another subject of controversy. Was it Shiite, as so many indications and some of his verses would lead us to believe?[5] Or was he a Kharijite, given the phrase (long considered the Kharijite *credo*) found on his flag and on his coins, or was he, more precisely, as some would have it Azrakite?[6]

I believe that it is really much more logical to see in the tendency to embrace different doctrines a powerful political tool of the revolt. Passing himself off as a Shiite was, for the Master of the Zanj, doubtless a means of attracting sympathy from the most powerful party in Islam. Claiming to be a Kharijite meant stroking the feelings of the great majority of his supporters, given Kharijism's egalitarian principles.

What is striking in the Zanj revolt, which was above all a social uprising, is the absence of a definite plan and a well-thought out social program:

> He reminded them, according to the Arab historian Tabarî, of the evil state in which they lived and claimed that 'God would save them from it through him and that he desired to raise their status and make them masters of slaves and wealth and dwellings.' The last words reveal a weakness of the movement—it had no real programme of reform, no general aim of abolishing slavery, but was rather a revolt of specific slaves to better their own position.[7]

It was, indeed, only a new state within a state, with the same foundations; but to be surprised that the Zanj revolt did not aim at abolishing slavery is perhaps asking too much. I do not see how it would have been possible, in the Muslim Middle Ages, to contemplate suppression of an institution that was tolerated by the Qur'an and accepted by custom.

The Zanj revolt was, therefore, a political (power struggle) and social (betterment of a certain class living conditions) revolt.[8] Nevertheless, I must insist on one very sensitive point: it was indeed *in part* a social revolt, but it was not, as some have said, a true (modern) social revolution with a definite plan. As for the role played by 'Ali b. Muhammad, his true sentiments and the limits of his real power in this or that circumstance, what knowledge we have does not allow us to form a definite opinion.

Our attention is also drawn to two other points: Ya'qûb b. al-Layth's rejection of the alliance proposed by the Master of the Zanj, and 'Alî b. Muhammad's fruitless discussion with Hamdân Qarmat.

It is strange, to say the least, that Tabarî does not even mention the famous correspondence that was supposedly exchanged between 'Alî b. Muhammad and Ya'qûb.

This is quite enough to place us in a quandary. It is, therefore, all the more reasonable not to attempt to interpret it. As far as Hamdân Qarmat's words are concerned, I admit that they are open to several interpretations.

The Consequences of the Zanj Revolt.—If, as we shall observe later, the Zanj revolt produced many results, there is, nonetheless, good reason to be suspicious of the overemphasis on the subject found in certain works.

The Zanj revolt greatly facilitated the establishment of the Tûlûnids in Egypt. It also aided, indirectly, the Saffarid movement and, apparently, even Byzantium's military undertakings. It was also of benefit to the Qarmats, some of whose followers, it seems, made their debut among the Zanj.

Although the economic and social consequences of the revolt are, obviously, much more difficult to grasp, they were not very profound. The revolt does not seem to have influenced, in any lasting way, the course of Islam's history nor brought about a radical change in social structure.[9] It does not seem to have greatly affected Lower Iraq's irrigation and agriculture.[10]

The most important consequence of 'Alî b. Muhammad's revolt is undoubtedly the abandonment of Lower Iraq's barren lands by the servile workforce and the definite disappearance of the large work sites. This necessarily brought about improvement in the living conditions of the slaves who had worked there previously.[11] Besides, the Zanj survivors were enrolled in the Abbasid army and not returned to their former servile condition.[12]

As to the death toll during these fourteen years, estimates vary between five-hundred-thousand and two and a half million victims. It is clearly impossible to make a definite statement on the number of dead, but Silvestre de Sacy had already written on the subject: "Fakhr-eddin also reports the same facts, in a brief statement, under Motamed's caliphate. It is claimed that 2,500,000 men perished in this war. I do not need to point out what is exaggerated in this account."

Here ends the presentation and modest analysis of the information that has come down to us on the slave revolt that occurred in Basra eleven centuries ago.

One book of history is always replaced by another and this one will surely be no exception to the rule. Others, including the present author perhaps, will revisit the subject with new interpretations and more solid conclusions based on more faithful sources. As Maxime Rodinson has noted, "We all are deplorably lacking in imagination in regard to tomorrow's findings. But the continual renewal of historical ideas—even when there is only a modest increase in documentation—perpetually defies this powerlessness of the mind."

NOTES

1. I admit readily, however, that I am impressed by Heinz Halm's reasoning. He sees in the Master of the Zanj a Persian *mawlâ* whose principal collaborators were also Persian *mawâlî*. Heinz Halm's theses are very interesting and his argumentation is as discerning as it is serious. The difficulty lies in the fact that our sources mention only Arabs as 'Ali b. Muhammad's ancestors and in the fact that we cannot see any major reason for these authors to invent (or support) an Arab ancestry for the Master of the Zanj, however biased they may be. For want of anything better, I still believe in the information provided by these sources, namely, that he lived in Persia in his youth, but was an Arab by birth, as were his parents and ancestors. If I am wrong, he was truly a sort of forerunner of Jamâl al-Dîn al-Afgânî.

2. Cf. Appendix IV. Some of them have been cited and subjected to comment by various authors.

3. Most authors do not even ask this question. Nöldeke, however, attempts to out find what might be said on the subject; Faysel al-Sâmir explains his opinion at length, while A. Olabi ventures into this area much less.

   For many reasons, it would be extremely interesting to analyze theatrical works about the Zanj revolt. Cf., for example, Mu'în Bisîsû's play, which premiered in Cairo in February 1970 (M.B., *Thawrat al-Zanj, masrahiyya shi'riyya,* Le Caire, 1970, 98pp. and illustrations), and the work of the Tunisian Ezzedine Madani (*al-Zanj wa thawrat shab al-homar,* 3rd edition, Tunis, STD, 1986, 190 pp.), which was the discovery at the Festival of Arab Theater in Rabat in March 1974 (cf. Paul Balta's article, *Le Monde,* Paris, March 21, 1974, p. 15). There will most probably be others, and the cinema will not lag far behind in embracing the subject.

4. I omit other details in his favor, pointed out by Tabarî, without speaking of 'Alî b. Muhammad's personal declarations in the same vein.

5. See *supra*, p. 85, the words that he is supposed to have uttered on learning of the execution of a Shiite poet. Diametrically opposed details do exist. (Cf. *supra*, p. 86, Mas'ûdî's passage). Heinz Halm considers him unquestionably a Shiite.

6. "His conduct proves that the accusation that he was a member of the Kharedjite sect called Azrakites is justified; he did indeed kill women, children and the elderly, all those whose lives should have been spared, which proves how legitimate is this accusation. We still have one of his speeches which begins with these words (the Kharedjite profession of faith): 'God is great, God is great; there is no other God but God, God is great; to God alone belongs the commandment'; moreover he held that all sin makes one an infidel." (al-Mas'ûdî). But Maurice Gaudefroy-Demombynes replies to that, when he writes: "An Arab historian recalling that he had women, chil-

dren and old people massacred, concluded that he was a Kharijite, which is a hollow insult . . . "

As for the phrase "*la hukma illâ lillâh* (there is no judgment except that of Allâh),"
it poses the seemingly inexplicable problem of reconciling dogmas as opposed to one another as Shiism and Kharijism. About the only place we find awareness of the situation is in a statement by P. Casanova: "It is rather strange to see the phrase of the Kharedjites, ʿAlî b. Abû Tâlib's enemies, on the coins of one claiming to be an ʿAlid. It is true that the *hâkemis* quarrel focused on an altogether special point. ʿAlî had accepted an arbiter to decide between him and his rival Moawia (first caliph of the Umayyad dynasty, he reigned from 661 to 681). The Kharedjites, more royalist than the king, declared that God alone was the arbiter, and that ʿAlî b. Abû Tâlib could not allow his rights to be debated. Two centuries after ʿAlî's death, then, it was easy to adopt this expression and recognize Alî and his family's claims."

In truth, it was, as D. Sourdel so subtly suggests, obviously something quite different: "For my part, I would be tempted to explain this curious coincidence by W. Montgomery Watt's hypothesis that such a phrase would not have been pronounced regarding the 'arbitration' at Siffîn (place where the famous battle took place in 657 between ʿAlî b. Abî Tâlib's partisans and those of the future Umayyade Caliph, Moʿâwiya, was fought. This battle was followed by the famous 'arbitration' concluded to ʿAlî b. Abî Tâlib's disadvantage), but to express the claims of ʿUthmân's enemies, that is to say, ʿAlî's oldest supporters; from then on, it would be essentially a Shiite and not a Khârîjite cry, and we can understand its reappearance at the time of the Zanj, who took an ʿAlid pretender as their leader. As a result, part of passage of Hilâl al-Sâbi's (reported by Heribert Busse, *Der Islam*, 44, June 1968, p. 270, 1. 27–29) is not to be considered."

7. Bernard Lewis, *The Arabs in History,* London, 1950, p. 104.

8. Is it a question of Zanj or of *mawâlî* in the first place?

9. This causes us to think of G. von Grünebaum's remarks in *Medieval Islam*, p. 210: "It cannot be said that the final suppression of this movement affected the position of the Negro in Muslim Society."

10. Cf. Claude Cahen and Bernard Lewis. Other authors are not of the same opinion; Nöldeke assumes that the cities and villages of the lower Tigris probably never recovered from the losses they suffered during this period. Müller claims that for fourteen years the entire southern part of Iraq and Khûzistân were transformed into a desert; and Maurice Gaudefroy-Demombynes writes, "After ten years of fighting and plundering, the slave revolt was spent. But it took a long and methodical effort to repair the material damage, dig the irrigation and drainage canals anew, rebuild the stables, recruit farmers: a task beyond the forces of the Baghdad government. The slave war,

which was a manifestation of the social and political disorder, was also a new cause of ruin for the caliphate."

11. 'A. 'A. al-Dûrî also reflects on the birth of a class attitude.

12. Heinz Halm believes, on the contrary, that the slaves were returned to their masters, which seems to me unlikely.

Annotated Chronological Bibliography

This bibliography contains only works that mention either 'Alî b. Muhammad or the Zanj revolt. The advantage of this criterion is that it provides a concrete and limited bibliography. The disadvantage is that it eliminates major works that make no mention of the revolt, but provide otherwise excellent information about the epoch, the milieu, etc. The authors are arranged chronologically so that the transmission of information can be followed better. As far as authors of the Middle Ages are concerned, they are arranged by the dates of death; for the authors of the last three centuries, they are listed by the publication date of their work. As far as the latter are concerned, there is some imprecision because it was not always possible to fix a date for the first edition of work. In these cases, it is the date of the reprinted edition consulted that is given. A few lines of commentary accompany the texts listed. It is evident that these comments concern only the information on the revolt or on the name of 'Alî b. Muhammad. To facilitate consulation of the *Encyclopédie de l'Islam,* articles in this work are grouped under the years 1913–1942 for the first edition and under the year 1956 for the second edition.

I. PRIMARY SOURCES

3rd/9th–10th Centuries

1. Ibn al Rûmî (d. 283?/896?), *Dîwân,*
   a) ed. Kâmil Kaylânî, Cairo, 1924, pp. 419–27 and 458;
   b) ed. Said Boustany, forthcoming.

The great poem on the capture of Basra and an allusion to Ibrâhîm b. al-Mudabbir's escape. Ibn al-Rûmî mentions the Zanj in many other places: Cairo ms., f. 41a, 49a, 66ab, 96b, 101b, 126b, 155b, 201b, 223b, 243b, 253a, 270ab, 271ab. Cf. Rhuvon Guest, *Life and Works of Ibn er-Rûmî*, London, Luzac, 1944; Said Boustany, *Ibn al- Rûmî, sa vie et son oeuvre*, Beirut, Imprimerie Catholique, 1967; and 'Abbâs Mahmûd al-'Aqâd, *Ibn al-Rûmî hayâtuhu min shi'rihi*, Cairo, 1357/1938, pp. 20–21 and 27.

2. Al-Buhturî (d. 284?/897?), *Dîwân,*
   a) Cairo edition, 1911, two books in one volume; I, pp. 14–16, 21–23, and 126–27; II, pp. 174–77;
   b) ed. Karam al-Bustânî, 2 vols. Beirut, 1381/1962;

c) ed. Hasan Kâmil al-Sayrafî, Cairo, 1963–64.

On Ibrâhîm b. al-Mudabbir's escape; on the merits of al-Muwaffaq; glorifying al-Mu'tamid; again on Ibrâhîm b. al-Mudabbir's escape.

3. Al-Ya'qûbî (d. 284/897), Ta'rîkh,
a) ed. Martijn Theodor Houtsma, Ibn Wâdhih, qui dicitur al-Ja'qûbî, Historiae, Leiden, E. J. Brill, 1883, 2 vols.; vol. II, pp. 620 and 622–24;
b) Baghdad edition, 1939, 3 vols.; vol. III, pp. 227 and 231.
Only a few lines.

4. Ibn Rustah (written in 290/903), Kitâb al-A'lâq al-nafîsa,
a) ed. Michael Jan de Goeje, Leiden, E. J. Brill, 1892 (BGA, t. VII);
b) trans. Gaston Wiet, Les atours précieux, Cairo, Publications de la Société de Géographie d' Égypte, 1955, p. 213.
Speaking of the city of Tahîthâ.

5. Ibn al-Mu'tazz (d. 296/908), Dîwân, I, pp. 126–45, ed., trans. and commentary by Carl Lang, Mu'tadid als Prinz und Regent ein historiches Heldengedicht von Ibn el-Mu'tazz, Leipzig, 1886–87, in ZDMG, 36 (p. 620), 40 (pp. 563–611), and 41 (pp. 232–79).
Poem in honor of al-Mu'tadid. Many details on the revolt and the exploits of Abû l-'Abbâs.

6. Ibn al-Mu'tazz, Tabaqât al-shu'arâ' al-muhdathîn,
a) ed. Abbâs Eghbâl, London, 1939, p. 185;
b) ed. 'Abd ad-Sattâr Ahmad Farrâj, Cairo, 1956, p. 392.
An anecdote concerning 'Alî b. Muhammad and Muflih that is not found elsewhere.

4th/10–11th Century

7. Wakî' (d. 306/918), Akhbâr al-qudât, ed. 'Abd al-'Azîz Mustafâ al-Maragî, 2 vols., Cairo, 1366/1947; vol. II, p. 181.

8. Al-Tabarî (d. 311/923). Kitâb Akhbâr al-rusul wa l-mulûk, ed. Michael Jan de Goeje, Annales quos scripsit Abû Djafar . . . , Leiden, E. J. Brill, 1879–1901; III/3, pp. 1742–87, 1834–38, 1842–58, 1859–72, 1874–80, 1883, 1888–89, 1898–1911, 1912–15, 1917–29, and 1932–37; III/4, pp. 1938–39, 1942–2026, 2028–37, 2040–83, 2085–2103, 2111, 2129–30, and 2135–36.

Cf. now David Waines's translation: al-Tabarî, The History (Ta'rîkh al-rusul wa'l-mulûk), vol. XXXVI: The Revolt of the Zanj, Albany (U.S.A.), State

University of New York Press, 1992, xvii + 229 pp.; and that of Philip M. Fields: al-Tabarî, *The History*, vol. XXXVII: *The 'Abbasid Recovery: The War Against the Zanj Ends*, Albany (U.S.A.), State University of New York Press, 1987, xv + 195 pp.

By far the best source from every point of view.

9. Eutychius (d. 328/940), *Nazm al-jawâhir*, ed. Edward Pococke, *Annales . . .*, Oxford, 1658, pp. 469–70.

Compilation. Erroneous dates.

10. Ibn al-Dâya (d. 330/941), *Sîrat Ahmad b. Tûlûn*, in *Fragmente aus dem Mughrib des Ibn Sa'îd*, ed. Karl Vollers, Berlin, E. Felber, 1894, p. 19.

11. Al-Balawî (written ca. 330/941), *Sîrat Ahmad b. Tûlûn*, ed. Muhammad Kurd 'Alî, Damascus, 1358/1939; pp. 19, 32, 81, 84, 282, 294, 301, and 317.

Verse by 'Alî b. Muhammad and known details.

12. Al-Sûlî (d. 385/946), *Akhbâr al-Buhturî*, ed. Sâlih Ashtar, Damascus, 1378/1958, pp. 113–14.

An allusion to Ibrâhîm b. al-Mudabbir's escape.

13. Al-Sûlî, *Kitâb al-Awrâq*.

Only a partially preserved work. Information came to us through al-Husrî; many authors have referred to it.

14. Al-Istakhrî (d. 340/951), *Kitâb al-Masâlik wa-l-mamâlik*,

a) ed. Michael Jan de Goeje, Leiden (*BGA*, t. I);

b) ed. Michael Jan de Goeje, Leiden, E. J. Brill, 1927.

In "Addenda and Emendanda," *BGA*, t. IV, p. 209. In speaking of Warzanîn.

15. Al-Nu'mânî b. Abî Zaynab (written in 342/953), *Gaybat al-Nu'mânî*, lith., ed.

Cited by Louis Massignon, in *EI*, 1, s. v. "Zandj."

16. Al-Mas'ûdî (d. 345/956), *Kitâb Murûj al-dhahab wa-ma'âdin al-jawâhir . . .*, ed. and trans. Charles Barbier de Meynard and Pavet de Courteille, *Les prairies d'or*, 9 vols., Paris, Imprimerie Impériale, 1861–74; vol. VII, pp. 404–405; vol. VIII, pp. 13, 31–33, 38–40, 45, 57–61, 64, 69, and 140; vol. IX, p. 297.

In spite of the small number of pages that deal with the revolt, al-Mas'ûdî provides a great many new details. They are anecdotal rather than historical.

17. Al-Mas'ûdî, *Kitâb al-Tanbîh wa-l-ishrâf,*
a) ed. Michael Jan de Goeje, Leiden, E. J. Brill, 1894, *BGA*, t. VIII, pp. 396–97; and pp. 392–93 for the verses.
b) trans. Bernard Carra de Vaux, *Le livre de l'avertissement et de la révision,* Paris, Imprimerie Nationale, 1897, pp. 471–72 and 498–99.
An uninteresting passage and seven verses from 'Alî b. Muhammad.

18. Al-Kindî (d. 350/961), *Kitâb Tasmiyat wulât Misr,* ed. Rhuvon Guest, *The Governors and Judges of Egypt,* London-Leiden, E. J. Brill, 1912, p. 225.

19. Hamza al-Isfahânî (d. between 350–360/961–971), *Tawârîkh sinî mulûk al-ard wa-l-anbiyâ',* ms. Leiden, Or. 767, p. 371.
A new version of 'Alî b. Muhammad's death.

20. Al-Maqdisî, al-Mutahhar b. Tâhir (d. 355/966), *Kitâb Bad' al-khalq wa-l-ta'rîkh,* ed. and trans. Clément Huart, *Le livre de la création et de l'histoire,* 6 vols., Paris, Publications de l École des Langues Orientales Vivantes, 1899–1919; VI, pp. 37 and 121–22.

21. Al-Isfahânî, Abû l-Faraj (d. 356/967), *Kitâb Maqâtil al-Tâlibîyîn wa akhbârihim,*
a) ed. lith. Teheran, 1307/1889–90, pp. 229 and 430;
b) ed. Najaf, 1353/1934–35, pp. 424 and 427–28;
c) ed. Ahmad Saqr, Cairo, 1949, pp. 672 and 689.
On an 'Alid by the name of 'Alî b. Muhammad, whose father died in prison under al-Musta'în, plus another note.

22. Ibn Hawqal (written ca. 367/977), *Kitâb al-Masâlik wa-l-mamâlik,*
a) ed. Michael Jan de Goeje, Leiden, 1873 (*BGA,* t. II), pp. 160–61;
b) ed. Johannes Hendrik Kramers, Leiden and Leipzig, E. J. Brill, 1938–39, p. 237.
Note of a copyist of the year 537/1142–43.

23. Al-Sîrâfî (d. 368?/979?), *Akhbâr al-nuhât al-basrîyîn,* Cairo edition, 1374/1955, pp. 70 and 80.
In speaking of al-Riyâshî and of al-Mubarrad.

24. Anonymous (written around 372/982), *Hudûd al-'âlam,* ed. Vladmir Minorsky, *The Regions of the World,* London, Luzac, 1937, pp. 138–39; 31b.

25. Al-Muqaddasî (written in 375/985), *Kitâb Ahsan al-taqâsîm fî ma'rifat al-aqâlîm,* ed. Michael Jan de Goeje, Leiden, E. J. Brill, 1877 (*BGA,* t. III), II, p. 406.

Al-Muqaddasî points out that in his time the inhabitants are still finding the Zanj's buried treasure.

26. Al-Malatî (d. 377/987), *Kitâb al-Tanbîh wa-l-radd,*
a) Damascus ms., Persian copy, p. 58;
b) ed. Sven Dedering, *Die Wiederlegung der Irrgläubigen und Neuerer,* Istanbul, 1936, pp. 26–27.
"He makes the leader of the Zanj a Zaidite, a political adversary of the Sayid and the Arabs." (Louis Massignon, *EI,* 1, s.v. Zandj).

27. Ibn al-Nadîm (written in 377/978–79), *Kitâb al-Fihrist,* Cairo edition, 1348/1929–30, p.184; suppl. p. 6.
A note on Shaylama and a verse from 'Alî b. Muhammad.

28. Al-Zubaydî (d. 379/990), *Tabaqât al-nahwîyîn wa l-lugawîyîn,* ed. Muhammad Abû l-Fadl Ibrâhîm, Cairo, 1373/1954, pp. 106 and 120.
In speaking of al-Riyâshî and al-Bâhilî.

29. Al-Tanûkhî (d. 384/994), *Nishwâr al-muhâdara wa-akhbâr al-mud-hâkara,* ed. and trans. in part by David Samuel Margoliouth, *The Table Talk of a Mesopotamian Judge*, 2 vols., London, Royal Asiatic Society, 1921; and in *Islamic Culture*, vols. III–VI, 1929–32; t. I, pp. 83–84 (77–78), pp. 137–38 (126), pp. 183–84 (167–68), and pp. 279 (268); t. VIII, pp. 232–34.
Previously unpublished details on the wounding of al-Muwaffaq, his operation, and the execution of Qirtâs. The rest is much less interesting.

30. Al-Makkî (d. 386/996), *Qût al-qulûb,* Cairo edition, 1310/1892–93, 2 vols.; vol. II, p. 71.

31. Al-Shâbushtî (d. 399/1008), *Kitâb al-Diyârât,* ed. Kurkîs 'Awwâd, Baghdad, 1951, pp. 17 and 66.
Previously unpublished anecdote concerning Muflih.

5th/11–12th Century

32. Al-Husrî (d. ca. 413/1020 or 453/1061), *Zahr al-âdâb,* ed. 'Alî Muhammad al-Bajâwî, Cairo 1953, 2 vols.; vol. I, pp. 286–88; vol. II, pp. 777–78.
Extremely valuable, it passes on a passage from al-Sûlî and seven verses from 'Alî b. Muhammad.

33. Al-Husrî (d. circa 413/1020 or 453/1061), *Jam' al-jawâhir*, ed. 'Alî Muhammad al-Bajâwî, Cairo 1372/1953, pp. 190–93.
Even richer than the previous work with forty verses from the Master of the Zanj.

34. 'Abd al-Jabbâr al-Hamadhânî (d. 415/1024), *Tathbît dalâ'il al-nubuwwa*, ed. 'Abd al-Karîm 'Uthmân, Beirut, n.d., t. II, pp. 341–42 and 395.
Strange passage that is not found elsewhere: an alleged discussion between the celebrated mu'tazilite Abû Ya'qûb al-Shahhâm and the Master of the Zanj.

35. Miskawayh (d. 421/1030), *Kitâb Tajârib al-umam wa-ta'âqib al-himam*, ms. Bibliothèque Nationale de Paris, Fonds Arabe, no. 5838 (coll. Shefer), f. 31b–35b, 41b–47b, 49a, 50b–51b, 52b–67b, 71b, and 72b.
Except for two sentences, this is a compilation of Tabarî's chronicle.

36. Al-Bagdâdî (d. 429/1037), *Kitâb al-Farq bayn al-firaq,*
a) ed. Muhammad Badr, Cairo, 1328/1910, p. 354;
b) trans. Abraham Halkin, *Moslem Schisms and Sects,* Tel Aviv, 1935, p. 229.
An accusation against 'Alî b. Muhammad.

37. Al-Tha'alibî (d. 429/1038), *Kitâb Latâ'if al-ma'ârif,*
a) ed. Pieter de Jong, Leiden, E. J. Brill, 1867, p. 85.
b) trans. Clifford Edmund Bosworth, *The Book of Curious and Entertaining Information,* Edinburg, Edinburg University Press, 1968.

38. Al-Bîrûnî (d. 440/1048), *Kitâb al-Âthâr al-bâqîya 'an al-qurûn al-khâliya,*
a) ed. C. Eduard Sachau, Leipzig, D. M. G. and Brockhaus, 1876–78, p. 332;
b) English trans., C. Eduard Sachau, *The Chronology of Ancient Nations,* London, Allen, 1879, p. 330.
A few lines of very great importance.

39. Hilâl al-Sâbî' (d. 448/1056), *Kitâb al-Wuzarâ',* trans. part., "Das Hofbudget des Chalifen al-Mu'tadid billâh (279/892–289/902)," in *Der Islam*, 43, 1967, pp. 11–36, cf. p. 16; *Der Islam*, 44, 1968, p. 270.
A new version of the Master of the Zanj's death.

40. Anonymous (mid-11th century?), *Târîkhe Sîstân*, ed. Muhammad Bahâr, Teheran, 1314/1936, pp. 235–36 and 242.

41. Abû l-'Alâ' al-Ma'arrî (d. 449/1057), *Risâlat al-gufrân,* ed. Bint al-Shâti', Cairo, 1950, pp. 385–86 and 539.

Very important. Nine of 'Alî b. Muhammad's verses and some information not found elsewhere.

42. Al-Najâshî (d. 450/1059), *Kitâb al-rijâl*,
a) ms. British Museum, Or. 7717; f. 44b;
b) ed. lith., Bombay, 1317/1900, p. 7071.
The first work in which we find a note on Shu'ûbî Ahmad b. Ibrâhîm b. al-Mu'allâ b. Asad al-'Ammî of Basra, author of the lost work entitled *Kitâb akhbâr Sâhib al-Zanj*.

43. Al-Qudâ'î (d. 454/1062), *Kitâb Nuzhat al-albâb*, ms. British Museum, add. 23.285; f. 33b.
Three of 'Alî b. Muhammad's verses and a few lines of no interest.

44. Al-Qudâ'î, *'Uyûn al-ma'ârif wa-funûn akhbâr al-khalâ'if*, ms. Bibliothèque Nationale Paris, Fonds Arabe, no. 1490 (1); f. 100a.

45. Ibn Hazm (d. 456/1064), *Jamharat ansâb al-'arab*, ed. Évariste Lévi Provençal, Cairo, 1948, pp. 50–52.
Absolutely unique information on 'Alî b. Muhammad and his family.

46. Al-Tûsî (d. 458/1066), *Fihrist kutub al-Shî'a*,
a) eds. Aloys Sprenger and Mawlawy Abd al-Haqq, *Tusy's List of Shy'ah Books and 'Alam al- Hoda's Notes on Shy'ah Biography*, Calcutta, 1853–55, pp. 21–22, no. 37;
b) ed. Muhammad Sadiq, Baghdad, 1937, p. 30, no. 80.
Note on Ahmad b. Ibrâhîm b. al-Mu'allâ.

47. Al-Khatîb al-Bagdâdî (d. 463/1071), *Ta'rîkh Bagdâd*, ed. Cairo, 1349/1931, 14 tomes in 7 vols.; t. II, p. 127, no. 518; t. VIII, pp. 446–47, no. 4556; t. XII, pp. 138–40, no. 6591.
In speaking of Zayd b. Akhzam and al-Riyâshî.

48. Nizâm al-Mulk (written in 484–5/1091–92), *Siyâset nâme*,
a) ed. and French trans., Charles Shefer, Paris, E. Leroux, 1893, pp. 285 and 290;
b) Russian trans., Boris Nikolaevich Zahoder, Moscow-Leningrad, Akad. Nauka, S.S.S.R., 1949, pp. 220, 223, 265, 298, 301, 341, 346, and 349.
A summary of the events and some fanciful remarks.

49. Al-Qayrawânî (5th–6th/11th–12th century), *Kitâb al-'Uyûn wa-l-hadâ'iq fî âkhbâr al-haqâ'iq*, t. IV,

a) ms. Tübingen, Or. Wetzstein II/342 (Wilhelm Ahlwardt, Kat. Berlin, IX, pp. 95–96, no. 9491, We. 342); f. 6a–12b, 13b, 14b, 16a, and 17a–30a;
b) critical edition by Omar Saïdi (forthcoming). Cf. *infra*, no. 215.
Compilation of Tabarî with a few new details.

6th/12th–13th Century

50. Al-Gazâlî (d. 505/1111), *Ihyâ' 'ulûm al-dîn*, IV, p. 255.
According to Louis Massignon, *La Passion* . . . , p. 32, no. 3, al-Gazâlî mentions Sahl al-Tustarî's presence in Basra during the revolt of the Zanj. The same information is found in al-Makkî; cf. *supra*, no. 30.

51. Al-Sam'ânî (d. 562?/1167?), *Kitâb al-Ansâb*, ed. David Samuel Margoliouth, London-Leiden, E. J. Brill, 1912, pp. 264b.
In speaking of al-Riyâshî.

52. Ibn 'Asâkir (d. 571/1176), *al-Ta'rîkh al-kabîr*, Damascus edition, 1329–30/1911–12, 7 vols.; vol. VI, p. 245.

53. Anonymous (written ca. 592/1196), *Mujmal al-tawârîkh wa-l-qisas* (in Persian), ed. Muhammad Bahâr, Teheran, 1318/1939, pp. 363 and 367.

54. Ibn al-Jawzî (d. 597/1200), *al-Muntazam wa multaqat al-multazam*, ed. Fritz Krenkow, Haydarabad, 1357–59/1938–40, 10 vols., 5/II, pp. 4–6, 8, 19, 21, 45, 49–50, 56, 58–59, 63, 66–67, 69, 74–75, 85, 112–13, 121, 136, and 141–42.
Although they are numerous, these pages are of little interest.

55. Ibn al-Jawzî, *'Ajâ'ib al-badâ'i'*, ms. Bibliothèque Nationale Paris, Fonds Arabe, no. 1567, f. 27a–b.

56. Pseudo-Muslim al-Lahjî (13th century?), *Ta'rîkh*, ms. Bibliothèque Nationale Paris, Fonds Arabe, no. 5982, f. 173a–b and 174a.
Known passages and seven verses by 'Alî b. Muhammad.

7th/13th Century

57. 'Alî b. Zâfir al-Azdî (d. 613?/ 1216?), *Kitâb Akhbâr al-duwal*,
a) ms. British Museum, Or. 3685; f. 29b and 131b–132a;
b) excerpts in Ferdinand Wüstenfeld, *Die Statthalter von Egypten*, Göttingen, Dieterich, 1875–76, p. 58.

58. Muslim b. Mahmûd al-Shayzarî (d. 626/1229), *Jamharat al-islâm dhât al-nathr wa-l-nizâm*, Leiden ms., Or. 287, f. 53a–54b.
Sixty-one of 'Alî b. Muhammad's verses and a passage from al-Mas'ûdî.

59. Yâqût (d. 626/1229), *Mu'jam al-Udabâ'*, ed. David Samuel Margoliouth, Leiden, E. J. Brill, 1907–31, 6 vols.; vol. I, p. 376; vol. IV, pp. 284–85; vol. VI, pp. 494–95.
Notes on Ahmad b. Ibrâhîm b. al-Mu'allâ b. Asad al-'Ammî, al-Riyâshî, and Shaylama.

60. Yâqût, *Mu'jam al-buldân,* ed. Ferdinand Wüstenfeld, Leipzig, Brockhaus, 1866–73, 6 vols.; vol. I, p. 410.
In speaking of Ahwâz.

61. Ibn al-Athîr (d. 630/1233), *al-Kâmil fî l-ta'rîkh,* ed. Carolus Johannes Tornberg, Leiden, E. J. Brill, 1851–76, 14 vols.; vol. IV, pp. 314–15; vol. V., pp. 340–41; vol. VII, pp. 139–47; 163–64, 166–71, 173–80, 188, 190–91, 200–204, 212–13, 216–18, 223–24, 227–30, 233–51, 254–56, 260–76, 279–85, 294–95, 297, and 320.
With Tabarî and Ibn Abî l-Hadîd, Ibn al-Athîr has left the greatest number of pages on the question. He follows Tabarî in abridging him, often keeping the same phrases and the same words. Wherever we read "about" in Tabarî, he gives just the number or precedes it with "more than." Manuscript B makes the best reading.

62. Muhammad b. 'Alî b. 'Abd al-'Azîz b. 'Alî b. Barakât al-Hamawî (d. 631/1233), *Mukhtasar siyar al-awâ'il wa-l-mulûk wa-wasîlat al-'abd al-mam-lûk,* ms. Bibliothèque Nationale Paris, Fonds Arabe, no. 1507, f. 162a–b.

63. Sibt Ibn al-Jawzî (d. 654/1257), *Mir'at al-zamân fî ta'rîkh al-a'yân,*
a) ms. British Museum, Or. 4618; f. 190b–191a, 195b–196a, 197a–198a, 201b–202b, 205b, 212a, 213–214a, 215a, 215b, 217b–218a, 219b–223b, 224b–229b, 2316b, 237a, 239a, 241b–242a, and 250b.
b) ms. Bibliothèque Nationale Paris, Fonds Arabe, no. 1505; f. 188a–b, 197b, 200a, 201b–202a, and 212b.
Compilation that does not always follow Tabarî's version. The Paris manuscript is clearly less complete.

64. Ibn Abî l-Hadîd (d. 655/1257), *Sharh nahj al-balâga,*
a) Cairo edition, 1329/1911, 20 t. in 4 vols.; vol. II, pp. 310–20 and 341–62, for pages 321–40 do not exist;
b) Beirut edition, 1955, vol. II, pp. 488–540, with the same defect in pagination.

With Tabarî and Ibn al-Athîr, our principal source. He is a source of ines-timable value, for though he copies Tabarî he gives us details that are not found in the *Annales*. That would lead us to suppose that the text he used is not the one we know.

65. Ibn al-Abbâr (d. 658/1260), *I'tâb al-kuttâb,* ed. Salih Ashtar, Damascus, 1961, p. 162.
In speaking of Ibrâhîm b. al-Mudabbir.

66. Ibn al-'Adîm Kamâl al-Dîn (d. 660/1262), *Zubdat al-halab min ta'rîkh Halab,*
    a) ed. Georg Wilhelm Freytag, *Selecta ex Historia Halebi,* Paris, Typografia regia, 1819, pp. 23, 30, 97, note no. 144;
    b) ed. Sâmî al-Dahhân, Damascus, 1951–54, 2 vols.; vol. I, p.79.
According to Ibn al-'Adîm, Lu'lu' personally killed the Master of the Zanj.

67. Al-Makîn (d. 672/1273), *Historia Saracenica,*
    a) ed. and trans. Thomas Erpenius, Lugd. Batavorum, Elzevier, 1625, pp. 162–73, whereas pages 167–68 do not exist.
    b) trans. Pierre Vattier, *Histoire Mahométane*, Paris, 1657, pp. 173–81.
Compilation with distorted proper names.

68. Ibn Sa'îd (d. 673/1274), *al-Mugrib fî hula l-Magrib*, ed. in part by Karl Vollers, *Fragmente aus dem Mugrib des Ibn Sa'îd,* Berlin, E. Felber, 1894, p. 19 (cf. *supra,* no. 10).

69. Ibn Hallikân (d. 681/1282), *Kitâb Wafâyât al-a'yân wa-anbâ' âbna' al-zamân,*
    a) ed. Ferdinand Wüstenfeld, Göttingen, R. Deuerlich, 1835–50, 3 vols.; vol. I, p. 97; vol. II, p. 9;
    b) trans. Mac Guckin de Slane, *Ibn Khallikan's Biographical Dictionary,* Paris-London, Firmin Didot, 1843–71, 4 vols.; vol. I, p. 154; vol. II, pp. 10–11; vol. III, p. 39; vol. IV, p. 334.
In speaking of Ahmad b. Tûlûn, of al-Riyâshî, of Ibn Durayd, and of Ya'qûb b. al-Layth al-Saffâr.

70. Barhebraeus (d. 685/1286), *Chronography,* ed. and trans. Ernest A. Wallis Budge, 2 vols., London-Oxford, Oxford University Press, 1932; ed. pp. 161–64; trans. pp. 147–49.

71. Barhebraeus, *Ta'rîkh mukhtasar al-duwal,* ed. Antun Sâlhânî, Beirut, 1890, p. 258.

72. Ibn al-Tiqtaqâ (written ca. 701/1301), *al-Kitâb al-fakhrî fî l-âdâb al-sultânîyya wa l-duwal al-islâmîya*, trans. Émile Amar, Paris, E. Leroux, 1910, pp. 50, 427, and 434–35.
A summary of events.

73. Hindushâh Ibn Sanjar Nakhjawânî (written ca. 724/1323), *Tajârib al-salaf*, ed. Abbas Eghbal, Teheran, 1934, pp. 187 and 189–91.
Persian translation of Ibn al-Tiqtaqâ with additions.

74. Baybars (d. 725/1325), *Zubdat al-fikra fî Ta'rîkh al-hijra*, ms. Bibliothèque Nationale Paris, Fonds Arabe, no. 1572; f. 15b–19b, 20b–22a, 23a, 26a–27a, 32a–33b, 38ab, 40b–42a, 44b–45b, 47a, 47b–49a, 50b, 51a–59a, 61a–62a, 64a–71a, 72a, 73b–77b, 86ab, and 103b.

75. Hamdallâh al-Mustawfî al-Qazwînî (written in 730/1330), *Ta'rîkh-i Guzîda*,
   a) ed. Edward Granville Browne, Leiden-London, E. J. Brill-Luzac, 1910, pp. 332–34;
   b) trans. abr., ed. Edward Granville Browne and Reynold Alleyne Nicholson, Leiden-London, E. J. Brill-Luzac, 1913, pp. 64–65.
The Master of the Zanj is mentioned under the name al-Burqu'î 'Alî b. Muhammad b. Ahmad al-Bâqir (?).

76. Abû l-Fidâ' (d. 732/1331), *Mukhtasar fî akhbâr al-bashar*,
   a) ed. Johann Jakob Reiske, *Annales Moslemici*, Copenhagen, 1789–94, 5 vols.; vol. II, pp. 228–29, 234–35, 238–41, 250–53, 256–61, 706, and 718;
   b) Cairo edition, 1325/1907–8, 4 tomes in 2 vols.; vol. I, t. 2; pp. 46, 48–49, and 51–53.

77. Al-Nuwayrî (d. 732/1332), *Nihâyat al-'arab fî fûnûn al-adab*, ms. Bibliothèque Nationale Paris, Fonds Arabe, no. 1576, f. 25a–47a.

78. Al-Dhahabî (d. 748?/1348?), *Kitâb duwal al-Islâm*, Hayderâbâd, 1364–65/1918, 2 vols.; vol. I, pp. 111, 113–14, and 116–20.

79. Al-Dhahabî (d.748 ?/1348 ?), *Ta'rîkh al-Islâm*, Leiden ms., Or. 2363; f. 47a–104a.
For our subject, see f. 47b–51a, 79a–84a, 104a and 106a, of European pagination. The Arabic pagination has been moved forward.

80. Al-Dhahabî (m.748?/1348?), *al-'Ibar fî khabar man gabar*, ed. Fu'âd Sayyîd, al-Kuwayt, 1960–61, 2 vols.; vol. II, pp. 8, 13–18, 21, 32, 34–35, 37, 39,

41–43, 59, and 76.
A summary of the events.

81. Ibn al-Wardî (d. 749/1349), *Tatimmat al-Mukhtasar fî akhbâr al-bashar*, Cairo edition, 1285/1868–69, 2 vols.; vol. I, pp. 233–35, 237, and 240.
An abridgment of the chronicle by Abû l- Fîdâ'.

82. Al-Safadî (d. 764/1363), *al-Wâfî bi-l-Wafayât,* ms. British Museum, Or. 6587, f. 140b–143b.
Unique information and thirty-five of 'Alî b. Muhammad's verses.

83. Al-Yâfi'î (d. 768/1367), *Mir'ât al-janân wa-'ibrat al-yaqzân,* ed. Hayderâbâd, 1334–39/1915–21, 4 vols.; vol. II, pp. 161, 166, 169, 176, 180–82, and 192.

84. Ibn Kathîr (d. 774/1373), *al-Bidâya wa-l-nihâya*, Cairo edition, 1351/1932, 14 vols.; vol. XI, pp. 18–19, 24, 28–32, 35–45, 47, and 50.
A summary of the events.

9th/15th Century

85. Ibn Khaldûn (d. 808/1406), *al-Muqaddima*, trans. Mac Guckin de Slane, *Prolégomènes*, 3 vols., Paris, Imprimerie Impériale, 1862–68; vol. I, p. 408.

86. Ibn Khaldûn, *Kitâb al-'Ibar wa-dîwân al-mubtadâ' wa-l-khabar*, ed. N. Hurînî, Cairo, 1284/1867–68, 7 vols.; vol. III, pp. 301–303, 306–308, 311–14, 316–28, 336, 339–44; vol. IV, pp. 18–22, 299, 303, and 324–26.
Ibn Khaldûn knew Ibn Hazm's passages concerning 'Alî b. Muhammad. (This is a very bad edition. Most of the proper names are unrecognizable).

87. Al-Fâsî (d. 832/1428), *Shifâ al-garâm bi-akhbâr al-balad al-harâm*, ed. Ferdinand Wüstenfeld, *Die Chroniken der Stadt Mekka,* 4 vols., Leipzig, Brockhaus, 1859; vol. II, pp. 198 and 240.

88. Ibn al-Jazarî (833/1429), *Qurra*, ed. Gotthelf Bergsträsser and Otto Pretzl, *Das biographische Lexikon der Koranlehrer*, 3 vols., Leipzig and Cairo, 1933–37; vol. II, p. 388.

89. Al-Maqrîzî (d. 845/1442), *al-Mawâ'iz wa-l-i'tibâr fî dhikr al-khitat wa-l-âthâr,* Cairo edition, 1270/1853–54, 2 vols; vol. I, p. 320.

90. Al-Maqrîzî (?), *Muntakhab al-tadhkira*, ms. Bibliothèque Nationale Paris, Fonds Arabe, no. 1514, f. 159b, 160a, 161a, 163ab, 164b, and 165a.
A few pages of no great interest. Nevertheless, he underlines Miskawayh's phrases concerning 'Alî b. Muhammad's genealogy.

91. Al-'Aynî (d. 855/1451), *'Iqd al-jumân fî ta'rîkh ahl al-zamân*, ms. Bibliothèque Nationale Paris, Fonds Arabe, no. 5761, f. 138a, 139b–141a, and 144a.
A brief summary of the events.

92. Ibn Tagrîbirdî, Abû l-Mahasîn (d. 874/1470), *Kitâb al-Nujûm al-zâhira fî mulûk Misr wa-l-Qâhira*, eds. Theodor Willem Jan Juynboll and Benjamin Frederik Matthes, Leiden, E. J. Brill, 1852–61, 3 vols.; vol. II, pp. 22, 25, 28–34, 37–45, 49, and 73.
Compilation. The editors are among the few who mention Emil Rödiger (*ZDMG*, XIV, p. 493 s.). See *infra*, no. 110.

10th/15th–16th Century

93. Mîrkhwând (d. 903/1498), *Ta'rîkh rawdat al-safâ*, ed. Teheran, 1960–61, 9 vols.; vol. III, pp. 492–95.

94. Al-Suyûtî (d. 911/1505), *Ta'rîkh al-khulafâ'*, eds. William Nassau Lees and Mawlawî 'Abd al-Haqq, Calcutta, 1875, pp. 372–73.

95. Khwândamîr (d. 942–3/1535–37), *Habîb al-siyar*, ed. lith., Teheran, 1271/1854, 3 tomes in 1 vol.; t. II, pp. 101–102.
We read everywhere: *Sâhib al-rîh* (!), "Master of the Wind"!

96. Khwândamîr, *Khulâsat al-akhbâr*, according to David Price. Cf. *infra*, no. 105.
This manuscript also mentions the revolt of the Zanj.

97. Qutb al-Dîn al-Makkî (d. 988/1580), *Kitâb al-I'lâm bi a'lâm bayt Allâh al-harâm*, ed. Ferdinand Wüstenfeld, *Die Chroniken der Stadt Mekka*, Leipzig, Brockhaus, 1859, pp. 135–36.

11th/17th Century

98. Qaramânî, Ahmad b. Yûsuf (d. 1019/1611), *Kitâb Akhbâr al-duwal wa-*

âthâr al-uwal, ed. lith., Cairo 1282/1865, pp. 163–64.

99. Al-Astarâbâdhî, Muhammad b. 'Alî (d. 1028/1619), *Manhaj al-maqâl,* ed. lith., Teheran, 1304/1886, p. 30.
A note on al-Shu'ûbî Ahmad b. Ibrâhîm b. al-Mu'allâ b. Asad al-'Ammî of Basra.

100. Hajjî Khalîfa (d. 1067/1657), *Taqwîm al-tâwarîkh.*
In his edition of Abû l-Fidâ'(*Mukhtasar fî akhbâr al-bashar,* 2nd ed., Copenhagen, 1789–94, t. II, p. 718, no. 224), Johann Jakob Reiske points out that Hajjî Khalîfa ('ad anno 270') mentions the revolt of the Zanj. It is most certainly a question of the work, *Taqwîm al-tawârîkh* (*Chronological Tables,* written in Turkish and Persian) and more precisely of the Leipzig and Dresden manuscripts. (Cf. *EI,* 1, s.v. Hadjdjî Khalîfa).

101. Ibn al-'Imâd (d. 1086/1679), *Shadharât al-dhahab,* Cairo edition, 1350/1931–32, 8 vols.; vol. II, pp. 129–30, 136–37, 139, 141, 147, and 151–56.

102. Al-Bagdâdî, Ahmad b. 'Abdallâh (d. 1102/1690), '*Uyûn akhbâr al-a'yân,* ms. British Museum, add. 23.309; f. 100 a–b and 101b.

II. MODERN STUDIES

103. D'Herbelot, *Bibliothèque Orientale ou Dictionnaire Universel;*
a) Paris, 1697;
b) new edition, Paris, 1781–83, 6 vols.; vol. III, pp. 60–62; vol. IV, pp. 298–300 and 366–67; vol. VI, pp. 503–505.
A summary of the events.

104. Anonymous, *Histoire des Arabes,* 8 vols.; ms. of the Bibliothèque de l'École des Langues Orientales (ms. bought from the Abbé de Tessan before (?) 1719. École Royale des Jeunes de Langues de Paris, registered in the Arab language catalogue no. 86), vol. VI, pp. 389, 399–402, 409, 411, 417, 419–20, and 424–26.
A chronological summary of the events. List of sources: vol. VIII, p. 465.

105. Major David Price, *Chronological Retrospect or Memoirs of the Principal Events of Mahometan History,* 3 vols., London, J. Booth, 1811–21; vol. II, pp. 162–65.
According to Khwândamîr's *Khulâsat al-akhbâr.*

106. Giovanni B. Rampoldi, *Annali Musulmani,* 11 vols., Milano, F. Rusconi, 1823; vol. IV, pp. 364-65 and 368; vol. V, pp. 28–29, 32–35, 38, 40–42, 44, 48, 50–55, 57–59, 66–67, and 368–70.

107. Roorda Taco, *Vita Amedis Tulonidis,* Leiden, Luchtmans, 1825, pp. 23–24, 34, 40, and 44–45.

108. Gustav Weil, *Geschichte der Chalifen,* 5 vols., Manheim-Stuttgart, F. Bassermann, 1846–62; vol. II, pp. 422–23, 441–43, 446, and 452–64.
A long summary based on Ibn al-Athîr and Ibn Khaldûn.

109. Charles Defrémery, *Mémoire sur la famille des Sadjides,* in *Journal Asiatique,* 1848, série 4, t. IX and X, pp. 4–6.
Very complete, according to Ibn al-Athîr, Baybars, and Ibn Khaldûn

110. Emil Rödiger, *Mittheilungen zur Handschriftenkunde,* in *ZDMG,* XIV, 1860, pp. 489–501. Cf. pp. 493–94.
The only one who points out the Master of the Zanj's verses that are found in al-Shayzarî's *Jamhara* (d. 626/1229).

111. Michael Jan de Goeje, *Mémoire sur les Carmathes du Bahraïn et les Fatimides,*
    a) Leiden edition, E. J. Brill, 1862;
    b) Leiden edition, E. J. Brill, 1886, pp. 16, 19, 26–27, and 36–37.
Relations between the Qarmats and the Zanj.

112. Gustav Flügel, *Geschichte der Araber bis auf den Sturz des Chalifats von Baghdad,* 2nd ed., Leipzig, W. Baensch, 1867, pp. 245–48.
A summary of the events.

113. Louis Marcel Devic, *Le pays des Zendjs ou la côte orientale d'Afrique au Moyen Age d'après les écrivains arabes,* Paris, Hachette, 1883, pp. 161–66.
The only work of such importance (280 pp.) on the question. Some details on the revolt. (Cf. also Jean Doresse, *Histoire . . . , infra.,* no. 214).

114. August Müller, *Der Islam im Morgen und Abendland,*
    a) Berlin edition. 2 vols., G. Grote, 1885–87; vol. I, p. 579s.
    b) Russian trans., Nikolai Mednikov, Saint Petersburg, Panteleev, 1895, 4 tomes in 2 vols.; vol. II, p. 280s.
The events seen from a personal angle.

115. Ignaz Goldziher, *Muhammedanische Studien,* 2 vols., Hale, Niemeyer,

1889–90; vol. I, p. 142.
On the subject of 'Alî b. Muhammad's genealogy.

116. William Muir, *The Caliphate, Its Rise, Decline and Fall,* London, The Religious Tract Society, 1891, pp. 540–43, 546, 550, 554, and 556.
A summary of the events.

117. Theodor Nöldeke, *Ein Sklavenkrieg in Orient,* in *Orientalische Skizzen,*
a) Berlin, Paetel, 1892, pp. 153–84;
b) English trans., John Sutherland Black, *Sketches from Eastern History,* London-Edinburgh, A. Black, 1892, pp. 146–75.
The first thorough study of the revolt of the Zanj. Cf. *supra,* p. 4.

118. Theodor Nöldeke, *Ja'kub the Coppersmith and His Dynasty,* in *Sketches . . . ,* English trans., John Sutherland Black, London-Edinburgh, A. Black, 1892, pp. 189–90, 192–93, and 196–97.

119. Paul Casanova, *Monnaie du chef des Zendj,* in *Revue Numismatique,* 1893, pp. 510–16.
Explanation of the coin in the Bibliothèque Nationale de Paris and a few remarks.

120. Michael Jan de Goeje, *Fin des Carmathes de Bahreïn,* in *Journal Asiatique,* 1895, pp. 6 and 26.
On 'Alî b. Muhammad's stay in Bahrayn.

121. Guy Le Strange, *Baghdad during the Abbasid Caliphate from Contemporary Arabic and Persian Sources,* Oxford, Clarendon Press, 1900, pp. 247–48 and 324–25.

122. Guy Le Strange, *The Lands of the Eastern Caliphate,* Cambridge, Cambridge University Press, 1905, pp. 45, 47–48, and 233–34.

123. Michael Jan de Goeje, *Carmatians,* article in *Encyclopedia of Religion and Ethics,* London, 1910; III, p. 223.
Hamdân Qarmat's interview with 'Alî b. Muhammad.

124. Aleksandr Adamov, *Irak arabskij* (in Russian), Saint Petersburg, 1912, pp. 290–94.
A summary of the events according to the texts of Gustav Weil and August Müller.

125. Clément Huart, *Histoire des Arabes*, 2 vols., Paris, Geuthner, 1912–13; vol. I, pp. 307–308.

126. Chauncy Hugh Stigand, *The Land of Zinj*, London, Constable, 1913, [2nd ed., 1996], p. 6.

127. *Encyclopédie de l'Islam* (French ed.), 1, 1913–42;
a) Maximilian Streck, *Abû l-Khasîb*, vol. I, p. 98;
b) Anonymous, 'Alî b. Muhammad, vol. I, p. 292;
a summary of the events;
c) Maximilian Streck, *al-Batîha,* vol. I, p. 692;
d) Maximilian Streck, *al-Maisân*, vol. III, pp. 153–62;
e) Louis Massignon, *Zandj*, vol. IV, p. 1281.

128. Muhammad al-Khudarî, *al-Dawlat al-'Abbâsiyya,*
a) Cairo, 1916;
b) 9th ed., Cairo, 1959, pp. 303–305 and 312.
A summary of the events.

129. Giuseppe Gabrieli, *Indice alfabetico di tutte le biografie contenute nel Wâfî bi-l-Wafayât di al-Safadî,* in *R. R. A. L.,* 5th series, vol. XXV, Milan, Accademia dei Lincei, 1916; p. 364, notice no. 2738.

130. J. Laurent, *L'Arménie entre Byzance et l'Islam depuis la conquête arabe jusqu'en 886*, Paris, 1919, pp. 231, 236, 238, and 254–55.
A brief summary based on a number of sources.

131. Ignatiï Krackovskij, *Pamyaty N. A. Mednikova*, in *ZVORAO*, XXV, 1919, p. 424.
Krackovskij points out that, on March 14, 1890, Mednikov lectured on "The Revolt of the Blacks in Basra."

132. Cornelius Van Arendonk, *De Opkomst van het Zaidietische Imamaat in Yemen,*
a) Leiden, E. J. Brill, 1919, pp. 96–97;
b) French trans., Jacques Ryckmans, *Les débuts de l'Imamat Zaidite au Yemen*, Leiden, E. J. Brill, 1960, p. 106.
Interesting passage concerning the Master of the Zanj's genealogy.

133. Maurice Gaudefroy-Demombynes, *Les institutions musulmanes,*
a) Paris, Flammarion, 1921;
b) 3rd ed., Paris, Flammarion, 1946, pp. 42, 142, and 191.

134. Adam Mez, *Die Renaissance des Islams,*
a) Heidelberg, Winter, 1922;
b) English trans., Salahuddin Khuda Bukhsh and David Samuel Margoliouth, London, Luzac, 1937, p. 166.
Mez mentions the Berlin manuscript of *Kitâb al-'Uyûn* (Cf. *supra*, no. 49).

135. Louis Massignon, *La Passion d'al-Hallâj, martyr mystique de l'Islam,* 2 vols., Paris, Geuthner, 1922; vol. I, pp. 20, 23, 32, 142–43, and 145.
Cf. the new edition in 4 vols., Paris, Gallimard, 1975, vol. I, pp. 63–64, 104–106, 112, 114, 120, 140, 180, 184, 187, 191, 193, 197, 210, 252, 254, 286, 298, 302, 304, 309, 326, 369, 379, 399, 467, 490, and 533; vol. II, pp. 18, 325, 352, and 408; vol. III, p. 269.
Personal comments on several questions.

136. Eduard de Zambaur, *Manuel de généalogie et de chronologie pour l'histoire de l'Islam,*
a) Hanover, Lafaire, 1927;
b) 2nd ed., Bad Pyrmont, Lafaire-Behrens, 1955, p. 41.

137. Reuben Levy, *A Baghdad Chronicle*, Cambridge, Cambridge University Press, 1929, pp. 114–17 and 133.
A summary of the events.

138. David Samuel Margoliouth, *Lectures on Arabic Historians*, Calcutta, 1930, pp. 66–68, 80, and 137–38.
In speaking of Ibn al-Mu'tazz, of al-Buhturî, and of al-Tanûkhî.

139. Zaki Mubarak, *Étude critique sur la lettre vierge d'Ibn el-Mudabber*, Paris-Cairo, Maisonneuve Fréres, 1931, p. 6.

140. Maurice Gaudefroy-Demombynes and Sergei Fedorovich Platonov, *Le monde musulman et byzantin jusqu aux Croisades*, Paris, de Boccard, 1931, pp. 291, 296, and 445–49.
A survey of the revolt of the Zanj and a few personal remarks.

141. Carl Heinrich Becker, *Islamstudien*, 2 vols., Leipzig, Quelle and Meyer, 1924–32, vol. II, p. 170.

142. Dwight Martin Donaldson, *The Shi'ite Religion, a History of Islam in Persia and Irak*, London, Luzac, 1933, pp. 255–56.
Some phrases according to al-Suyûtî.

143. Abbas Eghbal, *Les Nawbakht* (in Persian), Teheran, 1311/1933, p. 108.

144. John Walker, *A Rare Coin of the Zanj*, in *J.R.A.S.*, 1933, pp. 651–55 and pl. V.
Explanation of the Zanj coin of the British Museum, comparison with that of the Bibliothèque Nationale, as well as photographs. A summary of the events and some comments.

145. Zaky Mohamed Hassan, *Les Tulunides*, Paris, Busson, 1933, pp. 40–44, 58, 63–65, 79, 93–94, 105, 143, 147, and 315.
A summary of the events of the revolt and the insurrection's consequences for the Tûlûnids.

146. Hans Kindermann, "'Schiff' im Arabischen, Untersuchung über Vorkommen und Bedeutung der Termini," Zwickau i. Sa., thesis, Bonn University, 1934, pp. 42–43, 48, 54–55, and 102.
In explaining the words *sumayriyya, shadhâ, salga, and mi'bar.*

147. Abraham Naum Poliak, *Les révoltes populaires en Egypte à l'époque des Mamelouks et leur causes économiques*, in *Revue des Études Islamiques*, 8, 1934, pp. 251–52.
Follows Louis Massignon's notion on the growth of Jewish banks.

148. Charles Diehl and Georges Marçais, *Le Monde oriental de 395 à 1081*, Paris, Presses Universitaires de France, 1936, pp. 383–84.

149. Walther Hellige, "Die Regentschaft al-Muwaffaq's, eine Wendenpunkt in der Abbassidengeschichte," thesis, Berlin University, 1936, pp. 25–31 and 39–45.

150. Philip Khûri Hitti, *History of the Arabs*,
a) London, Macmillan, 1937;
b) 6th ed., London, Macmillan, 1956, pp. 445, 453, and 467–68.
A brief summary of the events, based on al-Mas'ûdî, Tabarî, and Nöldeke.

151. Louis Massignon, *Causes et modes de la propagation de l'Islam parmi les populations païennes de l'Afrique*,
a) *Convegno Volta*, Rome, October 1938, t. I, pp. 653–70;
b) *Opera Minora*, Paris, Presses Universitairies de France, vol. I, 1969, pp. 317–24, cf. 319–20.

152. Carl Brockelmann, *Geschichte der islamischen Völker*,

a) Berlin, Oldenbourg, 1939;

b) French trans., *Histoire des peuples et des États Islamiques,* Paris, Payot, 1949, pp. 120–22 and 131.

A summary of the events accompanied by a few comments.

153. Jean Sauvaget, *Introduction à l'Histoire de l'Orient musulman,*

a) Paris, Adrien Maisonneuve, 1943, p. 129;

b) Claude Cahen and Jean Sauvaget, Paris, Adrien Maisonneuve, 1961, p. 144.

154. Rhuvon Guest, *Life and Works of Ibn er-Rûmî,* London, Luzac, 1944, pp. 14, 16, 18, 20–21, 27, and 30.

A few phrases on the Zanj Revolt.

155. 'Abd al-'Azîz al-Dûrî, *Dirâsât fî l-'usûr al-'abbâsiyya al-mutâ'akhkhira,* Baghdad, 1945, pp. 6, 17, 20–21, 23, 29, 75–106, 115, 117, 160, and 178.

A study on the revolt based on a limited bibliography.

156. Ahmad Amîn, *Zuhr al-Islâm,* t. I, Cairo, 1945, pp. 70–72.

157. Hasan Ibrâhîm Hasan, *Ta'rîkh al-Islâm al-siyâsî,*

a) Cairo, 1945, 2 vols.;

b) 2nd ed., Cairo, 1948–49, 3 vols., vol. III, pp. 26–30, 87, 145–46, 221–24, 349, and 401.

A summary of the events based on several sources.

158. Gustave Edmund von Grünebaum, *Medieval Islam,* Chicago, University of Chicago Press, 1946, p. 210.

159. Taha Husayn, *Thawratânî,* in *al-Kâtib al-Misrî,* no. 8, vol. 2, May 1946, pp. 553–74.

A comparison between the revolt of Spartacus and that of the Zanj, written for a broad public.

160. Ernst Herzfeld, *Geschichte der Stadt Samarra,* Hamburg, Eckardt and Messtorff, 1948, pp. 250, 258, and 262–68.

A few remarks based on Tabarî's *Annales.*

161. 'Abd al-'Azîz al-Dûrî, *Ta'rîkh al-'Irâq al-iqtisâdî fî l-qarn al-râbî'al-hijrî,* Baghdad,1367/1948, pp. 1, 21, 62, 66–72, and 80.

The revolt of the Zanj from the economic and social point of view.

162 Bernard Lewis, *The Arabs in History,*

a) London, Hutchinson, 1950, pp. 103–106 and 110;
b) French trans., *Les Arabes dans l'histoire*, Neuchâtel, La Baconnière, 1950, pp. 94–97 and 100.
A summary of the events with personal remarks on the question.

162a. George Fadlo Hourani, *Arab Seafaring in the Indian Ocean in Ancient and Early Medieval Times*, Princeton, N. J., Princeton University Press, 1951, pp. 38 and 78–80.

163. Félix M. Pareja, *Islamologia*, Roma, Orbis Catholicus, 1951, pp. 108 and 112.
A brief summary of the events.

164. *Bolshaja Sovjetskaja Enciklopedija,* 2nd ed., 1952, t. XVII, pp. 91–92.
A new interpretation of the revolt of the Zanj.

165. Bertold Spuler, *Geschichte der Islamischen Länder*, Leiden, E. J. Brill, 1952, pp. 66–67.
A summary of the events in a few phrases.

166. Saleh Ahmed el-'Alî, *Khitat al-Basra*, in *Sumer*, VIII, Baghdad, 1952; I, p. 76; II, pp. 281, 298, and 302.

167. Bertold Spuler, *Iran in früh-islamischer Zeit*, Wiesbaden, F. Steiner, 1952, pp. 71, 73–74, 76, 78, 317, and 327.

168. Muhammad 'Abd al-Ganî Hasan, *Thawrât fî l-mujtama' al-islamî*, in *al-Kitâb*, vol. 12 (no. 1), January 1953, pp. 121–23.

169. Charles Pellat, *Le milieu basrien et la formation de Jâhiz,* Paris, Adrien Maisonneuve, 1953, pp. 5, 38, 41–42, 47–48, 80, 132, and 274.
A few details and some comments on the three revolts of the Zanj.

170. Faysal al-Sâmir, *Thawrat al-Zanj,* Baghdad, 1954, 165 pp.
A very complete study of the revolt of the Zanj. Cf. *Arabica*, vol. II, 1955, p. 125. Cf. the 2nd ed., Baghdad, 1971, 223 pp.

171. Louis Massignon, *Explication du plan de Basra*, in *Westöstliche Abhandlungen, Mél. R. Tschudi,* Wiesbaden, 1954, pp. 154–74; cf. above all pp. 157 and 164–65.
Personal comments.

172. Abdul Karim Khalifa, "Les sources de la révolte du Zendj, collecte des textes avec traduction annotée et une introduction sur ce mouvement révolutionnaire," thesis, University of Paris, 1954.

172. Louis Massignon, *Hoceïn Mansûr Hallâj, Dîwân*, Paris, 1985, pp. xv–xvi.
Massignon points out that the Karnabâ'iyya (the family of al-Hallâj's wife) had joined the revolt for political reasons.

174. H. A. R. Gibb, *The Caliphate and the Arab States*, in *A History of the Crusades*, Philadelphia, Penn., University of Pennsylvania Press, 1955, p. 84.

175. Claude Cahen, in Édouard Perroy, *Le Moyen Âge* (coll. *Histoire Générale des Civilisations*, Paris, Presses Universitaires de France, 1955), t. III, pp. 165 and 171.
A few phrases in a completely new type of study.

176. Gaston Wiet, *Islam*, in *Histoire Universelle*, (coll. *Encyclopédie de la Pléïade*, Paris, Gallimard, 1955), vol. II, pp. 90–93.
A summary of the events.

177. Claude Cahen, *L'histoire économiquie et sociale de l'Orient musulman médiéval*, in *Studia Islamica*, vol. III, 1955, pp. 112–13.
Personal comments on the revolt of the Zanj.

178. *Encyclopédie de l'Islam, Nouvelle Édition* (French ed.), 2, 1956 s.
a) Maximilian Streck, *Abû l-Khasîb* , vol. I, p. 137;
b) Laurence Lockhart, *al-Ahwâz*, vol. I, p. 315;
c) Bernard Lewis, *'Alî b. Muhammad*, vol. I, p. 400, very complete article;
d) George Rentz and W. E. Mulligan, *al-Bahrayn*, vol. I, p. 969;
e) Saleh el-Ali and Maximilian Streck, *al-Batîha*, vol. I, pp. 1126–30.

179. 'U. R. Kahhâla, *Mu'jam al-mu'allifîn*, Damascus, 1376–1380/1957–61, 15 vols.; vol. I, p. 134; vol. IX, p. 193.

180. Francesco Gabrieli, *Gli Arabi*,
a) Firenze, Sansoni, 1957;
b) French trans., Paris, Buchet-Chastel, 1963, p. 126.

181. Reuben Levy, *The Social Structure of Islam*, Cambridge, Cambridge University Press, 1957; pp. 420–22, 429, 435, 438, and 441–42.
Several details on the military organization of the Abbasid troops in the war against the Zanj.

181a. Gavin Maxwell, *A Reed Shaken by the Wind*, London, Longmans, 1957, pp. 17–20. (The same work appeared in 1975, under the title *People of the Reeds*, New York, Harper & Brothers).

182. Evgeniï Aleksandrovich Beljaev, in *Istorija stran zarubezhnego Vostoka v srednie veka*, Moscow, University of Moskau, 1957, pp. 216–17.
A short summary of the events.

183. *Vsemirnaja Istorija*, Moscow, 1957, vol. III, p. 120.
A summary of the events.

184. Claude Cahen, *Leçons d'Histoire Musulmane, VIIIIe–XIe siècles*, "Les cours de la Sorbonne," 3 fascs., Paris, Université de la Sorbonne, 1957; II, pp. 6–7, 23, 35, 54, 61, and 65; III, pp. 5 and 32.
A summary of the events and several personal comments.

185. Aleksandr Jur'evich Jakubovskij, in *Istorija Irana*, Leningrad, 1958, pp. 117–18.
The same summary, more or less, as the one published in *Vsemirnaja Istorija*, Moscow, 1957. Cf. *supra*, no. 183.

186. Ibrahim Artuk, *Abbasi ve Anadolu selçukilerine ait iki eshsiz dinar*, in *Annual of the Archaeological Museums of Istanbul*, Istanbul, 1958, pp. 44–45 and 86–87.
Explanation of the only known coin that comes from al-Muwaffaqiyya.

187. Ahmad Muhammad Hilmî Muhammad, *al-Khîlâfa wa-l-dawla fî al-'asr al-'abbâsî*, Cairo, 1959, pp. 104–105, 115, and 133.

188. Dominique Sourdel, *Le vizirat 'abbâside*, 2 vols., Damascus, Institut Français de Damas, 1959–60; vol. I, pp. 307–308 and 318.

189. George Carpenter Miles, *Trésor de dirhems du IXème siècle*, Paris, 1960, in *Mémoires de la Mission Archéologique en Iran*, t. XXXVII, pp. 68, 70–74, 112–13, 119, 122–24, 128, 131–33, and 135.
The Zanj pieces of money brought to light, with an important personal contribution. Cf. Dominique Sourdel's account in *Arabica*, IX/2, 1962, pp. 215–16.

190. Ahmed S. Olabi, *Révolte des Zanj et son chef Ali b. Mohammed* (in Arabic), Beirut, 1961, 140 pp.
A study of the revolt of the Zanj and its instigator, focusing mainly on interpretation of the facts. Cf. account by Claude Cahen in *La Pensée*, no. 98, July–August 1961, p. 149.

191. Louis Massignon, *Les nuages de Magellan*, *REI*, 1961; in *Parole donnée*, Paris, Julliard, 1962, pp. 421–37; cf. pp. 421–22 and 433.

191a. Howard S. Nelson, *An Abandoned Irrigation System in Southern Iraq*, in *Sumer,* XVIII/1–2, Baghdad, 1962, pp. 67–72. Cf. pp. 68–69 and 72.

192. Ergeniï Aleksandrovich, Beljaev, *Araby, Islam i arabskij halifat,* Moscow, Nauka, 1965, pp. 258–68.
A summary of the events.

193. Alexandre Popovic, *Quelques renseignements inédits concernant "Le Maître des Zanj"* 'Alî b. Muhammad, in *Arabica*, XII/2, 1965, pp. 175–87.

194. Heinz Halm, in *Die Welt des Islams*, n. s. XI, 1967–68, pp. 240–41; Heribert Busse, in *Der Islam*, 44, 1968, pp. 269–71.
Review of Alexandre Popovic's typewritten thesis, " 'Alî b. Muhammad et la révolte des esclaves à Basra," University of Paris, 1965.

195. H. Laoust, *Les schismes dans l'Islam*, Paris, 1965, pp. 131–33.
A summary of the events, based chiefly on Ibn Kathîr as a source.

196. Maxime Rodinson, *Islam et Capitalisme*, Paris, Éditions du Seuil, 1966, p. 82.

197. 'Alî Husnî al-Kharbûtlî, *Thawrat-Zanj . . . ,* in *al-Hilâl,* June 1967, pp. 24–37.
A particularly badly informed summary of the events. The author omits the works of Faysal al-Sâmir and Ahmed Olabi!

198. Gernot Rotter, "Die Stellung des Negers in der islamisch-arabischen Gesellschaft bis zum XVI. Jahrhundert," thesis, Bonn University, 1967; pp. 7, 21–25, 29, 35–37, 54–55, 57–58, 62–63, 66–67, and 105–111.
An important, very carefully documented work.

199. André Miquel, *La géographie humaine du monde musulman jusqu'au milieu du XIe siècle,* vol. I, Paris-The Hague, Mouton-EPHE, VIe Section, 1967, pp. 4, 130, 208, 218, and 338; vol. II, Paris-The Hague, Mouton-EPHE, VIe Section, 1975, pp. 167–73.

200. Heinz Halm, "Die Traditionen über den Aufstand 'Ali Ibn Muhammads, des 'Herrn der Zang,' eine quellenkritische Untersuchung," thesis, Bonn University, 1967, 142 pp.

Excellent study of the revolt and the most thorough as to the Master of the Zanj's personality. It was announced under a different title in *ZDMG*, 116, 1966, p. 1. Cf. *infra.*, no. 211.

201. Heribert Busse, *Das Hofbudget des Chalifen al-Mu'tadid billâh (279/892–289/902),* in *Der Islam*, 43, 1967, p. 16.
A new version of the Master of the Zanj's death.

202. Alexandre Popovic, *Encore quelques détails autour du problème des Zang,* in *Actas do IV Congresso de Estudos Arabes e Islâmicos (Coimbra-Lisboa, Setembro 1968)*, Leiden, E. J. Brill, 1971 [1975], pp. 367–71.

203. Claude Cahen, *Der Islam I, Vom Ursprung bis zu den Anfängen des Osmanenreiches*, Frankfurt am Main, Fischer, 1968, pp. 118, 137–8, 155, 202, 209, 213s., 237, 245, 247, and 258.

204. Xavier de Planhol, *Les fondements géographiques de l'histoire de l'Islam*, Paris, Flammarion, 1968, pp. 92–95 and 346–47.

205. Robert Mantran, *L'expansion musulmane (VIIe–XIe siècles)*, Paris, Presses Universitaires de France, 1969, pp. 41, 168, 176–77, 185–86, 205, and 289.
A summary of the events.

Among the studies that I was unable to use fully (because they appeared after the final editing of this book or were unknown to me at the time of writing), the following works should be given special attention:

206. Vasiliï Vasil'evich Struve, *The Problem of the Genesis, Development and Disintegration of the Slave Societies in the Ancient Orient*, in *Ancient Mesopotamia, Socio-Economic History* (a collection of studies by Soviet scholars); Moscow, Nauka, 1969, pp. 17–69, cf. p. 66.
It is a question of a 1933 article.

207. Claude Cahen, *L'islam, des origines au début de l'empire ottoman*, coll., *L'Aurige: Histoire universelle*, 14, Paris, Bordas, 1970, index s. v. "Zendjs."

207a. John Wansbrough, *Africa and the Arab Geographers,* in David Dalby (ed.), *Language and History in Africa*, London, Frank Cass, 1970, pp. 89–101. Cf. pp. 93–94 and 97–99.

Analysis of Tabarî's use of the word *zanj* (*zinj*) in his description of the revolt. According to Wansbrough, "it is almost certainly an ethnic description."

207b. John O. Hunwick, *Some Notes on the Term* zanj *and Its Derivatives in a West African Chronicle*, in David Dalby (ed.), *Language and History in Africa*, London, Frank Cass, 1970, pp. 102–108.

208. Ahmad Olabi, *Thawrat al-'abîd fî l-Basra*, in *al-Tarîq*, 2, Beirut, 1970, pp. 93–112.

208a. Muhammad 'Abd al-Fattâh 'Ilyân, *Qarâmita al-'Irâq fî al-qarnayn al-thâlith wa-l-râbi' al- hijrîyayn*, Cairo, 1970.
On the relations between the Zanj and the Qarmats, cf. pp. 38–40.

209. Bernard Lewis, *Race and Colour in Islam*, New York-London, Harper & Row, 1971, xi + 103 pp.; coll. *Harper Torchbooks*, no. 1590.
Cf. also the French translation, *Race et couleur en pays d'Islam*, Paris, Payot, 1982.
A less comprehensive version of this study appeared previously in *Encounter*, August 1970, pp. 18–36.

209a. Muhammad 'Abdul Jabbâr Begg (in reality: Beg), "The Social History of the Labouring Classes in 'Iraq under the 'Abbâsids (A.D. 750–1055)," thesis, University of Cambridge, 1971, pp. 344–76.

210. Maurice Lombard, *L'Islam dans sa première grandeur (viiie–xie siècle)*, Paris, Flammarion, 1971, p. 27 ss.

210a. Souhayl Zakkâr (ed.), Thâbit b. Sinân wa Ibn al-'Adîm, *Târîkh akhbâr al-Qarâmita*, Beyrouth, 1971, pp. 12 and 100.

211. J. Cristoph Bürgel's review of Heinz Halm, *Die Traditionen*, (cf. *supra*, no. 200), in *ZDMG*, 121/1, 1971, pp. 193–96.

212. 'Abd al-Jabbâr Nâjî, *Sâhib al-Zanj al-thâ'ir al-shâ'ir*, in *al-Mawrid*, I, no. 3–4, Baghdad, 1972, pp. 11–23.

213. Maurice Lombard, *Espaces et réseaux du haut moyen âge*, Paris-The Hague, Mouton-EPHE VIe section, 1972, pp. 72 ss and 215.

213a. Ahmad *'Olabî, Thawrat al-Zanj aw al-ta'rîf bi-thawrat tabaqiyya fî-l-islâm*, in *al-Tarîq*, Beyrouth, 1972/ no. 6, pp. 102–108.

214. Jean Doresse, *Histoire sommaire de la Corne orientale de l'Afrique*, Paris, Geuthner, 1972, pp. 78–79, 96–97, and 105–39.
An important chapter on the land of the Zanj and its early colonization by Arabs and Persians. It contains a great deal of information.

215. Omar Saïdi, *Kitâb al-'Uyûn wa-l-hadâ'iq fi akbâr al-haqâ'iq*, Chronique anonyme, I-II, Damascus, IFD, 1972–73. Cf. *supra*, no. 49.

216. Muhammad 'Abdul Jabbâr Beg, *A Contribution to the Economic History of the Caliphate: A Study of the Cost of Living and the Economic Status of Artisans in Abbasid Iraq*, in *Islamic Quarterly*, 16, London, 1973, pp. 140–67. Cf. p. 148.

217. Ahmad Jâsim al-Najdî, *Ash'âr Sâhib al-Zanj*, in *al-Mawrid*, III/no. 3, Baghdad, 1974, pp. 167–74.
On the Master of the Zanj's poetry.

218. Fârûq 'Umar, *al-Khilâfa al-'abbâsiyya fi 'asr al-fawdâ al-'askariyya*, Baghdad, 1974, pp. 106–18.
Analysis of the position the Zanj revolt holds in a larger context, that of opposition movements to Abbasid power.

219. Muhammad 'Abdul Jabbâr Beg, *The "Serfs" of Islamic Society under the 'Abbâsid Regime*, in *Islamic Culture*, 49, Hyderabad, 1975, pp. 107–18. Cf. p. 114.

220. H. Neville Chittick and Robert Irwin Rotberg (eds.), *East Africa and the Orient: Cultural Synthesis in Pre-Colonial Times*, London-New York, Africana Pub. Co., 1975.
Cf., s. v. *Zanj* and especially pp. 20–25 and 30–32 (H. Neville Chittick); pp. 71–72 (Vinigi L Grotanelli); pp. 87–88 (Paul Wheatley); and pp. 116–18 and 272–83 (John Spencer Trimingham).

221. 'Alî Hasan, *Ta'qîb "Ash'âr Sâhib al-Zanj,"* in *al-Mawrid*, IV/ no. 2, Baghdad, 1975, p. 289 ss.
On the Master of the Zanj's poetry.

222. Eliyahu Ashtor, *A Social and Economic History of the Near East in the Middle Ages*, London, Collins, 1976, pp. 115-21 and 345.
Important remarks on the reasons for the alliances formed between the rebels and the different classes of the populations of Lower Iraq (or the reasons for the nonexistence of such alliances).

223. Alexandre Popovic, *Mâdhâ yumkin al-qawl 'an thawrat al-Zanj,* in *Dirâsât 'arabiyya,* 12/ no. 8, Beyrouth, June 1976, pp. 96–107.

224. Ahmad Jâsim al-Najdî, *Hawla ash'âr Sâhib al-Zanj,* in *al-Mawrid,* V/ no. 2, Baghdad, 1976, pp. 302–304.
On 'Alî b. Muhammad's poetry.

225. Muhammad Abdulhayy Shaban, *Islamic History: A New Interpretation. 2: A.D. 750–1055 (A.H. 132–448),* Cambridge, Cambridge University Press, 1976, pp. 98, 99, 100–102, 107, 108, 110, 112, 126, 130, 133, and 166–67.
Contains very good reflections on the nature of the revolt and on the groups of the populations that participated.

226. Nikita Elisséef, *L'Orient Musulman au Moyen Age 622–1260,* Paris, A. Colin, 1977, pp. 146–47.

227. Gavin Young, *Return to the Marshes: Life with the Marsh Arabs of Iraq,* London, Collins, 1977, p. 46.

228. David Waines, *The Third Century Internal Crisis of the Abbasids,* in *Journal of the Economic and Social History of the Orient,* 20, Leiden, 1977, pp. 282–306. Cf. pp. 301–304.

229. Ghada Hashem Talhami, *The Zanj Rebellion Reconsidered,* in *International Journal of African Historical Studies,* 10/ no. 3, 1977, pp. 443–61.
Ideological remarks, based on documentation of secondary importance.

230. Emanuel Sivan, *Arab Revisionist Historians,* in *Asian and African Studies,* 12/ no. 3, Jerusalem-Haifa, 1978, pp. 283–311. Cf. p. 303.
Also concerns the way certain contemporary authors see the Zanj revolt.

231. Muhammad Manazir Ahsan, *Social Life under the Abbasids, 170–289 AH/786–902 AD,* London-New York, Longman-Librairie du Liban, 1979, pp. 136, 140, and 296.

232. Patricia Crone, *Slaves on Horses: The Evolution of the Islamic Polity,* Cambridge, Cambridge University Press, 1980, pp. 264–65.

233. Jere L. Bacharach, *African Military Slaves and the Medieval Middle East: The Cases of Iraq (869–955) and Egypt (868–1171),* in *International Journal of Middle East Studies,* 13, 1981, pp. 471–95. Cf. pp. 473–74 and 478.

234. Minoo Southgate, *The Negative Images of Blacks in Some Medieval Iranian Writings,* in *Iranian Studies,* 17, New York, 1984, pp. 3–36.
Contains many citations concerning the Zanj, drawn from medieval Iranian texts.

235. Ahmad 'Olabî, *Thawrat al-'abîd fî-l-Islâm,* Beyrouth, Dâr al-Adab, 1985.

236. Paulo Fernando de Moraes Farias, *Models of the World and Categorical Models: The "Enslavable Barbarian" as a Mobile Classificatory Label,* in John Ralph Willis (ed.), *Slaves and Slavery in Muslim Africa,* vol. I: *Islam and the Ideology of Enslavement,* London, Frank Cass, 1985, pp. 27–46. Cf. pp. 3–42.
On the word *Zanj.*

237. Habib Ben Abdallah, *De l'iqta' étatique à l'iqta' militaire: transition économique et changements sociaux à Baghdad, 247–447 de l'Hégire/861–1055 ap J.,* Upsala-Stockholm, Almquist and Wiksell, 1986, pp. 111, 197, and 200.

238. Murray Gordon, *L'esclavage dans le monde arabe: VIIe–XXe siècle,* Paris, R. Laffont, 1987, pp. 54–55, 71, 73, 103–107, 119–125, 139, and 242/ no. 4.
There is also an English-language edition, under the title *Slavery in the Muslim World,* New York, 1989.

239. Philip M. Fields (trans.), (annotated by Jacob Lassner), al-Tabarî: *The History of al-Tabarî,* vol. XXXVII: *The 'Abbâsid Recovery, The War Against the Zanj Ends,* Albany (U.S.A.), State University of New York Press, 1987, pp. 2–4, 6–27, 30–36, 39–47, 49–62, 64–67, 69–78, 80, 82–86, 88, 91–123, 125–26, 128, 130–39, 152, and 175–76.

240. Zakariyau I. Oseni, *The Revolt of Black Slaves in Iraq under the 'Abbâsid Administration in 869–883 C.E.,* in *Hamdard Islamicus,* XII/ no. 2, 1989, pp. 57–65.
The author considers this to be about a Kharijite revolt.

241. Bernard Lewis, *Race and Slavery in the Middle East,* New York, Oxford University Press, 1990. French trans.: *Race et esclavage en Proche Orient,* Paris, Gallimard, 1993. Cf. pp. 27–28, 53–57, 73, 75, 76, 79–84, 86–88, 131–32, 137–141, 143, 166/ no. 18, 170/ no. 13, 172/ no. 3, 176/ no. 9, 179/ no. 18, 181/ no. 12, and 197–99.
The most complete study on the subject.

242. David Waines (trans.), al-Tabarî, *The History* (*Ta'rîkh al-rusul wa'l-mulûk*), vol. XXXVI: *The Revolt of the Zanj,* Albany (U.S.A.), State University of New York Press, 1992, pp. xv–xvii, 29–67, 108–12, 120–35, 137–49, 152–56, 158–67, 174–81, 186–87, and 190–207.

243. Alexandre Popovic, *al-Mukhtâra,* in *Encyclopédie de l'Islam,* vol. VII, 1992, pp. 526–27.

The Zanj revolt has been taken up in many other texts that have appeared during the last twenty years, but it is impossible to mention them in detail here. Nevertheless, it should be pointed out that there have been no studies directly devoted to the subject. However, as I mentioned at the end of my conclusion, such studies will certainly appear, in the distant or near future, because there will be no end to research on the subject.

As for recent works on slavery in general (in the Muslim world and elsewhere), the interested reader will find an expanded bibliography in many works, among which I will cite a few titles here: David Brion Davis, *The Problem of Slavery in Western Cultures,* Ithaca, N.Y., Cornell University Press, 1966 (2nd ed., 1969); Allan George Barnard Fisher and Humphrey J. Fisher, *Slavery and Muslim Society in Africa*, London, Hurst, 1970; Orlando Patterson, *Slavery and Social Death: A Comparative Study,* Cambridge, Mass.-London, Harvard University Press, 1982; James de Vere Allen and Thomas H. Wilson (eds.), *From Zinj to Zanzibar: Studies in History, Trade and Society on the Eastern Coast of Africa* (Essays in honor of James Kirkman), Wiesbaden, F. Steiner [*Paideuma*, 28], 1982; Paul E. Lovejoy, *Transformations in Slavery: A History of Slavery in Africa,* Cambridge, Cambridge University Press, 1983; David Brion Davis, *Slavery and Human Progress,* Oxford-New York, Oxford University Press, 1984; John Ralph Willis (ed.), *Slaves and Slavery in Muslim Africa,* vol. I: *Islam and Ideology of Enslavement,* vol. II: *The Servile Estate,* London, Frank Cass, 1985; Paul E. Lovejoy, *Africans in Bondage: Studies in Slavery and the Slave Trade* (Essays in honor of Philip D. Curtin), Madison, Wisc., University of Wisconsin Press, 1986; Abdallah Fadel, *Islam, Slavery and Racism: The Use of Strategy in the Pursuit of Human Rights,* in *American Journal of Islamic Social Sciences,* 4/ no. 1, 1987, pp. 31–50; Bernard Lewis, *Race and Slavery in the Middle East: An Historical Enquiry*, Oxford-New York, Oxford University Press, 1990; J. C. Miller, *Muslim Slavery and Slaving: A Bibliography*, in Elizabeth Savage (ed.) *The Human Commodity: Perspectives on the Trans-Saharan Slave Trade*, London, Frank Cass, 1992, pp. 249–71.

Maps

There are few useful maps for the region and the period that interest us. The city of al-Mukhtâra appears on some of them, particularly in the following works:

G. Le Strange, *The Lands of the Eastern Caliphate,* Cambridge, 1905;

Faysal al-Sâmir, *Thawrat al-Zanj,* Baghdad, 1954;

Vsemirnaja Istorija, Moscow, 1957;

Sûsâ (Ahmad), *al-Dalîl al-jugrâfî al-'Irâqî,* Baghdad, 1958;

Heinz Halm, *Die Traditionen . . . .,* Bonn, 1967.

By far the best of the maps are those drawn according to Halm's texts. The author was kind enough to allow me to reproduce them here. I am truly thankful to him.

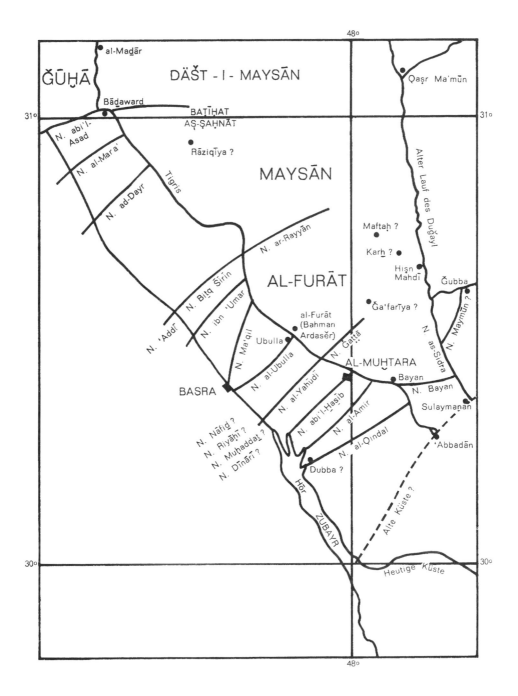

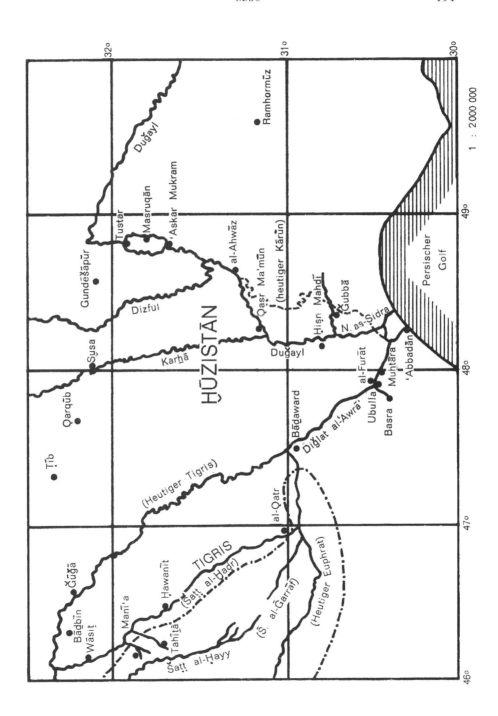

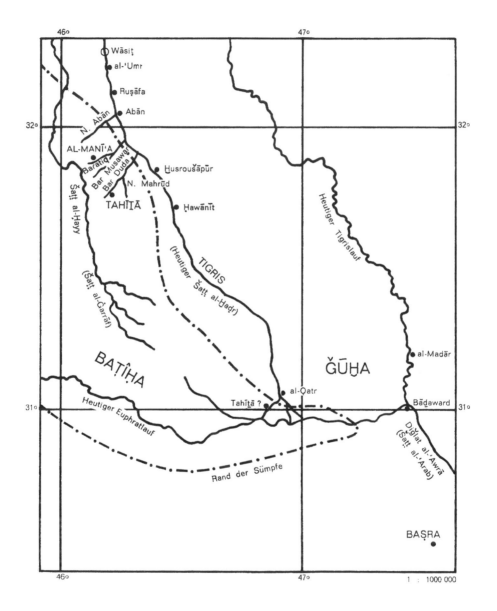

The Different Names of
'Alî b. Muhammad

a) Bernard Lewis agrees with Ibn al-Jawzî and accepts Bihbûdh as the Master of the Zanj's true name. I am little inclined to believe this, in spite of a host of historians who have followed Ibn al-Jawzî's lead. I am convinced that it is rather a question of one of his generals, the famous Bahbûdh b. 'Abd al-Wahhâb (who died in *Rajab* 268/February 882). The way historians who came after al-Tabarî used his Chronicle and arbitrarily cut it, often with no concern for the continuity of the text, and the unwitting mistakes of copyists have convinced me, in more than one instance, that Ibn al-Jawzî's statement is extremely suspect.

b) Al-Bîrûnî states that he was known under the name *al-Burqû'î* "the veiled one." Since al-Bîrûnî's assertion, this name has often been taken up by other authors. The surname is sometimes found in the form of al-Mubarqa'. Al-Tabarî does not give it, nor does he mention the wearing of a veil. Besides, veiled persons are numerous in Muslim medieval history: Muqanna', who revolted in Transoxiane from 159 to 167/775–784; Mubarqa', who revolted in Syria in 840 (of our era); Aswad, called 'Ayhala (or according to others 'Abhala b. Ka'b, Dhû l-Khimâr, etc. . . .).

c) Al-Khabîth "evil, vile" is an epithet used very often by al-Tabarî and by many subsequent authors. Through a substitute entry it became *Habîb* for a number of ancient Orientalists. The phrase we often encounter is the following: "He took the name Habîb because he wanted to be loved by all the members of the sect . . . "

It is not al-Tabarî's only epithet for him, but it is the most frequent. The others are: *al-Khâ'in* "traitor"; *al-Fâsiq* and *al-Fâjir* "a debauched person," *al-Mâriq* "heretic," and *al-La'în* "damned."

d) By far his most common surname is *Sâhib al-Zanj* "the Master of the Zanj." Since Khwândamîr it is sometimes seen in the form of *Sâhib al-Rîh* "Master of the Wind" [sic].

e) He is also often called *'Alawî* "the 'Alid" or *'Alawî al-Basrî* the 'Alid of Basra, in conformance with his link to 'Alî.

f) In Balawî's work and in the Anonymous *Târîkhe Sîstân*, his surname is given as *al-Nâjim*. It is found also in Ibn Abî l-Hadîd's work.

Genealogy of 'Alî b. Muhammad

a) Most authors do not believe he was an 'Alid and consider him a pre-varicator. Some go even further and show that these genealogies are false.

b) A great many Orientalists hesitate to express an opinion. As for Heinz Halm, he believes that the Master of the Zanj was a Persian *mawlâ* and that his supposed 'Alid genealogy is false.

The Different Versions of 'Alî b. Muhammad's Death

On the subject of, 'Alî b. Muhammad's death, Nöldeke writes:

> We do not quite know how he died. We can perhaps rely on information claiming that he poisoned himself. According to other information, he met with an accident during his flight. One fact tends to prove that he did not fall in battle. Despite the abundance of information, there is no mention of any soldier having demanded a legitimate reward for having killed the chief of the rebels. Suicide seems to us to be the end most befitting this man.

Opinions on his death are so divided that they have to be classified in order to see them more clearly.

a) Most authors rely on Tabarî's account: "One of Lu'lu''s soldiers galloped up carrying 'Alî b. Muhammad's head," or give no details ("was killed"). G. Weil also adds a note claiming that his death occurred on 3 and not 2 *Safar* 270. As for Mas'ûdî, he writes: "It is the same Loulou who later sought refuge with the government of Baghdad; welcomed by Mouaffak who was waging war on the leader of the Zendj, he took part in this war and in the death of the chief of the Zendj, as we have related in our preceding works. We have also said that rivalry broke out between Loulou's troops and those of Mouaffak about this leader's murder, for which both claimed responsibility, and that it almost led to a break between the two parties, until the soldiers in Mouaffak's camp sang the following verse: Speak as much as you like; the victory is due only to Loulou."

b) It is a short step from having been killed by one of Lu'lu''s soldiers to the claim that he was killed by Lu'lu' himself.

c) Others claim that he was captured and executed:
"Mowaffak who had caused him to die"; "At the end, Mouwaffaq, brother of the Caliph Moutamid, used a ploy to take him prisoner. All the Zendjs were massacred and Aly ibn Mohammed Borqouy who was taken to Baghdad was tied to the gallows"; "'Alî b. Muhammad was hanged in Baghdad"; "He was made prisoner and executed A.H. 270"; "It was not until *Safar* 270 (August 833 A.D.) that the Abbasids under al-Muwaffaq succeeded, after repeated campaigns, in capturing and executing the leader, 'Alî the Sâhib al Zanj."

d) For some, he was killed in Khûzistân:
" . . . was forced to take refuge in Ahwâz province where having fought his last battle he left his life." "Who finally reached him in the province of Ahwaz, he was taken prisoner and shortly afterwards, his head was severed."

e) According to a statement by Hilâl al-Sâbi', the Master of the Zanj was killed by his own soldiers. This is a tempting hypothesis.

f) The most plausible solution is suicide. Hamza al-Isfahânî writes on this subject: "He sucked the poison that was under his ring and died, then his head was severed." This caused Claude Cahen to say, without hesitation, "while he committed suicide."
Apart from all that, there is another piece of information that is extremely troubling: Three lines after having given Tabarî's well-known

version, Ibn Abî l-Hadîd, describes how 'Alî b. Muhammad fought his last battle, saber in hand. He fell when closed in and struck by several swords and was decapitated by one of Lu'lu' 's soldiers. All according to Ibn Abî l-Hadîd's usual expression, "Qâla Abû Ja'far ("Abû Ja'far [Tabarî's name]) writes!" Once more, we must wonder to what extent the *Annals* have come down to us mutilated.

Poetic Fragments from the Master of the Zanj

a) A verse in al-Balawî (written around 330/941).

b) Seven verses in al-Mas'ûdî (d. 345–46/956).

c) A verse in Ibn al-Nadîm (written in 377/987–88).

d) Forty-seven verses in al-Husrî (d. 413/1020 ?).

e) Nine verses in Abû l-'Alâ' al-Ma'arrî (d. 449/1057).

f) Three verses in al-Qudâ'î Abû 'Abdallâh Muhammad B. Salâma (d. 454/1062).

g) Sixty-one verses in al-Shayzarî (d. 626/1229).

h) Ten verses in Ibn Abî l-Hadîd (d. 655/1257).

i) Seven verses in the Pseudo-Muslim al-Lahjî (13th century).

j) Thirty-six verses in al-Safadî (d. 764/1362).

k) Two verses in Hindûshâh b. Sanjar Nakhjawânî (14th century).

l) Three verses in al-Dhahabî (d. 748/1348 ?).

Chronological Table[1]

? Birth of 'Alî b. Muhammad in Warzanîn.

? His departure for Samârrâ.

249/863–64: His departure for Bahrayn.

254/868: Return to Iraq, first sojourn in Basra, departure for Baghdad.

Ramadân 255/August–September 869: Return to the Basra area.

26 *Ramadân* 255/September 7, 869: Beginning of the revolt.

End of *Ramadân* 255/September 869: The Nahr Maymûn sermon.

Shawwâl 255/September–October 869: The Zanj's first victory.

12 *Dhû'l-Qa'da*, 255/October 22, 869: Great Zanj defeat.

13 *Dhû'l-Qa'da*, 255/October 23, 869: Gathering of the rest of the troops.

14 *Dhû'l-Qa'da*, 255/October 24, 869: Great Basrian defeat.

Rajab 256/June 870: Sa'îd al-Hâjib replaces Ju'lân.

25 *Rajab*, 256/June 28, 870: Capture of al-Ubulla.

12 *Ramadân*, 256/August 13, 870: Capture of Ahwâz.

Rajab 257/ May–June 871: Zanj defeat on the Nahr Murgâb.

10 *Shawwâl*, 257/August 31, 871: Meeting of Basrians in the house of Burayh.

14 *Shawwâl*, 257/September 871: Lunar eclipse.

17 *Shawwâl*, 257/ September 7, 871: Capture of Basra.

20 *Shawwâl*, 257/ September 10, 871: Massacre of the inhabitants of Basra.

1 *Dhû' l-Qa'da*, 257/ September 20, 871: Muhammad b. al-Muwallad leaves Samârrâ.

1 *Rabî' II*, 258/ February 15, 872: al-Muwaffaq and Muflih are put in

charge of the war against the Zanj.

18 *Jumâdâ I*, 258/April 1, 872: Wounding of Muflih who died the next day.

10 *Rajab*, 258/May 22, 872: Execution of al-Bahrânî.

Sha'bân 258/ June–July 872: al-Muwaffaq returns to Wâsit.

26 *Rabî' I*, 259/January 30, 873: al-Muwaffaq returns to Samârrâ.

6 *Rajab*, 259/May 873: Second occupation of Ahwâz.

17 *Dhû' l-Qa'da*, 259/September 14, 873: Mûsâ b. Bûgâ is given responsibility for the war against the Zanj.

260/873–74: 'Alî b. Zayd al-'Alawî is killed by the Zanj.

261/874–75: Third occupation of Ahwâz.

Sha'bân 261/May–June 875: Masrûr al-Balkhî is put in charge of the war against the Zanj.

20 *Dhû' l-Hijja*, 261/September 25, 875: Masrûr leaves Samârrâ.

9 *Rajab*, 262/April 8, 876: Ya'qûb b. al-Layth's defeat at Dayr al-'Aqûl.

11 *Rajab*, 262/April 10, 876: Ya'qûb b. al-Layth rejects an alliance.

Jumâdâ I 264/January–February 878: Sulaymân b. Jâmi' returns to al-Mukhtâra.

End of *Rajab* 264/April 878: Sulaymân b. Jâmi' carries off the booty to al-Mukhtâra.

Sha'bân 264/April–May 878: Sulaymân b. Jâmi' defeats Abbasid troops.

Dhû' l-Qa'da 264/July–August 878: Sulaymân b. Jâmi' takes al-Rusâfa.

5 *Dhû' l-Hijja*, 264/August 8, 878: Sulaymân b. Jâmi' leaves for al-Mukhtâra.

28 *Dhû' l-Hijja*, 264/August 31, 878: Sulaymân b. Jâmi' returns from al-Mukhtâra.

Dhû' l-Hijja 264/August–September 878: Capture of Wâsit.

9 *Shawwâl*, 265/June 4, 879: Death of Ya'qûb b. al-Layth.

Rabî' II 266/November–December 879: Abû l-'Abbâs undertakes the offensive.

Ramadân 266/April–May 880: Agartmish replaces Takîn al-Bukhârî.

11 *Safar*, 267/September 880: al-Muwaffaq assembles a new army.

2 *Rabî' I*, 267/October 11, 880: al-Muwaffaq leaves al-Firk.

28 *Rabî' I*, 267/November 6, 880: The two armies advance towards the Zanj.

8 *Rabî' II*, 267/November 16, 880: Capture of al-Manî'a.

18 *Rabî' II*, 267/November 26, 880: al-Muwaffaq arrives in Bardûdâ.

20 *Rabî' II*, 267/28 November 880: al-Muwaffaq leads the troops to Tahîthâ.

26 *Rabî' II*, 267/December 4, 880: Death of Ahmad b. Mahdî al-Jubbâ'î.

27 *Rabî' II*, 267/ December 5, 880: Capture of al-Mansûra.

1 *Jumâdâ II* 1, 267/January 7, 881: al-Muwaffaq's departure for the Khûzistân.

15 *Rajab*, 267/February 19, 881: Regrouping on the Nahr al-Mubârak.

20 *Rajab*, 267/ February 24, 881: al-Muwaffaq approaches al-Mukhtâra.

24 *Rajab*, 267/February 28, 881: al-Muwaffaq chooses the Nahr Jattâ for his camp.

14 *Sha'bân*, 267/ March 20, 881: al-Muwaffaq launches a new appeal to the insurgents.

15 *Sha'bân*, 267/March 21, 881: Construction of al-Muwaffaqiyya.

17 *Sha'bân*, 267/March 23, 881: Bahhûdh burns the camp of Abû Hamza.

2 *Ramadân*, 267/April 6, 881: Death of Sandal-al-Zanjî.

Shawwâl 267/May–June 881: Great defeat of the Zanj.

Dhû' l-Qa'da 267/ June–July 881: The insurgents' fleet forbidden to move out of al-Mukhtâra.

24 *Dhû' l-Hijja*, 267/July 26, 881: First attack on al-Mukhtâra.

29 *Dhû' l-Hijja*, 267/July 31, 881: Rayhân b. Sâlih deserts.

1 *Muharram*, 268/August 1, 881: Ja'far b. Ibrâhîm deserts.

16 *Rabî' II*, 268/ November 13, 881: Second attack on al-Mukhtâra.

Rajab 268/January–February 882: Death of Bahbûdh b. 'Abd al-Wahhâb.

Muharram 269/July–August 882: al-Hârûn the 'Alid rejoins the ranks of the Abbasids.

25 *Jumâdâ I*, 269/ December 10, 882: Qirtâs wounds al-Muwaffaq.

Sha'bân 269/February–March 883: al-Muwaffaq returns to the fighting.

18 *Sha'bân*, 269/March 2, 883: Muhammad b. Sam'ân deserts.

19 *Sha'bân*, 269/March 3, 883: 'Alî b. Muhammad's palace on fire.

20 *Sha'bân*, 269/March 4, 883: Death of Nusayr Abû Hamza.

10 *Shawwâl*, 269/April 22, 883: Attack on the bridge (stones).

14 *Shawwâl*, 269/April 26, 883: Attack on the first bridge (boats).

22 *Shawwâl*, 269/May 4, 883: Attack on the second bridge (boats).

7 *Dhû' l-Qa'da*, 269/May 18, 883: Concentration of Abbasid troops.

8 *Dhû' l-Qa'da*, 269/May 19, 883: Attack on the eastern section of al-Mukhtâra.

Dhû' l-Hijja 269/June 12, 883: Sâ'id b. Makhlad brings reinforcements.

2 *Muharram*, 270/July 12, 883: Lu'lu' rejoins al-Muwaffaq's ranks.

3 *Muharram*, 270/July 13, 883: Lu'lu' and his officers are received by al-Muwaffaq.

27 *Muharram*, 270/ August 6, 883: Next to last attack on al-Mukhtâra.

2 *Safar,* 270/August 11, 883: Death of 'Alî b. Muhammad.

Jumâdâ I 18, 270/November 23, 883: Abu l-'Abbâs's triumphal entry into Baghdad.

Shawwâl 272/March–April 886: Execution of the leaders of the Zanj army.

23 *Shawwâl*, 272/April 2, 886: Crucifixion of bodies.

7 *Muharram*, 280/March 29, 893: Death of Shaylama, Muhammad b. al-Hasan b. Sahl.

---

1. The concordances were established according to H. G. Cattenoz, *Tables de concordance des ères chrétienne et hégirienne,* 3rd ed., Rabat, 1961.

Index